Sustainable development for a democratic South Africa

Sustainable development for a democratic South Africa

Edited by Ken Cole

from Routledge

First published by Earthscan in the UK and USA in 1994

This edition published 2013 by Earthscan

For a full list of publications please contact:

Earthscan
2 Park Square, Milton Park, Abingdon, Oxon OX14 4RN
Simultaneously published in the USA and Canada by Earthscan
711 Third Avenue, New York, NY 10017

*Earthscan is an imprint of the Taylor & Francis Group,
an informa business*

A catalogue record for this book is available from the British Library

ISBN: 978-1-85383-230-7 (pbk)

Copy-edited and typeset by Selro Publishing Services, Oxford
Biddles Ltd, Guildford and King's Lynn

Contents

PART III
Education and the Media

PART IV
Sustainable Development: An Overview

The Contributors

Charles Abugre trained as an economist in Ghana and the Netherlands and worked with ACORD (a UK-based consortium of European and Canadian NGOs) as a Research and Policy officer. In this capacity he has travelled and worked extensively in Africa enabling him to distil lessons that could cross-fertilize projects across the continent. He is currently with Third World Network (based in Malaysia) working on macro-economic adjustment issues, trade and commodities, and the economics of environmental management.

Jesmond Blumenfeld is senior lecturer at Brunel University (West London), where he has been teaching since 1978. He grew up in South Africa and studied economics at the Universities of Natal and Rhodes. He has written extensively about South Africa's international economic relations and its political economy. His most recent book is *Economic Interdependence in Southern Africa: From Conflict to Cooperation*.

Lionel Cliffe is professor of politics at the University of Leeds. He has worked on, or in, independent Africa for 30 years and was a founding editor of the *Review of African Political Economy*. As a specialist in agrarian reform and rural development, he has written a special report for the UN Food and Agriculture Organization (FAO) and the Zimbabwe government on 'Policy Options for Agrarian Reform in Zimbabwe', and worked on land tenure and agrarian reform with the FAO in Rome. He is author, with Colin Stoneman, of *Zimbabwe: Politics, Economy and Society*.

Ken Cole teaches at the School of Development Studies at the University of East Anglia (UK). He specializes in development economics and the ideological dimension of development theory. He has worked in Honduras, Nicaragua, Peru and Swaziland and has directed specialist training courses on South African development. He is co-author of *Why Economists Disagree*.

François du Bois studied law at the Universities of Stellenbosch and Oxford. As well as being an advocate of the Supreme Court of South Africa he teaches law at the School of Oriental and African Studies (UK). His research interests include law and the environment in Africa and

Asia, in particular constitutional rights in post-apartheid South Africa and comparative environmental law.

Robert Fine is senior lecturer in the Sociology Department at the University of Warwick, where he has worked since 1973. His main research interests are in democracy, the state and labour. He has written extensively on South Africa, including *Democracy and the Rule of Law*, and *Beyond Apartheid: Labour and Liberation in South Africa*.

Paul Fordham is honorary professor at the University of Warwick (UK) and director of the International Centre for Education in Development. He has taught at the universities of Makerere (Uganda), Nairobi (Kenya), Southampton and Nottingham (UK) and has worked as an educational consultant for UNESCO, British Council, Overseas Development Administration, Commonwealth Secretariat, Action Aid and the European Commission. He has published extensively, including *Participation, Learning and Change*.

David Johnson is a lecturer in Education at the University of Bristol (UK) and director of the Education Management and Policy Project for Post-Apartheid South Africa. He has worked in education in South Africa, Botswana, Zimbabwe and the UK.

Leo Katzen trained at the University of Witwatersrand and the London School of Economics. He has taught development economics at the Universities of Natal, Cape Town and Leicester. He has a special interest in the economics of South Africa with particular reference to labour issues. Publications include *Gold and the South African Economy*.

John Kirkby is a senior lecturer in the Department of Environment at the University of Northumbria (UK). He has worked extensively in eastern and southern Africa. His research is focused on sustainability in peasant land-use systems.

John Macdonald has for the past 12 years been setting up and coordinating primary health care (PHC) courses in UK universities. He has also evaluated PHC and set up PHC courses in a number of countries in Africa, Asia and Latin America. He is currently coordinator of PHC courses at the School of Education, University of Bristol (UK). He is the author of *Primary Health Care: Medicine in its Place*.

Barry Munslow is a reader in the School of Politics and Communication at the University of Liverpool (UK). He has acted as an adviser to governments in southern Africa and to the Southern African Development Community on sustainable development policy issues. He taught in earlier years at the Eduardo Mondlane University in Mozambique. He has published extensively on southern Africa.

Phil O'Keefe has had field experience as a consultant in over 26 countries worldwide, and has taught at universities in Britain, Africa, Sweden and the USA. He is currently professor of environmental management at the University of Northumbria (UK). His extensive publications include most recently *The Tears of the Crocodile: From Rio to Reality in the Developing World*.

Chris Peters has worked in Botswana and Kenya and, as a consultant in Lesotho, worked on the provision of community services by local government. He has recently completed a master's degree in development studies at the University of East Anglia (UK) and is to return to southern Africa to work on local government and the provision of services.

Benjamin Pogrund was born in Cape Town and educated at the Universities of Cape Town and Witwatersrand. He was deputy editor of the *Rand Daily Mail* until the newspaper was closed in 1985. He is currently in the foreign department of *The Independent* in London and is the author of *How Can Man Die Better: Sobukwe and Apartheid*.

Steve Randall is a team leader of the Trade Union and Basic Education Project in Manchester. He works closely with black and other community groups devising and designing learning programmes appropriate to their needs. He has considerable experience in organizing day schools, conferences and seminars on issues of current concern to the black minority in Britain.

Colin Stoneman is an economist at the Centre for Southern African Studies at the University of York. He is editor of the *Journal of Southern African Studies* and a member of the editorial working group of the *Review of African Political Economy*. He has published extensively on Zimbabwe and writes the quarterly report on Zimbabwe for the *Economist Intelligence Unit*. He is currently working on the prospects for industrialization in the Southern African Development Community (SADC) countries, and in post-apartheid South Africa.

Alan Whiteside is a senior research fellow in the Economic Research Unit at the University of Durban. He has worked extensively on industrialization and the economic prospects for post-apartheid South Africa. He is co-editor (with Sholto Cross) of *Facing Up to Aids: The Socio-Economic Impact in Southern Africa*.

Preface

In August 1992 the Overseas Development Group and the School of Development Studies at the University of East Anglia were approached to mount a short (three-month) course for 11 activists from South Africa, all of whom had extensive experience in community organization and had been active in the mass democratic movement. The course, entitled 'Sustainable Development for a Post-Apartheid South Africa', was intended to introduce the participants to a range of academic understandings of, and techniques for, analysing processes of sustainable development, so that they might better fulfil their role in the development process.

The course, which ran in the spring of 1993, culminated in an international conference on 25/26 March. The aim of the conference was to bring together a range of experts from outside the University of East Anglia to help equip the course members to tackle the crucial issues and debates that will face South Africa as it moves towards democracy. This book is made up of the presentations at this conference.

The originality of this collection of readings is that it looks forward to the issues that will figure large in any move in South Africa towards sustainable development. To this end, experience from elsewhere in Africa is addressed in an attempt to consider the alternatives, as South Africa enters the uncharted waters of one-person-one-vote.

Acknowledgements

Ian Cherrett and Phil O'Keefe of ETC Foundation (UK) were the main motivating forces behind the course which I organized and which led to the conference and this book. The 11 community activists and development workers on the course itself were Dudu Nkosi, Padi Matlala, Themba Mavimbela, Mzwai Msoki, Japhet Ngubane, Stone Sizani, Hans Ramharak, Andre Nzima, Vincent Mogane, Richard Clacey and John Kgori. Their enthusiasm, experience and wit made these three months the most exciting and worthwhile of my teaching career.

A book such as this is the product of many people. For help in turning the drafts submitted by authors into a book, I would like to thank Jane Kingswell, Sally McAleese and Josh Bailey of the Overseas Development Group, and Ingrid Barriskill and Jill Wyatt of the School of Development Studies. I would also like to thank the authors for keeping to the guidelines for the various drafts and observing deadlines.

The conference on which the book is based attracted speakers from the USA, South Africa, 13 British universities, and four non-governmental organizations (NGOs) and over 120 participants. A partial contribution from the Economic and Social Research Council (ESRC) seminar grant, 'African Environments: Building the Future', is gratefully acknowledged, since it provided help towards financing the conference and the publication.

Ken Cole
Norwich, February 1994

Acronyms

ACORD	UK-based consortium of European and Canadian NGOs
AIDS	Acquired Immune Deficiency Syndrome
ANC	African National Congress
AZAPO	Azanian People's Organization
BCP	Basotho Congress Party
BOS	Bureau of Statistics
CA	Communal Area
CBOs	community-based organizations
CACE	Centre for Adult and Continuing Education
CNA	Central News Agency
CODESA	Congress for a Democratic South Africa
COSAG	Concerned South African's Grouping
COSATU	Congress of South African Trade Unions
CPS	Current Population Survey
CSSAEIF	LSE Centre for the Study of the South African Economy and International Finance
DBSA	Development Bank of South Africa
EPZ	export-processing zone
ERF	export-revolving fund
ESAP	economic structural adjustment
ESRC	Economic and Social Research Council
ESCOM	the national electricity corporation
EU	European Union
FAA	Forcas Armados Angolanas
FAO	United Nations Food and Agriculture Organization
FCR	Foundation for Contemporary Research
FFF	food supplements, female education and family planning
FRELIMO	Frente de Libertaçao de Mozambique
GASCOR	the South African gas utility
GATT	General Agreement on Tariffs and Trade
GDP	gross domestic product
GNP	gross national product
GOBI	growth monitoring, oral rehydration, breast feeding, immunization
GOL	Government of Lesotho
GOZ	Government of Zimbabwe
GPA	Global Programme on AIDS
HIV	human immunodeficiency virus

HSRC	Human Sciences Research Council
ID	institutional development
IDF	Institute for Forest Development
IDS	Institute of Development Studies, University of Sussex
IDT	Independent Development Trust
IMF	International Monetary Fund
ISI	import-substitution industrialization
IUCN	International Union for Conservation of Nature and Natural Resources
JSC	Judge of the Supreme Court
JWG	Joint Working Group
LHWP	Lesotho Highlands Water Project
LNDC	Lesotho National Development Corporation
LPG	liquefied petroleum gas
LSCF	large-scale commercial farm
LSPP	Lands, Surveys and Physical Planning
LSE	London School of Economics and Political Science
MCC	Maseru City Council
MDP	Maseru Development Plan
MICARD	Ministry of Interior, Chieftainship and Rural Affairs
MPLA	Popular Movement for the Liberation of Angola
MSC	Manpower Service Commission
NAFTA	North American Free Trade Agreement
NCS	National Conservation Strategy
NEAC	National Environmental Awareness Campaign
NECC	National Education Coordinating Committee
NEPI	National Education Policy Investigation
NFE	non-formal education
NGOs	Non-governmental organizations
NICs	newly industrializing developing countries
NLC	National Land Commission
NPPHCN	National Progressive Primary Health Care Network
NR	Natural Region
NTI	new training initiative
OD	organizational development
ODA	Overseas Development Agency
OECD	Organization for Economic Cooperation and Development
PAC	Pan-Africanist Congress
PHC	primary health care
PTSA	parent–teacher–student association
PWV	Pretoria–Witwatersrand–Vereeniging
RA	Resettlement Area
RENAMO	Mozambique National Resistance
REPLAN	adult unemployed programme
RSA	Republic of South Africa
SABC	South African Broadcasting Corporation

SACP	South African Communist Party
SACU	Southern African Customs Union
SADC	Southern African Development Community
SADCC	Southern African Development Coordinating Conference
SADF	South African Defence Force
SAHSSO	South African Health and Social Services Organization
SARB	South African Reserve Bank
SASOL	oil from coal production plant
SD	Sustainable Development
SECC	Soweto Education Coordinating Committee
SIDA	Swedish International Development Agency
SPHC	selective primary health care
SPP	Surplus People Project
STD	Sexually Transmitted Disease
TAU	Technical and Advisory Unit
TAZAMA	Tanzanian–Zambian pipeline company
UCL	University College, London
UCT	University of Cape Town
UGA	Urban Government Act
UK	United Kingdom
UN	United Nations
UNCED	United Nations Conference on Environment and Development
UNDP	United Nations Development Programme
UNEP	United Nations Environmental Programme
UNESCO	United Nations Educational, Scientific and Cultural Organization
UNICEF	United Nations (International) Children's (Emergency) Fund
UNITA	National Union for the Total Independence of Angola
USA	United States of America
USIT	Urban Sanitation Improvement Team
USRP	Urban Sector Reorientation Project (Urban II)
UWC	University of the Western Cape
UWDC	urban ward development committees
VAT	value added tax
VIPs	Ventilated Improved Pit Latrines
WASA	Water and Sewage Authority
WCEFA	World Conference on Education for All
WHO	World Health Organization
YTS	Youth Training Scheme

Introduction

Sustainable Development for a Democratic South Africa

Ken Cole[1]

The prospect of a new, non-racial, democratic South Africa is on the political horizon, but how this potential is to be realized is far from clear. The direction of South Africa's future development critically will depend upon policy choices made now, and it is to this policy debate that this book (and the conference which was its precursor) attempts to contribute, by addressing key policy issues on which a sustainable future will rest.

Although the first democratic election in South Africa's history is provisionally set for 27 April 1994, it is uncertain what the future direction of post-apartheid South Africa will be. But at least it is a signal that a corner has been turned, that change is irreversible.

A historic compromise was reached between President F W de Klerk and Nelson Mandela, and between the National Party and the African National Congress (ANC), with the new post-apartheid constitution being agreed in principle. Of the 26 negotiating parties, 20 voted in favour and six against: the six being united in trying to protect privileges acquired under apartheid (or their minority interests) in the future South Africa. The dissenting group, Concerned South African's Grouping (COSAG), which was led by Mangosuthu Buthelezi's Inkatha Freedom Party, included the right-wing white extremist Conservative Party and the leadership of the nominally independent 'homelands' of Ciskei and Bophuthatswana. COSAG became the Freedom Alliance — a collaboration between the white right-wing and three black Bantustan leaders. At the time of writing (early November 1993), the Freedom Alliance seems to be virtually all that stands between the negotiation process and a new democratic constitution.

The alliance comprises Dr Hartzenberg, a white hardliner who inherited the leadership of the Conservative Party after the death of Andries

1 . I would like to acknowledge the useful and incisive comments by Alan White-side on a previous draft. Remaining deficiencies are my responsibility.

Treurnicht; General Viljoen and some retired generals, who in May 1993 launched the Afrikaner Volksfront to give political leadership to right wing Afrikaners who find the Conservative Party too reserved; President Lucas Mangope of Bophuthatswana, who has banned and ruthlessly suppressed the ANC in the homeland; Oupa Gqozo, the Ciskei dictator — shortly to go on trial for the murder of one of his henchmen, General Charles Sebe; and the kingpin of the alliance, the Inkatha Freedom Party president, Chief Mangosuthu Buthelezi.

The Freedom Alliance, and COSAG before it, has fought to postpone the election for the constituent assembly until after detailed constitutional negotiations, because after the first one-person-one-vote election their negotiating power, and influence, will reflect their (small) share of the vote. Indeed, at the beginning of July, Buthelezi pulled his negotiators out of the multi-party negotiating council, which was considering the interim constitution, protesting that no decision could be made without his party's agreement. When an agreed constitution was nevertheless drawn up, Buthelezi boycotted the presentation (26 July 1993) and objected to the scheduling of 27 April 1994 for the election. He even took his case to the Supreme Court, claiming that there were irregularities in the negotiating council's procedure. The claim was subsequently dismissed.

In an effort to placate the detractors and get them back round the negotiating table, the government re-emphasized that the document could not be regarded as any more than a first draft. But right-wing elements in de Klerk's cabinet saw Buthelezi as their primary ally against the ANC, to whom the government's negotiating team had conceded too much in their efforts to compromise and strike a deal. To appease such conservative ministers, at the end of July President de Klerk endorsed the appointment of Lieutenant-General Georg Meiring, the most conservative and discredited member of the general staff, as the new chief of South Africa's defence force. The ANC objected to this appointment.

Chief Buthelezi has defiantly presented his own constitutional plan for Kwazulu homeland/Natal province. It is secessionist and aims to preserve the one-party state, where dissent is not tolerated. To this end he has found willing allies in the white, conservative extremists, with their demand for a separate Boer state, even though there is no area in South Africa where Afrikaners are in the majority. At least Buthelezi has ambitions to control a coherent geographical area — but his electoral support is diminishing. One third of his voters are white, and increasingly the ANC is the most popular party among Zulus.

The Freedom Alliance asserts that the draft constitution has destroyed all hope of a peaceful negotiated settlement. In this context Buthelezi's waning political support is dangerous. No election will satisfy his ambition. He has raised the spectre of civil war, which is potentially consequent upon violent political destabilization by the far right and militants of the Inkatha Freedom

Party. The grenade and gun attack on a predominantly white Cape Town church congregation (25 July 1993), in which 11 people were killed and over 40 injured, brought the violence of the townships into the white heartland and underlined the helplessness of the government. A failure to uphold law and order upsets the delicate balance between black and white in the negotiating process. The standing of the National Party amongst the white constituency suffers, strengthening the cause of right-wing extremism. And the violence continues in the townships unabated. At the end of July 35 people were killed near a hostel in Tembisa, a township near Johannesburg. The hostel dwellers, who were Inkatha supporters, were fighting township residents, who overwhelmingly backed the ANC. Comment from the ANC (*The Guardian*, 2 August 1993) was that the killings were part of a deliberate strategy 'to prevent the negotiated transition to a democratic and non-racial society.'

The National Party and the ANC have made it clear that they have little patience with Buthelezi's personal political ambitions (or with aims of extremist Afrikaners to preserve apartheid within internal state boundaries) and have continued to work towards a compromise constitution. To this end the negotiators have worked towards a reconciliation of black aspirations and white fears. The original demand of the ANC was for simple majority rule, which fuelled the fears of the white minority that the blacks would do to the whites what the whites had done to the blacks. And to check any potential 'tyranny of the black majority' the National Party had demanded a federal system of power-sharing, with entrenched white minority vetoes.

In the compromise, the government has yielded on compulsory power-sharing, and the ANC has accepted a voluntary 'government of national unity' for the first five years of the new constitution, shifting its ground from straight majority rule.

The intended social democratic compromise calls for patience, under-standing and an awareness of a shared national interest on behalf of the black majority, and a willingness by the white minority to forego some of the privileges hitherto subsidized by black disadvantage and suffering.

But how long will those who have been deprived wait for retribution? This is especially a problem when people receive political double messages, for negotiators, leaders and representatives have to be sensitive to problems in their opponent's constituency and work towards compromise. At the hustings, however, to garner electoral support, they have to appear to fight for their constituencies' advantage and exploit heterogeneity.

In any political democracy, political differences will inevitably surface and any compromise will have to convince the various constituencies of the soundness of the final policy. But the bedrock of social democracy, the political centre, is weakening. After more than three years of negotiation, with no let-up in political extremism and racial violence, the extremes of the white right and the black left are growing in strength. For example, the white minority is fearful that President de Klerk has gone soft and is tempting the government to resort to strong-arm tactics, such as swooping on the Pan African Congress (May 1993) or appointing Lieutenant-General Georg Meiring as chief of the defence force. While such moves might do something to shore up the government's support base, they exacerbate the impatience of the ANC's constituency — an impatience born of the lack of tangible improvement in the lives of the black majority.

In the short term, setting a (provisional) date for the long dreamed of one-person-one-vote election may help to offset the disillusionment and violence born of decades of government intransigence. But there is a danger of even greater disenchantment should political enfranchisement fail to make any difference to people's life styles, or, more importantly, fail to give people a hope of better fulfilling their individual potential in the future. Political commitment is built upon ambitions, and the black majority has had no experience of personal fulfilment through the ballot box; why should its attitudes and intuitions change now? If democracy is to have any semblance of legitimacy, and the development process is to be sustainable, there is a pressing need to extend participation in the political process to the disadvantaged black majority, and for political empowerment to produce palpable benefits.

Development implies that people change their social behaviour to make it compatible with higher levels of social productivity. Sustainable development requires that social interaction is organized to take account of the natural implications of new forms of social life. Of fundamental importance is the institutional environment through which resources are distributed — which is essentially a political question. For instance, the Land Acts of 1913 and 1936 only reserved 13 per cent of the land for the black majority. And the 1948 Nationalist government institutionalized apartheid with the creation of self-governing homelands — effectively labour reserves for white-owned farms, industries and mines. With the repeal of the Pass Laws and the Urban Areas Act in 1986, laws that had been intended to restrict black habitation to the overcrowded and economically non-viable homelands, the floodgates of black urbanization opened, with an average of over 1000 people a day moving into urban areas (see Ramphele 1991: Chapter 1).

Squatter settlements in metropolitan areas mushroomed. With scarcely any provision of basic amenities — housing, sewerage, refuse collection, tarred roads, drainage, communications, social services, or electricity — people's lifestyles were inevitably damaging to the environment. Such environmental unsustainability can only be addressed by redressing the economic disadvantage and political disempowerment of the black majority. A process which will take generations, as people and politicians move from crisis management to stay alive, to participation and political empowerment in the face of opposition from politically vested interests.

Under apartheid the black majority had an unambiguous common enemy — the white minority. Now the priorities are less clear. South Africa is entering uncharted waters. Racial divisions will be eclipsed by political relations based on wealth and control of the economic resources that beget political power. And this will not be, and increasingly is not, solely a white preserve. With blurred social and political divisions the transition will be unpredictable and uncertain. In considering the possible scenarios and pitfalls of development in South Africa, lessons may be learnt from experiences elsewhere in Africa where there has been a transition to black majority rule. Various chapters in this book address such processes and try to draw lessons that are relevant to the case of South Africa.

How easily can the liberation movement move from opposition to government? This will depend on what opportunities (and abilities) people have to express democratically their needs, priorities and aspirations, and on how readily the state accedes to these demands. A whole range of policy issues have to be addressed, urgently and publicly.

Of fundamental importance is the economy, which is addressed in Part I. In a country with the greatest recorded inequality of any country in the world, according to the World Bank, and with over two-thirds of its black majority living below the minimum living level, defined to cover basic needs (see Ramphele 1991: Chapter 1), economic growth must provide the resources with which to raise black living standards if political optimism is not to be disappointed. There has to be economic recovery if the anger of the disadvantaged is to be diffused.

In Chapter 1 Jesmond Blumenfeld examines the economic potential of South Africa for losing its pariah status in the world and the lifting of economic sanctions. However, the restructuring of the economy to take advantage of increased exports, inward foreign investment, outward South African investment and the possibility of foreign loans to finance development projects is likely to conflict with the need to redress existing economic imbalances and inequalities. The need to compensate the economically and socially disadvantaged for past deprivation will be prejudiced, thus heightening the disillusionment of the black majority with political democracy. Development will be fraught with conflict and potentially politically unsustainable.

In Chapter 2 Colin Stoneman argues that there can only be meaningful poverty alleviation with substantial job creation and economic growth. The neo-liberal economic orthodoxy, ideologically dominant since the late 1970s, understands that economic growth emanates from the efficacy of the 'invisible hand' of market forces. This dogma has been enshrined in the ubiquitous 'structural adjustment' policies sponsored by the World Bank and the International Monetary Fund (IMF). Stoneman argues that such policies will prove disastrous, and that any real impact on South Africa's economic problems calls for imaginative and radical solutions. And in this regard lessons might be learnt from the experience of Zimbabwe.

In Chapter 3 Robert Fine considers the neo-liberal economic orthodoxy in reconciling the 'rage of the poor'. Neo-liberal and structural adjustment policies in other parts of the world have led to coercion and suppression of the poor and disadvantaged. Fine argues that this scenario will only be avoided in South Africa if the social demands of labour are recognized as legitimate, implying an interventionist, social democratic, economic and political regime, rather than the free-market, politically conservative social environment encouraged by the policies of the World Bank. In such a pluralist ambience the labour movement has to represented by a political party for the 'rage of the poor' to be heard, and for political democracy to have social legitimacy — a necessary condition for sustainable development.

In Chapter 4 Leo Katzen returns to the fundamental question of job creation, and looks at the contribution of the informal sector, especially important given the trend towards increased capital intensity consequent upon the lifting of international economic sanctions. Protection from international competition, occasioned by high tariffs, has perpetuated anachronistic, inefficient techniques in the manufacturing sector. So even though South Africa is a low-wage economy, labour costs are relatively high. To become internationally competitive there has to be an industrial strategy, intended to promote particular sectors, including investment in education to produce a skilled labour force. It is not a question of *should* the state intervene in the economy, but *how* economic relations will be managed if there is to be sustainable development.

In Chapter 5 Phil O'Keefe and John Kirby look at the wider regional dimension in considering South Africa's economic relations, particularly with regard to the production and supply of energy. As they are presently constituted, the institutional structures of SADCC (Southern African Development Coordinating Conference — the regional economic grouping of Botswana, Lesotho, Swaziland, Mozambique, Zimbabwe, Malawi, Zambia, Namibia, Tanzania and Angola — which has now become SADC, the Southern African Development Community), and of the South African economy, cannot address the energy and, therefore, economic needs of South Africa. Of particular relevance here is the nature of the mineral complex in South Africa, the provision of electricity to townships, and the possibility of a regional grid.

Apart from questions of economic growth, international economic sanctions, employment, regional economic integration and redistribution, the agricultural sector and sustainable agricultural development have particular requirements. One of these is land reform. In Chapter 6 Lionel Cliffe considers the issues of sustainability, agricultural development and land reform in South Africa in the light of the experience of Zimbabwe.

Cliffe starts by examining the agricultural structure inherited from apartheid. It is similar to that of Zimbabwe and is characterized by massive inequalities — large-scale commercial farms and semi-arid, over-crowded labour reserves (homelands) engaged in subsistence agriculture. The deleterious environmental consequences of such inequalities call for land reform. Techniques of 'population-resource balance' have become an ideological weapon with which to block agrarian reform; and the experience of Zimbabwe highlights how large amounts of land can be redistributed so that land is used more intensively and produces enough of a return to pay for the programme.

Central to environmentally sustainable development is the relief of social disadvantage. And, in a democratic society, people's recourse to legal protection of their rights is fundamental. François du Bois opens Part II on 'The State, NGOs and Social Policy' by examining how far the South African legal system allows people to participate in the pursuit of environmentally sustainable social development by empowering them to assert their rights.

The alternative to greater private recourse to the law is greater public provision of services. In Chapter 8 Chris Peters draws upon his experience of working in Lesotho to consider democratic, local authority social-service provision. The problems are discussed and the question of devolved service sourcing considered, along with the issue of an individual's social empowerment.

If people are to participate in helping to determine development paths it is essential that their *own* analyses of their conditions, needs and constraints are voiced and heard. Here civil society, the way people organize themselves outside the state to pursue social goals, is important. In this regard NGOs have a crucial role to play.

Charles Abugre (Chapter 9) addresses the majority of NGOs in South Africa, which grew out of the anti-apartheid struggle. This complex web of civil organizations, which includes neighbourhood structures, has a clear political affiliation, but faces immense problems in working towards building a new society. The challenges are made all the greater by the comparative lack of trust and of indigenous implementation skills, and dispute resolution and accountability mechanisms, as well as by the difficulties of turning the attentions of protest organizations to development promotion. Such deficiencies have to be addressed if international aid is to be used effectively.

In Chapter 10 John Macdonald looks at the provision of a particular social service, primary health care, as a contribution towards the future sustainability of the development process. The problems of equity, participation and intersectoral collaboration are addressed, as well as the strengths that could generate energy to overcome these constraints.

Although the epidemiology of AIDS (Acquired Immune Deficiency Syndrome) is perhaps, historically, the most studied and researched of any disease, its social and economic effects are only just beginning to be identified and understood. In Chapter 11 Alan Whiteside assesses the implications for development of the growing AIDS epidemic in South Africa. The data on HIV and AIDS, and the response to the epidemic, are examined, including information from sero-surveys carried out over the past two years.

South Africa is at special risk, it is argued, due to the socio-economic structure of the society and the legacy of apartheid that may combine to encourage the spread of the disease. The demographic, financial, macro-economic, social and political implications are considered. Data from South African sources are compared to examples from other countries in the region. There has, as yet, been little success in slowing the pace of the spread of the disease and the chapter concludes by suggesting possible policy responses.

Participation and empowerment are fundamental to effective sustainable development, but South Africa is a long way from this ideal, though parliamentary democracy (one-person-one-vote) is a step on the way. A distinct political culture is called for. Grassroots participation challenges traditional political power; direct popular involvement is politically volatile and implies a more sophisticated democratic political culture than parliamentary democracy. Such a culture evolves out of people's experiences and frustrations, which, in turn, provide the motivation to struggle to participate in the control of social existence. To this end conflict is not dysfunctional. As Wisner (1988: 15) put it, 'The poor learn from these conflicts; if the group can stay together, or — as often happens — dissolves only to regroup around another concrete basic need, it and its members will grow in consciousness and political power.'

An informed population is fundamental to the evolution of a participative political culture. Education is crucial. In Part III, 'Education and the Media', Steve Randall argues that education for empowerment — people's education — is in danger of being eclipsed by a 'skills paradigm', in which education is hierarchically controlled by 'experts' and divorced from the kinds of democratic controls that can ensure that a curriculum is relevant to the people's needs, interests and experiences. In other words, education becomes merely concerned with skills training for employment and fails to take on the wider challenge of helping pupils understand their social, economic and political environment.

In Chapter 13 David Johnson considers the implications of democracy for educational provision and argues for the democratization of school governance. Current practice reflects the policies of the National Party, namely limited participation of parents, which, in turn, led to the parent–teacher–student associations of the mid-1980s. The potential of this movement to work towards greater democracy and participation in education is considered.

In Chapter 14 Paul Fordham looks at post-school education and at the links between adult education, social activism and social justice. The recent emphasis on increasing non-white access to adult educational programmes (including literacy), as well as to undergraduate and postgraduate programmes in universities, can potentially work towards more effective political empowerment. A future educational strategy for sustainable development, based on the 1992 meeting of university-based adult educators is discussed.

Another dimension of an informed, participative political culture is a free press. In Chapter 15 Benjamin Pogrund, who is himself a distinguished and experienced South African journalist, argues that there are three fundamental requirements — a right-to-know statute giving journalists access to government information; more extensive training for journalists; and a greater awareness of the monopoly control of the established press. But it is equally important to encourage a vigorous alternative press, where there is generally a shortage of both capital and expertise. An innovative method of funding is suggested: the printing of government publications is currently controlled by two Afrikaans groups. These plants should be vested in the press, with a proportion of the income used to subsidize the alternative press. Also a role in radio and television is discussed.

The book concludes (Part IV) by considering the implications of the concept of 'sustainable development'. In Chapter 16 Barry Munslow looks at Mozambique and Angola, both of which have been ravaged by war for 30 years. Any future democratically elected government in South Africa has an enormous moral debt to the people of Mozambique and Angola. Their support for the anti-apartheid struggle turned their lands into killing fields as a result of the white minority government in South Africa's 'total strategy' of regional destabilization.

Apart from this obligation, an absolute priority for making compromises to secure sustainable development is peace. Armed groups within South Africa have to be diffused and given a role within the democratic process. For there to be sustainable development the natural resource base has to be managed in the social interest. People have to be empowered to participate in the political process, and enlightened through education to appreciate the priorities and organizational requirements of social life. Mechanisms of democratic representation and the provision of education are fundamental to achieving sustainable development.

In the final chapter, Chapter 17, Ken Cole considers policy making for sustainable development as a political process, which cannot be regarded simply as a logical, rational exercise effected by the appropriate institutions. For Cole people do not share the same social and economic priorities, and do not agree over what is, or should be, sustainable development. The dominant understanding of social objectives and organization, and of development and economic priorities, is a question of who holds the reigns of power.

Cole considers three different perspectives on sustainable development, each of which rests upon assumptions that structure research priorities, and each of which has a distinct political and ideological dimension. The implications of each of these conflicting theoretical frameworks is examined for South Africa.

However the constraints to sustainable development are defined — environmental, economic, social or political — in South Africa, the contradictions of 40 years of apartheid are fundamental. Its demise is testimony to its unsustainability. While the collapse of apartheid has piled more distress and hardship on an already overburdened people, it is also the harbinger of opportunity. The parameters of development may be politically defined, but how these opportunities are exploited to enable a desperately repressed people to begin to fulfil their potential is a question of considering the alternatives.

The balance between what is desirable and what can be, between expectations and possibility, can only be struck after careful deliberation of developmental priorities and alternatives. This book is offered as a contribution to the ongoing political process of development.

REFERENCES

Ramphele, M (ed) (1991) *Restoring the Land*, London, Panos
Wisner, B (1988) *Power and Needs in Africa*, London, Earthscan

PART I:
THE ECONOMY

Chapter One

Sustainable Growth after Sanctions: Opportunities and Constraints

Jesmond Blumenfeld

The decision to hold South Africa's first non-racial election in April 1994 means that the formal ending to the era of white minority rule, and especially the era of apartheid, is now in sight. In addition, it heralds an early end to the remaining economic and financial sanctions facing the country, and therefore raises hopes that economic recovery may once again be in prospect. South Africa does indeed have enormous economic potential, and it is a matter of common cause and observation that this potential has not been realized, that the majority of the population has been excluded from the benefits of economic growth and development, and that the need for a sustainable and more equitable pattern of growth is urgent.

It is universally accepted that agreement on a new political order is a necessary precondition for attaining both of these objectives. Whilst there is much room for debate as to whether the overall rate of economic growth would have been greater in the absence of apartheid (Lipton 1985; Lewis 1990), there is no doubt whatsoever that the highly unequal distribution of the fruits of that growth was predetermined by the white monopoly on political power. There is also no doubt that the continuing uncertainties generated by the slow, if inexorable, decline in the old political order, extending over at least the last decade, has been economically damaging. Without a political settlement, therefore, a healthy economy will remain out of reach. It is arguable that mutual recognition of this fact has been one of the major factors sustaining the political negotiations process through all the ups and downs of the past couple of years.

The ending of sanctions constitutes another precondition for full exploitation of the benefits of international economic linkages. Although the economy remained in many respects remarkably 'open' to the rest of the world even at the height of the sanctions period, the full develop-ment of many important linkages was undoubtedly inhibited. Freedom from these politically motivated constraints on South Africa's full partici-pation in the world economy must therefore bring many new oppor-tunities for foreign trade, foreign investment, and foreign economic assistance. Indeed, the lifting of sanctions is seen in many circles as providing the ultimate key to South Africa's future prosperity.

Unfortunately, however, neither the ending of apartheid nor the lift-ing of sanctions will, in themselves, be enough to ensure that growth is restored. There are far too many other factors which also have a bearing on whether South Africa can deliver on its promise and fulfil its poten-tial, and the outcome of these is still in doubt. One reason for this is the uncomfortable fact that democratization is not always a panacea for political and economic uncertainty and instability. Another reason is that the very fact of interdependence with the international economy renders every country hostage to events and forces which are beyond its control, and which can complicate or thwart the achievement of desirable objec-tives. But the primary reason is the nature of the macroeconomic inheritance which the 'old' South Africa is bequeathing to its 'new' incar-nation. This inheritance will place a number of serious objective constraints upon the options available to future policy makers, and will confront them with some immensely difficult dilemmas and conflicts.

The purpose of this chapter is to elucidate these potential difficulties and to warn against the complacent assumption that the lifting of sanctions means that sustained economic growth and, hence, a more acceptable distribution of its benefits, can be taken for granted. The message is not that these outcomes cannot be achieved. It is rather that false assumptions, and the consequent diversion of attention and effort away from necessary actions and choices, could well be instrumental in undermining the means for achieving them.

UNDERSTANDING THE CHALLENGE[1]

The expectation that the ending of South Africa's international economic isolation will create many new opportunities is both understandable and valid. The opportunities, which embrace increases in both trade and capital flows, are already yielding some important benefits. On the trade front, for example, the progressive erosion, and subsequent lifting, of most trade sanctions over the past few years has not merely allowed for

---

1 . Many of the issues touched upon in this section are dealt with more exten-sively in Blumenfeld (1993).

re-entry to traditional markets, especially in Europe and North America, where sales of South African products were inhibited by sanctions in the mid-1980s, but has also opened up the possibility of developing new export markets all over the world and which hitherto have been closed to a greater or lesser extent to South African producers for political reasons.

On the investment front, the multitude of exploratory visits from foreign corporations is testimony to the potential that they perceive not only for bi-directional trade with, but also for investment in, post-sanctions South Africa. No less important have been the investigative missions from a wide range of international financial and economic organizations seeking to identify potential targets and programmes towards which external development loans and technical assistance can be directed once the remaining financial sanctions have been lifted. These bodies include the International Monetary Fund, the World Bank, the African Development Bank, the Commonwealth Development Corporation, the US Agency for International Development and the whole family of UN agencies concerned with promoting economic and social development throughout the non-industrialized world.

If the opportunities are there, so also is the imperative for exploiting them to the full. Economic performance in South Africa has been on a declining trend since the early 1970s, with output growth, investment and especially employment all faring badly.[2] The average annual rate of growth of GDP fell from a creditable 4.9 per cent in 1947–74 to less than 1.7 per cent in 1975–92. In the past decade, the growth rate has dropped to a mere 0.8 per cent per annum With population still growing at some 2.5 per cent per annum, the stagnation of output growth means that real GDP per capita has retreated to the levels last registered in the mid-1960s. The growth rate of real gross fixed investment increased from an average of 4.8 per cent per annum in 1947–62 to 9.6 per cent in 1963–75, but then plummeted to register an average annual decline of 1.4 per cent between 1976 and 1992. In terms of the proportion of total output devoted to fixed investment, this has fallen from a post-war average of some 28 per cent to barely 16 per cent in 1992, implying that — after allowing for depreciation — virtually no net increase is now taking place in the capital stock. In employment, the rate of net job creation in the formal sector averaged 2.6 per cent per annum between 1947 and 1974, and less than 0.6 per cent per annum in 1975–92. Indeed, in 1990–92, total employment in the formal sector actually fell in absolute terms at the rate of 1.5 per cent per annum With private sector enterprises now

---

2 . The data in this paragraph are derived from Smit (1992) and from SARB(a) (various dates).

shedding jobs virtually across the board, the proportion of the labour force without formal sector employment is fast approaching 50 per cent.

The striking thing about this record of decline is not merely its depth, but also its length. Whatever may have been the precise impact of sanctions, it is abundantly clear that the onset of South Africa's downward economic spiral long predated the sanctions era. If only for this reason, any expectations that the lifting of sanctions will be sufficient to restore the impetus for growth are likely to be severely disappointed.

Nor is this simply a matter of the self-evident need to restore confidence in South Africa's political and economic prospects. Sustained domestic economic recovery and full realization of the benefits of the lifting of sanctions will remain elusive without the achievement also of major structural economic changes, the adoption of appropriate and consistent economic policies and incentives, and a strong political commitment to work for the desired ends. In the process, it will be necessary to reverse several long-standing and fundamental adverse economic trends and to abandon a number of policies which effectively have rendered the task of reintegration into the world economy much more difficult.

The requisite changes will be neither costless nor painless. Despite their general aspiration for closer economic integration with the rest of the world, South Africans have often also exhibited ambiguous attitudes and adopted ambiguous policies towards more extensive and more open external economic relations. Whether in the public or private sectors, or whether in their capacities as administrators, employers or workers, many economic actors in South Africa have long harboured — often for very different reasons — some significant suspicions and fears of foreign trade and foreign investment. For example, the deep-seated historical antipathy of the Afrikaner community towards 'imperial capital' (which was perceived as a threat to its nationalist aspirations) frequently found expression in the protectionist attitudes and policies which were instrumental in fostering the development of a domestic industrial base. More recently, the wider white community has viewed international trade and capital flows as a double-edged sword. Whilst recognizing their potential benefits, they have also been seen as providing a potential for unwelcome political leverage in the form of sanctions and disinvestment. Meanwhile, at least some of the business interests which profited both from the protectionist policies which flowed from these perceptions, and from the market opportunities which they created, are likely to have their own self-interested reservations about freer and more open links with the international economy, notwithstanding their rhetoric to the contrary.

Such ambivalence is not, however, confined to one part of the political spectrum. Other groups have shared the worldwide intellectual hostility which characterized left-wing attitudes, especially in the 1960s and 1970s, towards the prevailing international economic order in general, and the 'exploitative' role of direct foreign investment in particular. The sanctions and disinvestment debates revealed that, for many blacks, particularly in the trades unions, foreign trade and foreign investment were perceived simultaneously as the instruments of oppression and of liberation.

It would be naïve to assume that all these perceptions and reservations will disappear at a stroke simply because the political context has changed. On the contrary, they will need to be addressed and overcome at the levels of both government and individual enterprise, and the outcomes will need to be reflected in observable changes in attitudes, actions and policies. Moreover, the changing political and economic environment will bring new perceptions of the balance between threats and opportunities relating to international economic linkages. Amongst other things, therefore, if the benefits are to be maximized, it may well prove necessary to confront (or to compensate) the substantial political and economic interest groups that derive benefit from the current situation and that might therefore prove resistant to change.

But policy and attitudinal changes alone will not suffice. There is also the need to resolve three distinct, but interrelated, structural problems in the South African economy. One of these problems manifests itself in the form of a balance of payments constraint; the second as an employment problem; and the third as an inappropriate production technology (or 'factor proportions') problem.

Put simply, the balance of payments problem is that South Africa's exports of goods and services have never been sufficient to pay for its import requirements on a sustained basis.[3] Moreover, increased economic growth invariably seems to exacerbate rather than diminish the imbalance, the reason being that, on average, production processes in South Africa make very extensive use of imported goods and services (Kahn 1991: 67–72). The main implication is that the balance of payments acts as a constraint on economic growth, in the sense that growth cannot be sustained for any length of time unless sufficient inflows of foreign capital can be secured to bridge the rising gap between the foreign

---

3 . This statement is unambiguously valid for the period since the Second World War. It is also unambiguously true of the balance between total imports and *non-gold* exports in the pre-war period. However, for the majority of years in the 1920s and 1930s, total exports *including* gold did exceed total imports (Central Statistical Service 1988: Table 16.3).

currency costs of imports and the foreign currency earnings from exports.

The employment problem, as the record indicates, has been reflected in the long-term decline in the capacity of the economy to create employment on a scale sufficient to absorb the growing labour force. This has been partly the result of the declining rate of investment, since — outside the state bureaucracy — investment is the primary means for creating jobs. But it is also due to the 'factor proportions' problem which exists in the sense that the degree of capital-intensity (as opposed to labour-intensity) in production technologies in South Africa has always seemed inappropriately high, given the country's evident labour-abundance (Levy 1992: 3).

The three problems are interlinked, not least via their external economic dimensions. Resolution of the balance of payments problem demands that South Africa produce many more goods for export, whilst reducing the growth rate of imports. In seeking to achieve these outcomes, however, there are also risks of conflicts with attempts to resolve the employment and factor proportions problems. The latter problems demand that investment be resumed on a major scale in labour-intensive industries, so that many new jobs will be created and more labour will be utilized per unit of capital than has been the case in the past. The difficulty is, however, that South Africa's export strengths have traditionally lain in sectors that are highly capital-intensive. Thus, an emphasis on expanding exports would create relatively little employment (Harvey and Jenkins 1992: 25–6, 31–2).

Conversely, concentrating scarce investment resources in more labour-intensive activities could also prejudice the balance of payments both directly and indirectly: it could divert resources away from production of tradable towards non-tradable goods, causing production of both exports and import substitutes to fall; and it could reduce South Africa's competitiveness if the technologies adopted for tradable goods production were not best-practice technologies, thus leading to higher unit costs of production relative to costs in other producer countries. These adverse balance of payments effects would be compounded if the labour-intensive activities concerned also proved to be relatively highly import-intensive. This is no idle danger, since there is only a limited domestic capacity to produce capital goods of any degree of sophistication (Kaplan 1991).

Indeed, the heavy reliance of South African production in general on imported capital goods, intermediate goods and raw materials suggests that, even in seeking to expand exports, an initial — if only temporary — worsening of the balance of payments constraint may be unavoidable, on account of the prior need to increase imports of these inputs. In principle, it is possible to borrow the foreign currency needed to finance the extra imports, and to repay the loans out of the subsequent enhanced export earnings. But, in practice, even here there are potential constraints.[4] Moreover, as is discussed further below, the obstacles to the expansion of exports on the required scale may be greater than is commonly appreciated.

There is, of course, no a priori reason why all these conflicts and adverse consequences should materialize. But the converse also holds: there is no automatic mechanism to guarantee a favourable outcome. Moreover, South Africa starts from the de facto position in which there is already a conflict between exports and employment. This is evident not only from the observable fact that past export growth has not been accompanied by employment growth, but also from the fact that many of South Africa's existing producers of tradable and potentially exportable goods are relatively inefficient and, hence, internationally uncompetitive. The classic example of this is to be found in the garment and textile industries, which have grown up behind protective barriers which have shielded producers from foreign competition (Levy 1992). In the interests of increased exports, therefore, it may well yet prove necessary to destroy many existing jobs in these firms to enable them to survive in world markets.

This dilemma is by no means unique to South Africa: many different firms and governments in many different countries face the same dilemmas, usually all for much the same reasons. But the dilemma seems particularly cruel in South Africa's case, where the legacy of apartheid would seem to demand that as many jobs as possible should be preserved. In principle, the process of adjustment should lead eventually to increased employment and greater prosperity as economic efficiency increases and scarce resources, especially of investment capital, become better utilized. However, the affected workers in existing firms are likely to prefer some jam today rather than the promise of more jam tomorrow, not least because the extra jam cannot be guaranteed and because they may not be the recipients. If only for these reasons, implementing

---

4. On the one hand, South Africa is now widely regarded as being 'under-borrowed', in the sense that the ratios of its total foreign debt to such variables as GDP and annual exports are low by comparison with those of many other borrowing countries. On the other hand, the existing stock of $17 billion of foreign debt which has to be serviced and repaid places clear limits on the capacity for additional borrowing in the short term (CSSAEIF November 1992: 10–11).

'structural adjustments' of this nature is bound to be a politically sensitive matter.

In short, all three of the balance of payments, employment and factor proportions problems are of very long standing, extending back in time to the origins and nature of modern economic development in South Africa. In that sense, they are 'structural' problems, the existence of which cannot be attributed directly to — though, in different ways, all three were aggravated by — the existence of apartheid and of sanctions. Thus, as with the low propensity to invest, none will be resolved simply by the elimination of apartheid or the lifting of sanctions. Instead, to overcome them, South Africa will need to devise and implement policies and achieve structural economic changes that will simultaneously promote exports, reduce imports, create employment, and change the technological bias in production, and all on a hitherto unprecedented scale. As noted earlier, the required tasks, though daunting, are not impossible to achieve. Moreover, the political changes now taking place offer the opportunity for all these problems to be tackled with renewed vigour and without the added complications and encumbrances of arbitrarily imposed political obstacles either at home or abroad. The remainder of this chapter is therefore devoted to exploring and illustrating some of these opportunities and difficulties in the specific case of exports.

THE EXPORT CHALLENGE[5]

Whilst the creation of jobs is likely to be the most critical domestic economic policy issue for the new South Africa, the key challenge on the international front will probably lie in the imperative of finding ways to strengthen exports. Economic growth in the past has frequently been export-led and, given the balance of payments constraint, export performance will remain one of the most crucial determinants of growth.

Traditionally, South Africa has relied heavily on exports of minerals, especially gold, for the bulk of its export earnings. Indeed, there have been several occasions when fortuitous increases in the international price of gold have afforded much-needed relief from serious balance of payments difficulties. In the past decade, however, the role of gold has declined markedly. Previously, gold typically accounted for some 30 to 35 per cent of total (ie visible plus invisible) export earnings. By 1992, however, earnings from gold exports had fallen to less than 23 per cent of total export revenues. More importantly, in absolute terms, the foreign

---

5 . See Blumenfeld (1992, 1993) for further discussions of the export dilemma.

exchange earned from gold exports in 1992 was barely half the $13 billion earned at the height of the gold boom in 1980. Though gold clearly will remain the single largest export earner for some time to come, further gold bonanzas, whilst not impossible, are certainly improbable. Thus South Africa needs to adjust to a permanently lower proportionate, if not also absolute, contribution to foreign currency earnings from gold sales.

The inescapable implication of the above figures is that non-gold merchandise exports will have to increase at an even more rapid pace than in the past. Broadly speaking, non-gold exports can be divided into two distinct categories, namely commodities and manufactures. Post-sanctions, South Africa indisputably has the opportunity to improve its export performance in each of these categories.[6] However, the increase in opportunity seems least prominent in the case of commodity exports, most of which were largely unaffected by sanctions.[7] Whilst the opening up of new market possibilities, for example for minerals and mineral products in South and East Asia, will certainly help it remains true that the market for commodity exports is concentrated in the major industrialized countries. Consequently, export growth in this broad category will continue to be determined primarily by the rate of growth in the industrialized world, rather than by the presence or absence of sanctions. As is well known, the outlook for the world economy is currently relatively subdued, implying the likelihood of relatively slow growth in world demand for commodities, at least in the short term.

Moreover, there are two other considerations which may limit any increase in export earnings from this source. The first is the potential for

---

6 . There is, of course, a further source of export earnings in the form of services (such as tourism, insurance and freight) and other non-merchandise 'invisible' earnings (such as dividend and interest remittances on foreign investment and foreign lending). It is widely acknowledged that South Africa's tourist potential is still relatively undeveloped, especially in the lucrative developed country markets. Equally, as South Africa's *rapprochement* with the rest of Africa intensifies, it has the potential to act both as a major regional, even sub-continental, centre for the provision of financial and other business services, and as a major supplier of capital, especially in the form of fixed investment. Undoubtedly, therefore, there exists considerable scope for increased earnings from these sources. Valuable though these additional earnings will be, they are unlikely to make more than a relatively small overall contribution to net export earnings in the foreseeable future.

7. Only iron and steel products, agricultural products and gold coins were seriously affected by import bans in Europe and North America. Coal exports also suffered, but more on account of the 'political discount' which South African exporters had to offer to retain their market shares than as a result of actual sanctions.

competition from the former Eastern Bloc countries, which produce many of the same commodities as does South Africa. The second is the 'terms of trade problem', reflected in the general tendency for increases in world commodity prices to lag behind the increases in prices of industrial goods. Despite some important exceptions, for example in the case of diamonds and some strategic minerals, this rule applies also to South Africa's terms of trade, as measured by the ratio of the index of all export prices, excluding gold, to the index of all import prices. Taking 1985 as the base year, the index of South Africa's non-gold terms of trade has fallen from 165 in 1960 to 104 in 1992 (SARB(b): Table 4). The effect of a decline in the terms of trade is to require an ever-larger increase in export volumes in order to pay for the same volume of imports. The implication of this combination of circumstances is that, important though they will remain, commodity exports alone are unlikely to produce increases in export earnings on a scale anywhere near sufficient to relieve South Africa's balance of payments constraint. This conclusion will apply with even greater force if a resumption of economic growth in South Africa leads, as would be expected, to a large increase in the demand for imports.

It follows that hopes for future export growth must rest to a significant extent on the ability to diversify the export base. In essence, this means the expansion of manufactured exports. South Africa's policy makers have long harboured hopes that the country would one day join the select ranks of the so-called NICs — the newly industrialized developing countries, typified by South Korea, Taiwan, Singapore, Hong Kong and Brazil — which have all become major exporters of manufactures by pursuing deliberate strategies of export promotion. But, despite several past policy initiatives, South Africa still lags well behind the NICs in respect of the share of manufactures in total exports (Lewis 1990: 57–8). Indeed, manufactured exports have performed relatively poorly in the past two decades, having fallen from 37 per cent of total visible exports (including gold) in 1968 to 29 per cent in 1981, before recovering to 37 per cent again by 1987 (Kahn 1991: 72–3). In short, in proportionate terms, exports of manufactures are still in the minority and have — at best — stood still over the last 25 years.

One obvious route to raising the profile of manufactured exports is via further minerals 'beneficiation', namely the achievement of higher value-added through pre-export processing of minerals into semi-processed products. The much-vaunted Columbus stainless steel and Alusaf aluminium smelter schemes clearly fall into this category.

On paper, the potential for such projects is considerable, but they need to be seen as part of a long-term solution, rather than as some form of 'quick fix', and they are not without their risks. Whilst the Columbus scheme is in the fortunate position of being able to make use of some existing productive capacity, beneficiation schemes in general can be expected to require very substantial capital investments. The latter, in turn, will not only involve high financing costs (probably including large-scale borrowing from abroad), but are likely to generate very big increases in imports whilst creating relatively few jobs. Thus, their benefits will be derived largely from their export earning potential. If South Africa can demonstrate a long-term competitive advantage in the processing of minerals, then such investments will clearly make good sense. Unfortunately, many world minerals markets currently have excess production capacity — a fact which makes investments in new capacity even more risky. There is no question but that South African producers must — and will — seek to travel the local processing route, but given the scale of the investment needed, and the likely political and economic risks involved, it would be a mistake to rely on early materialization of the benefits.

An alternative route to diversification would be via the increased manufacture and export of finished consumer goods and capital goods. In many respects, it is in this direction that South Africa's biggest challenge lies. On the one hand, as the experience of those countries that have successfully made the transition to NIC status shows, the opportunities would seem to be almost limitless. South Africa's modern industrial sector, technological capabilities and efficient infrastructure should enable it to establish secure footholds for manufactured exports in many world markets, especially once any lingering inhibitions due to sanctions have finally disappeared.[8]

On the other hand, there are some major obstacles to be overcome in realizing these potentials. First, creeping protectionism in the industrialized countries over the past decade has made it harder for new producers to penetrate many developed country markets. This hurdle would be partly overcome if the long-running multilateral GATT (General Agreement on Tariffs and Trade) negotiations could be brought to a successful conclusion, since this would reinforce the earlier presumption that inter-

---

8 . It is often argued that South Africa's location in relation to the rest of Africa, and its understanding of the needs and problems of other semi-industrialized countries, also make it an ideal potential large-scale supplier of manufactures to many of these markets in the absence of trade sanctions. Whilst the underlying reasoning is correct, the short-term growth potential has probably been overstated, not least because — especially in the case of Africa — significant volumes of covert trade were already taking place before the lifting of sanctions. See Blumenfeld (1993) for further discussion of this point.

national trade should be conducted on a largely non-discriminatory basis. But with the developed world now organizing itself into major regional trade blocs, most notably the European Union (EU) and the North American Free Trade Agreement (NAFTA), market access for countries like South Africa has become increasingly contingent upon separate, often bilateral, negotiations which are less firmly based on non-discriminatory principles. Whilst this fact clearly does not preclude South Africa from entering, and successfully concluding, such negotiations, it does mean that there are significant diplomatic hurdles which could take some time to clear, with the outcomes being highly uncertain. Moreover, negotiations presuppose the existence of a legitimate government with an agreed and coherent set of policies towards the conduct of foreign trade (Page and Stevens 1992). Regrettably, South Africa is still some way — possibly a long way — from being in this position.

An even more fundamental handicap derives from the legacy of prior economic and political policies within South Africa itself. As noted earlier, much of South Africa's industry was developed behind protective barriers and, as a result, is inefficient by international standards. Low productivity and high unit labour costs of production have made exports uncompetitive. One index of this lies in the small proportion — only one-eighth — of total manufacturing output that is exported (Levy 1992: Table 2.8). This situation was aggravated by the labour policies of the apartheid era which, in seeking to deliver supposedly 'cheap' labour, severely prejudiced the productivity of the workforce by depriving it of skills, training, motivation and a stake in the system (amongst other things). Moreover, by concentrating wealth in the hands of the few, apartheid also had an adverse impact on efficiency in that production was necessarily restricted to a small scale due to the limited size of the domestic markets.

It is this competitiveness problem which is likely to prove most daunting in the battle to improve export performance in manufactures. Improving efficiency in manufacturing industry poses both political and economic challenges even in the best of circumstances, but threatens to create some especially painful dilemmas for policy making in post-apartheid South Africa. Increased competitiveness requires a reduction in production costs per unit of output, or greater productivity per unit of input (or both). South Africa's poor productivity record during the apartheid era clearly offers enormous scope for improvement, but this is likely to require substantial prior investment, both in new technologies and in training.

On the cost side, there are both political and economic conflicts to be resolved. Wage increases cannot be allowed to run ahead of productivity increases. Yet the inequalities and depredations of the past have accorded political urgency to the need to raise the real wages of black workers. Indeed, this has been a primary objective of the black trades unions, and one in which they have so far had considerable success: the index of hourly compensation in manufacturing in South Africa rose from 100 in 1975 to 550 in 1987, far outstripping the comparable figures for virtually all the OECD (Organization for Economic Cooperation and Development) countries. But the faster rise in wages has not been matched by larger increases in productivity. Over the same period, the corresponding rise in labour productivity was significantly lower in South Africa. Convincing the unions that achieving a reversal of these trends will have to be a priority for future policy is therefore likely to require considerable political adroitness.

In theory, an improvement in international competitiveness in manufacturing could be achieved by allowing the rand to depreciate against foreign currencies and then ensuring that the consequent cost advantages are not eroded through increases in wages in the relevant industries. But this strategy would be fraught with difficulties. A devaluation would increase the profits from minerals and other commodity exports, and workers in these sectors would surely resist any efforts to restrain their earnings. Moreover, a devaluation would raise the cost of imported goods and services and, because of the high import content of domestic production, would thereby quickly raise the cost of living for all workers. Manufacturing employees would thus have to be persuaded to accept a fall in their absolute levels of real wages as well as a fall relative to workers in the traditional export sectors.

Yet none of these changes would be of lasting value unless they were accompanied by meaningful reductions in the level of protection accorded to South Africa's manufacturing industries. However, as noted earlier, exposing existing inefficient producers of tradable goods to greater competition from abroad necessarily involves putting substantial numbers of jobs at risk. In circumstances in which employment creation is already at a premium, it would require a brave — some might say foolhardy — government to pursue such a strategy. This point, perhaps more than any other, neatly encapsulates the dilemmas involved in seeking to take advantage of the new opportunities which will be presented by the ending of sanctions.

CONCLUSION

The restrictions which were placed on the participation of South African enterprises in the international economy under sanctions were primarily the result of external political pressures arising from the existence of apartheid. However, the common belief that sanctions and apartheid were the main sources of South Africa's disastrous economic perform-ance in recent years and, hence, that their removal is all that is needed to guarantee a return to prosperity, is erroneous.

Against this, after such a long period of economic stagnation and decline, the need to extract the maximum potential gains from uninhibi-ted commerce with the world economy is indeed urgent. To the extent that establishment of the necessary conditions will depend crucially on domestic actions and policies, both sustained recovery and full interna-tional reintegration are realistically attainable objectives. But achieving these outcomes is unlikely to prove easy and certainly cannot be taken for granted. At the minimum, they will require a reasonable degree of political stability, sensible and realistic policies, and wise and deter-mined leadership.

Nor can it really be expected that the outside world will bear more than a small part of the underlying political and financial burdens of undertaking the necessary adjustments. Those who consider that the international community was complicit in imposing the burden of apart-heid on black South Africa and that it therefore owes the victims a living are likely to be sorely disappointed by the scale of assistance that will be forthcoming in practice. Whatever the moral force of their argument, the reality is that the 'new' South Africa will have to earn its own place in the sun.

REFERENCES

Blumenfeld, J (1992) 'The international dimension', in Schrire, qv

—— (1994) *South Africa in the World Economy*, Johannesburg, South African Institute of International Affairs

Central Statistical Service (1988) *South African Statistics 1988*, Pretoria, Government Printer

CSSAEIF (LSE Centre for the Study of the South African Economy and International Finance) (1992) *Quarterly Report*, November

Gelb, S (1991) *South Africa's Economic Crisis*, Cape Town, David Philip

Harvey, C and Jenkins, C (1992) 'The Unorthodox Response of the South African Economy to Changes in Macroeconomic Policy', *IDS Discussion Paper*, no 300, Institute of Development Studies, University of Sussex

Kahn, B (1991) 'The Crisis and South Africa's Balance of Payments', in Gelb, qv

Kaplan, D (1991) 'The South African Capital Goods Sector and the Economic Crisis', in Gelb, qv

Levy, B (1992) 'How Can South African Manufacturing Efficiently Create Employment? An Analysis of the Impact of Trade and Industrial Policy', Informal Discussion Papers on Aspects of the Economy of South Africa, Paper No 1, Southern Africa Department, World Bank

Lewis, S R Jr (1990) *The Economics of Apartheid*, New York, Council on Foreign Relations

Lipton, M (1985) *Capitalism and Apartheid*, Aldershot, Gower Publishing Company

Meth, C (1990) 'Capital Goods, "Dependence" and Appropriate Technology', in Nattrass and Ardington, qv

Nattrass, N and Ardington, E (1990) *The Political Economy of South Africa*, Cape Town, Oxford University Press

Page, S and Stevens, C (1992) *Trading with South Africa: The Policy Options for the EC*, London, Overseas Development Institute

SARB(a) (South African Reserve Bank), *Quarterly Bulletin*, various issues

—— (b) (South African Reserve Bank), 'South Africa's Balance of Payments 1946–1992', supplement to *Quarterly Bulletin*, June 1993

Schrire, R (1992) *Wealth or Poverty? Critical Choices for South Africa*, Cape Town, Oxford University Press

Smit, B (1992) 'Secular Trends in South African Macroeconomic Data', in Schrire, qv

Chapter Two

The World Bank, Income Distribution and Employment: Some Lessons for South Africa

Colin Stoneman

Even with significant state intervention to realign spending in South Africa in favour of black education, health, housing, and to some extent job creation, most black people will remain miserably poor for the fore-seeable future under orthodox economic policies. This can be stated with confidence — unless a sustained growth rate of the order of 10 per cent per annum can be achieved — a very unlikely possibility.

The cost of 'creating a job' that will be internationally competitive in South Africa is probably about R100,000. With an increase in the work force of about 3.3 per cent per annum, about 800,000 per year, it would require new investment of R80 billion (that is about 36 per cent of GDP) merely to employ the annual increment — plainly an impossibility.

Orthodox policies, as currently being presented as 'the only alternative' by the World Bank, the International Monetary Fund (IMF) and the National Party, will prove disastrous for all but the elites (including a new one). To make a real impact on South Africa's economic problems requires imaginative and radical solutions. There are some pointers to the dimensions of an alternative approach in the record of Zimbabwe in the period between 1984 (when it rejected IMF policies) and 1990, when social spending was maintained and GDP growth averaged over 4 per cent a year.

ECONOMIC ORTHODOXY

'Structural adjustment' sounds to be a good idea in the face of the horrors of an apartheid-structured society or the corrupt, inefficient, one-party, state-dominated dictatorships so common in Africa until recently, and still not extinct. But I would argue that such cases merely provide a pretext for imposing a single economic strategy worldwide, irrespective of whether countries were actually this unacceptable socially, or unsuccessful economically. Having been freed of the fear of Stalinist totalitarianism, we are now faced with the actuality of a worldwide market totalitarianism to which no exceptions are tolerated.

All markets are interfered with by governments (and other actors), and what is new about the 'new world order' is that for the first time there is a single unchallenged authority with the financial power to lay down *which* interventions are acceptable. Policies previously regarded as purely the business of individual countries and not the outside world, such as infant-industry protection, subsidies on basic foods, the balance between the state and the private sector, funding policies for education, health and other social services, to say nothing of trade and exchange-rate policies, are now routinely regarded as subject to influence if not outright determination by the World Bank and the IMF. This is not just a matter of denying countries the right to make their own mistakes, to prefer different choices to outsiders, it is also denying them the right to use the very policies of import-substituting industrialization, protection, subsidization and state intervention that are widely accepted to have been instrumental in bringing about the success of late developing countries, such as Germany in the last century, and the newly industrialized countries (NICs) in this.[1]

The metaphor of 'pulling up the ladder after us' may seem apt, until it is pointed out that the powerful are still using these policies: the Japanese and South Korean markets are still very closed to imports and investment, the Multi-Fibres Agreement (which places quotas on textile and clothing imports from Third-World countries) is still in force, and Europe still subsidizes its farmers — but then tells Zimbabwe that it must reduce its subsidies (which are in any case necessary mainly because of the dumping of excess European grain on the world market).

But what were those failed policies that structural adjustment is seeking to reverse, and why were they instituted? In fact they derive from post-colonial attempts to restructure economies away from the inherited colonial structures which featured extreme inequalities of wealth and income internally and external relations that were characterized by free trade with a metropolitan power.

---

1 . This was for some time denied by World Bank ideologists, but in the face of the evidence they appear to have dropped the issue. For South Korea see Amsden (1989); for Singapore see the *Financial Times* 'Survey on Singapore', 29 March 1993, p. 1.

This was the course most ex-colonies embarked on when they eventually obtained independence. To be sure, many of them failed to break the colonial pattern, and some even created worse structures involving corruption, repression and destitution for the majority of their populations. But some succeeded.

The wholesale imposition of structural adjustment should thus best be seen as a return to the former colonial relationship, this time taking a multilateral form, but no less disadvantageous to the peripheral countries. It is in this sense that some analysts have begun using the term 'recolonization' to describe the impact of structural adjustment in the 1980s and early 1990s.

It Has Also Been Largely Unsuccessful

The new policy shift began with the publication in 1981 of the 'Berg Report' (World Bank 1981), which argued that the problems of sub-Saharan African countries were largely self-inflicted, through an over-emphasis on the state, neglect of agriculture, suppression of markets, over-valued currencies and corruption. Only in the sequels (World Bank 1984 and 1989) was the influence of deteriorating terms of trade, rising oil prices, and the debt crisis given more than passing reference.

Few would now claim that defence of currencies at ten or more times their value on the world market is sensible policy, nor that states — least of all states with scarce resources of skills — should try to substitute for the market across a wide range of economic activities rather than making strategic interventions.[2] But the package contains other elements, including the liberalization of the trade and foreign exchange regimes, privatization, an end to subsidies (even if affordable), and a general minimization of the state's role. And of course they have been forced on countries like Zimbabwe, which already had a good record on the earlier less contentious parts of the package, as well as on countries that did not.

The result has been that the record of structural adjustment has been dubious at best and in some countries disastrous, despite the sensible ingredients. In the late 1980s the World Bank, having proclaimed that success for the policies had been demonstrated by Ghana[3] and later

---

2. However, it did not take the World Bank to tell this to even the most state-oriented countries such as Angola and Mozambique. The latter's president, Samora Machel, made his famous 'The state does not sell matches' speech in 1981 before the Berg Report was published.
3. As Ghana was seen to be growing at 5 per cent per annum on the basis of net inflows of 5 per cent of GDP, it is pertinent to ask whether it was the new policies or the reward for adopting them that was producing the growth. As after five years Ghana was still not in a position to repay the accumulated debt,

Tanzania, decided that wider demonstrations were needed and published a continent-wide survey (World Bank/UNDP 1989), which after omission of special cases showed a small average increase in GDP growth for adjusting countries. The United Nations Economic Commission for Africa reworked the World Bank figures with different (and in my view more plausible) criteria as to which were non-adjusters or adjusters, and as to which were special cases, and got the opposite result. The issue is therefore unresolved, and in no way can the World Bank claim that the statistics clearly support its case (Parfitt 1990). Clearly a number of World Bank personnel have lost faith in structural adjustment, and much press comment has been along the lines of how much the World Bank needs an unequivocal success story.

Zimbabwe was chosen for this role for two reasons: first it was an embarrassing advertisement for alternative policies, with even the US ambassador to Zimbabwe, James Rawlings, speaking in September 1988 of the USA's 'recognition that Zimbabwe's economy is healthy and dynamic with the potential for greater growth based on the successes of the past' (Economist Intelligence Unit 1988: 26); second this very success, especially the balance of payments surplus and the manageable debt, meant that structural adjustment would be applied in a context with fewer problems than was usual in adjusting countries. Zimbabwe therefore came under severe pressure to liberalize in the late 1980s as we see below. In March 1991, after it began what it claimed was a 'home-grown' economic structural adjustment programme (known locally as ESAP), the World Bank resident representative in Zimbabwe, Christian Poortman, incautiously argued that because of its earlier dynamic economic performance 'Zimbabwe could be the first to succeed with such reforms' (Economist Intelligence Unit, 1991: 13).

Successful alternatives have been largely ignored or drummed into line
That the main impetus for forcing countries to reform is ideological rather than economic or democratic is supported by two examples relating to Zimbabwe. The British government was widely criticized in 1988 for advancing large sums to the military dictatorship in Nigeria, whilst denying any programme aid to Zimbabwe, despite its better political, economic and human rights record. The response of Margaret Thatcher's government was twofold: Nigeria had promised to reform in five years'

---

it had the loans rescheduled and continued receiving net flows worth 5 per cent of GDP. Two further questions are posed: how long must this process continue before the country can begin to service its own debts? And how does this experience differ from the profligate borrowing to sustain earlier policies so criticized by the World Bank?

time;[4] and Zimbabwe did 'not have an IMF programme'. The latter point discloses the real motivations. Zimbabwe had no IMF programme because, like Botswana (which was not under pressure), it did not need one, although it did need programmes of development-oriented finance then denied it by both Britain and the USA and restricted by the World Bank.

The second example in fact concerns the World Bank, which in 1982 had lent Zimbabwe US $70 million to set up an export-revolving fund (ERF)[5] to promote exports of manufactured goods, no doubt seeing this as part of a process of reintegrating Zimbabwe into the world market. Unfortunately for its strategic aims, Zimbabwe made a great success of manufactured exports in a context which, after March 1984, reverted to being one of controlled trade. Negotiations for an expanded fund went through all the technical stages easily. But after a long delay in Washington, without any technical problems being raised, nor any doubts being cast on the potential of Zimbabwe to benefit from the loan, it was finally vetoed for ideological reasons at the highest levels of the bank. The last thing that the World Bank wanted to happen was for Zimbabwe to succeed with 'the wrong policies'.[6] Only when Zimbabwe agreed to liberalize trade would it get the funds (although in such a context such funds become irrelevant). The 'threat of a good example' (Melrose 1985) was diminished.

CONSEQUENCES: THE 50 PER CENT SOLUTION

What Open Market Policies Imply for Economic Development

As well as enforcing prudent economic policies, structural adjustment brings an end to most areas of discretion in economic policy, whether revolutionary experimentation, reactionary projects like apartheid, or even cautious attempts to change structures through the state in time-

---

4. In fact in 1992 after six years of structural adjustment its total external debt at US $29 billion was 113 per cent of GDP, debt-service arrears were US $3.4 billion and there was a debt-service ratio of about 70 per cent before rescheduling (*Financial Times*, 'Survey on Nigeria', 1 April 1993). Meanwhile elections between two parties approved by the military are scheduled for 1993.

5. ERFs ensure that potential exporters do not fail to produce because they have inadequate foreign exchange to purchase needed inputs. Whatever the general foreign exchange constraint, a firm export order wins the right to import essential inputs, the foreign exchange costs of which are then reimbursed from the export earnings.

6. Relations between Zimbabwe and the World Bank are discussed in more detail in Stoneman (1989).

honoured fashion. Policies that will be constrained include programmes of regional integration, because component states will have little scope for reducing tariff barriers to each other, or giving other preferences, if they have already been obliged to open up to world markets. Similarly it will be harder to protect infant industries, escape from primary-product dependence and create new comparative advantages, for these things involve looking ahead to future markets and the prices they would throw up, whereas obeying today's market signals means accepting today's comparative advantages in what are usually relatively unprofitable areas (that is what it means to be underdeveloped) and today's comparative disadvantages in profitable areas.

What Open Market Policies Imply for Investment and Employment

It is popularly claimed on the basis of neo-classical theory[7] that acceptance of world prices will promote foreign investment that is keen to exploit the resources — in particular cheap labour — of developing countries. To some extent this is true, as shown by the experience of some export-processing zones (EPZs) like Mauritius. Yet out of over 200 EPZs worldwide, the number of clear successes can be counted on the fingers of one hand. This shows that there is probably a market only for a tiny fraction of the type of goods that very cheap labour could produce, and with the entry of India and China into this area it is decreasingly likely that any African country could gain significant benefits from this market.

In fact most foreign investment promotes what it is most familiar with, namely modern capital-intensive technology. This technology is designed in rich countries, where US $50,000 is the average cost of an internationally competitive job. The process of bringing it into poor countries may be necessary if the latter are to compete in export markets where high quality and consistency are essential.

But if open policies therefore require investment with First-World technology and capital–labour ratios in export industries, they also impose them in the domestic market. To achieve employment for the annual increment to the labour force by these means would imply spending R100,000 on each of some 800,000 new workers or R80 billion, some 36 per cent of GDP — or 48 per cent if we add the 12 per cent or so needed to make good depreciation. This high an investment ratio is plainly an impossibility. Even if we assume that each 'international' job creates two others for a quarter the cost in related downstream and

---

7 . In particular the Hecksher–Ohlin theorem.

service industries (ie the average cost per job falls to R50,000), an investment ratio of 30 per cent is still needed. It is in fact extremely optimistic to expect that a 30 per cent investment ratio would indeed produce enough jobs (it would also imply a steady growth rate of at least 6 per cent annually), but it is also over-optimistic to believe that 30 per cent would be achievable at a time of expectations of much higher educational and health expenditure. Note furthermore that even this huge effort would merely stop unemployment rising above the present unacceptable levels. The actual outcome is much more likely to be closer to what actually occurred in both South Africa and Zimbabwe in the 1980s when barely 10 per cent of school leavers found jobs.[8]

Why a '50 per cent' Solution is Likely

Thus even employing 50 per cent of school leavers would be a startlingly good result for orthodox economic policies, and reading their strategy documents[9] it is clear that they would see it as such. The other 50 per cent (or they might well be two-thirds as in Latin America) would be thrown back onto subsistence in the rural areas, the Bantustans, the urban informal sector, or simply unemployment and crime.

Lewis's elegant model (Lewis 1954) has not come about in practice; indeed how can the market deal with a problem that lies outside it?[10] If unemployed people receive no income and exert no effective demand, the market has no information on whether they constitute 50 per cent of the population, or 60 per cent, or 90 per cent. So the equilibrium it reaches may be optimal for the lucky 50 per cent (or 40 per cent or 10 per cent) who happen to be inside already, but clearly not for the population as a whole. Investment to provide the right type of affordable jobs for the whole population is therefore primarily a *political*, not an economic, decision.

Alternatives: Some Lessons from the Experience of Zimbabwe

In the face of a situation in which a bankrupt orthodoxy nevertheless holds nearly all the levers of power, alternative policies need to be

---

8 . Although in South Africa the ratio was falling to 7 per cent, whilst in Zimbabwe it was rising to about 20 per cent.
9 . Such as McGregor (1990). However, the recent Nedcor–Old Mutual report (Tucker and Scott 1990) takes the measure of the scale of the problem, although its proposals for a solution involving a 'job corps' are very limited.
10 . The only linkage is through the supposed effect of the unemployed driving down wages so that profits and investment rise and new jobs are created. Clearly the leakages from this benign cycle have proved nearly complete in practice.

carefully tailored. It is not enough to show that alternative strategies are both theoretically possible and historically successful (which I attempt to illustrate in the next section); in addition the basic agenda of the international financial institutions — to create a single world market — needs to be confronted.

The Success of Zimbabwe in the 1980s

Zimbabwe's economic success in the 1980s provides good evidence for the existence of an alternative to the orthodoxy. During the 1980s GDP growth in Zimbabwe averaged over 4 per cent, about three times that in South Africa or in Africa as a whole. Furthermore, it was if anything faster in the second half of the decade, so, contrary to some suggestions, there is little evidence that the experiment was 'running out of steam'.[11] Over the decade, and particularly since March 1984 after the decision to terminate an IMF programme, Zimbabwe diversified exports in the direction of manufactures, repaid its debts without resort to rescheduling, expanded education and health services, created food security sufficient to enable it to ride out the devastating drought of 1987 without imports — and all this in face of a daunting battery of constraints, including destabilization, rigged export markets, donor hostility and four drought years.

Nevertheless, it is not the intention to claim that the Zimbabwean record is wholly positive.[12] The successes were coupled with a failure to create enough jobs, to implement redistribution, especially of land, to plan meaningfully, to work out fully government's role in industrial and trade policy, and to respond quickly and appropriately to shocks.[13] The constraints were serious enough, but mistakes were made in responding to them that often made their consequences worse than they need have been.

Depackaging Structural Adjustment

How then do we explain this significant (albeit somewhat mixed) success in such difficult circumstances? It is not simply a matter of Zimbabwe being a non-adjuster; in some respects it followed very conservative financial policies after the initial profligacy of the first three years. The over-borrowing did not at the time seem inappropriate in view of the

---

11 . This is not to say that reforms were not needed (Riddell 1990: 395).
12 . The first three years of Zimbabwe's independence saw serious over-borrowing, much of it unproductive in the short run, resulting in the debt crisis of the late 1980s, when the debt-service ratio approached 40 per cent.
13 . The importance of the last factor was pointed out to me by Carolyn Jenkins.

initial growth rate of 10 per cent, but when this declined with the world slump and the beginning of the drought of 1982–84, a balance of payments crisis forced the signing of an IMF programme in 1982. But as the economic situation worsened (1983 showed a 3.6 per cent decline in GDP), so did the balance of payments, and in March 1984 Zimbabwe returned to direct foreign exchange controls knowing that this would bring an end to the IMF facility after only a third of it had been drawn down. It then pursued a home-grown structural adjustment programme, which soon restored external balance. From then on the Reserve Bank of Zimbabwe maintained a realistic value for the Zimbabwe dollar by relating it to a 'trade-weighted basket' of imports and exports,[14] and a substantial trade surplus was engineered by tight import controls so as to repay the earlier debts. New borrowing was tightly monitored so that the debt-service ratio was reduced from nearly 40 per cent to under 25 per cent.

Although the state continued to play an active role, controlling prices and wage levels, most enterprise remained in private hands, and markets continued to operate in wide areas of the economy. For instance the Zimbabwe Stock Exchange flourished in the late 1980s, with its industrial index rising in real terms faster than any in the world for two years.

But if it can therefore be seen that, although Zimbabwe accepted the first half of a structural adjustment package — basically the stabilization part which amounts to little more than a prudent adaptation to external realities — it set its face firmly against later parts. In particular, it continued to control imports and foreign exchange, which can be seen as an essential part of a policy of import-substitution industrialization (ISI), and also (as in South Korea) part of a policy of developing export industries. The other part of the export policy included an export subsidy and other measures such as the export-revolving fund described above, and although modestly funded it was very successful. Subsidies on foodstuffs were reduced, but parastatals continued to require subsidies, largely, though not entirely, for external reasons. For instance, the Grain Marketing Board's deficit derived in large part from a combination of paying decent prices to farmers and the costs of storing surplus maize that could not be sold profitably on the world market because of the dumping of similarly surplus maize by the European Union and the USA. Other major costs that had been squeezed under the pre-1984 IMF

---

14 . The currency was deliberately kept slightly overvalued; the World Bank from time to time estimated it as being between 10 and 20 per cent high. Black market rates suggesting 50 to 100 per cent overvaluation did not accurately reflect underlying economic realities, but rather the premium that some individuals were prepared to pay at the margin to get trapped funds out.

programme were those arising in education, health and defence (in the face of destabilization by South Africa). All were protected after March 1984, although this meant that few areas were left in which major savings could be made in government expenditure.

Despite the impeccable payments record and an economy often rightly described as dynamic by outside observers, Zimbabwe received little credit. The pressure for liberalization continued to mount with aid programmes being squeezed on flimsy pretexts, as in the case of Britain (see above) and the USA (which stopped its aid programme in 1986 because of the criticism made on 4 July of US policy in Angola).

The bottom line, however, was that despite a net outflow of over 5 per cent of GDP occasioned by debt-service, Zimbabwe still continued to grow at 4 per cent, while Ghana, the World Bank's prime African example of adjustment success, was growing at 5 per cent on the basis of net inflows of 5 per cent of GDP. What would Ghana have managed with an outflow at Zimbabwe's level? Alternatively, at what rate might unadjusted Zimbabwe have grown with a 5 per cent net inflow?

Zimbabwe was thus not forced into structural adjustment by financial imbalances or the pressure of debt, as in so many other case; it had already confronted and overcome these problems. Nor had it 'run out of steam' or 'hit the buffers'. Insofar as economic factors were behind the shift to liberalization, it was desirable to relax the foreign-exchange constraints, worsened by the limits to aid imposed by the international financial institutions. Much more important than the economic factors, however, were political factors, as interests with external links were strengthened relative to domestic interests following the changes in Eastern Europe.

CONCLUSIONS — WHAT
SOUTH AFRICA CAN LEARN

The obvious lessons from the above are that considerable pressures will be applied to the future South Africa to follow the new orthodox open-market policies. The outcome will be a range of constraints against the undoing of the inequalities of income and property engineered by apartheid.[15] As in Zimbabwe, a new black elite will be welcomed into the existing elite, thereby moderating its egalitarian fervour.

We know that alternative policies do exist, and that they must be closely related to the successful policies followed by the late industrializers of the nineteenth and early twentieth centuries and by the NICs

---

15 . These issues have been discussed by Padayachee (1992).

and Zimbabwe more recently. Unfortunately we also know that such policies are now deemed by the new totalitarianism to be wrong.

How then can the future South Africa gain room for manoeuvre, avoid the blind alley that the orthodoxy will send it up, and adopt proven policies without antagonizing the financial powers that would undoubtedly defeat it in a head-on confrontation? If there is an answer, it must draw on two elements: the uncertainties and divisions within the World Bank; and the specificities of its own situation.

On the first point, it is no secret that the public certainties on the merits of structural adjustment hide profound uncertainties and controversy inside the World Bank in the face of the lack of visible success of its policies in Africa. On the second point, the high expectations of the population and likely social disruption in the event of disappointment are well appreciated. The African National Congress (ANC) could use this, together with the risk of finding itself outflanked by more militant forces in the Congress of South African Trade Unions (COSATU), the South African Communist Party (SACP), the Pan-Africanist Congress (PAC), the Azanian People's Organization (AZAPO) and the comrades in the townships to strengthen its bargaining position and obtain a range of exceptions to the usual package. South Africa and southern Africa as a whole need access to world markets without being denied the right to protect their own infant industries; this is what is in fact available to signatories to the Lomé Convention. They also need interventions to undo the past interventions of apartheid and colonialism, to promote exports, and to create labour-intensive jobs meeting the basic needs of the population.

Finally it may be remarked that one of Zimbabwe's major mistakes was to proclaim that it was building socialism while it was manifestly doing nothing of the sort (Davies 1988; Stoneman 1988). In this way it alienated much support from the major capitalist powers, while failing to gain significant support from socialist ones or being able to emulate their success in job creation. It was prepared to lose aid as a result of rhetoric, as when it attacked the USA over its policy in Angola and the Soviet Union over Afghanistan. But it was not prepared to risk the loss of aid through implementing land redistribution policies that were desperately needed for both human and economic reasons.

Perhaps the chief lesson for South Africa in this area therefore is that its actions need to be much more radical than Zimbabwe's, while its rhetoric should be less so.

REFERENCES

Amsden, A (1989) *Asia's Next Giant* Oxford, Oxford University Press

Campbell, B and Loxley, J (eds) (1989) *Structural Adjustment in Africa,* London, Macmillan

Centre for Development Research (1992) *Beyond Apartheid,* Copenhagen, CPR

Davies, R (1988) 'The Transition to Socialism in Zimbabwe: Some Areas for Debate', in Stoneman, qv

Economist Intelligence Unit (1988) *Country Report: Zimbabwe/Malawi, no. 4.,* London, The Economist

—— (1991) *Country Report: Zimbabwe/Malawi, no. 2,* London, The Economist

Lewis, W A (1954) 'Economic Development with Unlimited Supplies of Labour', *The Manchester School of Economics and Social Studies,* vol 22

McGregor, A (ed) (1990) *Economic Alternatives,* Johannesburg, Juta

Melrose, D (1985), *Nicaragua: The Threat of a Good Example?,* Oxford, Oxfam

Padayachee, V (1992) 'The IMF and World Bank in Post-Apartheid South Africa', in Centre for Development Research, qv

Parfitt, T W (1990) 'Lies, Damned Lies and Statistics', *Review of African Political Economy,* no 47

Riddell, R C (1990) *Manufacturing Africa,* London, James Currey

—— (1988) 'The Economy: Recognizing the Reality', in Stoneman, qv

—— (ed) (1988) *Zimbabwe's Prospects,* London, Macmillan

—— (1989) 'The World Bank and the IMF in Zimbabwe', in Campbell and Loxley, qv

Tucker, B and Scott, B R (eds) (1990) *South Africa: Prospects for Successful Transition,* Kenwyn, Juta

World Bank (1981) *Accelerated Development in Sub-Saharan Africa: An Agenda for Action,* Washington, World Bank

—— (1984) Towards Sustained Development: A Joint Programme of Action for Sub-Saharan Africa, Washington, World Bank

—— (1989) *Sub-Saharan Africa: From Crisis to Sustainable Growth,* Washington, World Bank

World Bank/UNDP (1989) *Africa's Adjustment and Growth in the 1980s,* Washington, World Bank

Chapter Three

Toward a Socialist Critique of Neo-Liberalism: Agenda Setting for Post-Apartheid South Africa

Robert Fine[1]

The Economist (20 March 1993) began its special review of South Africa with the triumphant comment that,

> ... it has been South Africa's good luck (though there is more to it than luck) that the ruling National Party gave up on apartheid at about the same time that Communism collapsed; that the transition to majority rule coincides not only with the emergence of a free-market orthodoxy in economics but also with a period during which economic power has come to rest with lenders rather than borrowers.

The 'lenders' are of course the bankers, and the 'borrowers' in this case will be the more or less democratically elected government of South Africa. *The Economist* goes on to announce that 'the leadership of the ANC [African National Congress] has pretty much adopted the prevailing orthodoxy,' regardless of a few rhetorical flourishes to the left, and that in any case it will perforce end up having to recognize the authority of the bankers. As *The Economist* put it, 'a government which tried to implement the old solutions, would sooner or later collide with the disciplines of the IMF [International Monetary Fund] and the World Bank.'

1 . I should like to acknowledge the help and advice of Robin Cohen and Lolo Ditshego and thank the Overseas Development Group at the School of Development Studies, University of East Anglia for the opportunity to present these ideas and receive responses to them at its conference on 'Sustainable development of post-apartheid South Africa', March 1993.

We are witness here to the contemporary self-confidence of neo-liberalism. It is as if socialism is dead, utopianism is dead, revolution is dead and neo-liberalism is the only truth: it is as if recognition of this truth has entered the minds, if not the hearts, of the opposition movement itself. A complacent tone of self-satisfaction runs throughout the survey.

The Economist's analysis of the economic crisis facing South Africa follows standard neo-liberal lines.[2] It sees the crisis as the product of wrong governmental policies: what it calls 'economic mismanagement'. First, it blames protectionism and import substitution policies for the development behind high tariff walls of inefficient industries with low productivity. Second, it argues that exchange controls resulted in those firms unable to spend abroad buying up domestic competitors instead; this resulted in the monopolistic concentration of capital and the stifling of competition and innovation. Third, it identifies 'over-government' in the form of the growing state bureaucracy as a factor sucking the nation dry. Lastly, it blames state subsidies for allowing firms to relocate to the homelands and build Potemkin factories with outdated machinery and more or less imaginary employees, but still to pocket the state grants.

The neo-liberal remedies follow inexorably from its diagnosis. What *The Economist* calls 'sound government' will be one that does away with, or at least limits, protectionism, tariffs, exchange controls, controls on the repatriation of profits, over-government, bureaucracy, state subsidies and state regulation. Once the new rulers have learnt the lessons of 'modern economics', then and only then will the future of post-apartheid South Africa be secure. This is called economic realism.

On the basis of these presuppositions, the question posed by *The Economist* is this: what are the prospects for neo-liberal policy being introduced? What are the obstacles to its fulfilment? Now *The Economist* is not worried about the ANC leadership. It writes condescendingly about Mandela's change of heart and mind on the question of nationalization after attending the World Economic Forum at Davos. It cites ANC economic policy statements stressing the need for a mixed economy and a dynamic private sector. It is heartened by ANC participation in the National Economic Forum and its exposure to the 'normative integrated economic model' as its 'introduction to modern thinking on economics'. It quotes Trevor Manuel, head of ANC economic planning, speaking of the need to oppose a 'culture of entitlement' and to increase competition through anti-Trust measures, and the late Chris Hani as speaking of a

---

2. For discussions on neo-liberalism, see Colclough 1991; Loxley 1989; Tarp 1992.

'reconstruction pact' according to which taxes will not be raised so high as to cause an exodus of the middle classes and foreign investment will be encouraged by allowing full repatriation of profits.[3]

The Economist's real concern, however, is not the ANC leadership, about whose neo-liberalism it is so confident, but about the poor. Its concern is not so much the poverty of the poor but rather the rage of the poor and whether this rage will upset 'sound government'. The problem in a nutshell is that, although GDP per head in South Africa is quite high by African standards — about the same as Hungary or Argentina — for the black population of South Africa it is of course quite low, ie more normal by African standards. With well over 42 per cent unemployment (that is, over six million people unemployed in the formal sector), with burgeoning shanty towns, with over seven million people having no access to any proper sanitation, and with over 1.5 million schoolchildren out of school, well might *The Economist* be concerned about the rage of the poor.

The Economist's basic argument is that in the immediate future nothing much can be done to alleviate poverty. Cutting expenditure on five million whites will not do much for a black population of 29 million rising at a rate of 2.5 per cent per annum. Equalization of state expenditure for black people at a level with whites would be prohibitively expensive; for example, equalization of expenditure on black education at white levels would increase the education budget's share of the GDP from 5.5 per cent to 15.5 per cent. Even to begin reducing employment would require a growth rate of 3.5 per cent a year, while in 1992 the GDP shrunk by about 2 per cent.

So with a state budget already of about one-third of the GDP, with the taxable part of the population (mainly whites) already heavily taxed, and with an already over-inflated state bureaucracy whose officials are being guaranteed their jobs and pensions by both the government and the ANC, the message is clear: there is precious little room for social spending and the development of welfare services, ie spending that will address the social question of the people.

The only rational answer in *The Economist's* eyes is to make redistribution dependent on prior growth, with growth itself being dependent on a free market, neo-liberal policy. This is a version of what is optimistically called the 'trickle down' effect. In the meantime, the poor will have to tighten their already tight belts and the political leaders will have to tell

---

3. For the ANC's formal economic policy documents, see ANC 1990, 1991, 1992 and ANC/COSATU 1990. See also Harris 1990. For critical perspectives on these policies, see Bond 1991b and Nattrass 1992b.

them to wait patiently. The implicit message is that the rage of the poor will have to be met by the other side of 'sound liberal government', which is constraint and coercion. The key to the whole scenario, then, is to develop the political will among the new leaders to restrain by all means necessary excessive expectations among the 'people'.

TOWARDS A CRITIQUE OF NEO-LIBERALISM IN SOUTH AFRICA

Neo-liberalism is right to highlight the serious economic difficulties facing South Africa.[4] In its particular diagnosis and remedy, however, most of the elements are present of the 'Washington Consensus' of the 1980s, which was so highly recommended for Latin American countries — deregulation, privatization and marketization; and opposition to excessive bureaucracy, protectionism, inefficiency and to the economic populism which allegedly leads to the inability of governments to control fiscal debt, inflation and recession.

Deregulation sounds good in relation to apartheid regulations, but state regulation also exists to protect the weak — workers as producers and consumers — and to respond to popular pressures from below for legal frameworks to guarantee such things as working conditions, food quality, the prescription of drugs, the rape of the environment and maternity leave for women. How far state regulation performs this social function depends on the strength of democracy in the country; something of course suppressed for black people under apartheid. But 'deregulation' as such represents a no less pernicious suppression of democracy than apartheid regulation.

What happens when these neo-liberal ideas are put into effect? In Latin America the track record of neo-liberalism has been none too good. After ten years of more or less neo-liberal policies in Latin American countries, the per capita income was on average about 9 per cent lower than it had been in 1980. In some countries, like Bolivia and Argentina, the decline was very much greater — up to about 20 per cent. In the 1980s GDP grew by about 10.3 per cent per annum, ie negative growth, given the population rise. In the bad old days of 'economic populism' and state intervention in the 1960s and 1970s, annual growth was around 5–6 per cent.

The difference was particularly marked in relation to the poor. In the 1960s and 1970s some progress was made in reducing the official numbers of 'poor' from 51 to 35 per cent. In the 1980s there are now well

---

4 . For an alternative analysis, see Gelb 1991; Cassim 1988; Nattrass 1992a.

over 40 per cent designated 'poor', that is well over 200 million people. There has been a drastic reduction in the social expenditure in social services, health and education provided by public authorities, the catastrophic effects of which were in no way compensated for by private health care, education and the like. There was a shift in taxation from indirect taxes to direct taxes like VAT (value added tax), which hit the poor directly and rose from anywhere between 0.6 and 4 per cent in 1980 to 20 per cent in 1990.[5]

I do not wish to suggest that this economic disaster for the poor — and economic recession for capital — was the consequence of the policies pursued in Latin America under the pressure of the Washington Consensus. Of course not. But the idea that neo-liberalism provided any kind of a solution also bears little historical scrutiny.

But then there is the great exception, Chile: neo-liberalism's apparent success story. Certainly growth rates in Chile have been and remain dramatic. In 1991/2 it achieved after China perhaps the highest growth rate in the world at a little under 10 per cent. This growth, fed by foreign investment, has been mainly in the agricultural and mining sectors (the latter being particularly interesting in that the main mining company nationalized by the Allende government remains nationalized), and in banking, insurance and retail sectors which are themselves now penetrating other Latin American countries. Chile was a particularly good candidate for neo-liberal economic policies — perhaps for some of the same reasons that South Africa is now considered a good candidate: not least because of the existence of a well established entrepreneurial class and a modern, efficient state administration.

But we should not forget that in Chile the 'trickle-down' effect worked no better than elsewhere. The standard of living of the middle classes improved greatly, but there is now about 40 per cent of the population who live in poverty and 30 per cent who are destitute: a considerable increase on the 1970s. Let us not also forget that the condition of implementing neo-liberalism in Chile was the wilful suppression of labour in particular and democracy in general and that the present democratization of government has been introduced on the backs of a defeated and demoralized working class.[6]

Worldwide there is a trend toward an increase in the number of the poor as well as their consolidation. Some European social scientists have

---

5. An interesting though dated introduction to the comparison between South Africa and Latin America in terms of redistribution may be found in Moll 1988.
6. See Whitehead 1993; Cammack 1990; Diamond et al 1989, Lowenthal 1991; and O'Donnell et al 1986 for the debate on democracy and inequality in Latin America.

spoken of the emergence of a two-third society with one-third excluded, chronically unemployed. In Latin America and South Africa it begins to look more like a 50–50 society. Apart from its inhumanity, this represents a vast waste of economic resources and vast reservoir of instability for the future. How much investment is there going to be in South Africa if there is war on the streets?

The key question is whether a democratic order is compatible over time with such grossly and increasingly inegalitarian social structures. The entire tradition of democratic political thought to which we are heirs — from Aristotle to Rousseau to Marshall — posits the necessity of some relationship between political democracy and economic equalization. There is nothing sacred about democracy: if it does not deliver the goods then it can be abandoned.

The sub-text of the neo-liberal attitude typified by *The Economist* seems to me to say that democracy must, as it were, impose itself by force against the rage of the poor: suppressing it, deflecting it, turning it against itself, making it wild and impotent. Neo-liberalism is a toughened, hardened, galvanized form of liberalism whose relation to democracy is, as the Chilean success story shows, at best equivocal and at worst absolutely hostile.

TOWARDS A SOCIAL DEMOCRATIC ALTERNATIVE TO NEO-LIBERALISM

The conception of the economy according to which the social demands of labour and the poor appear simply as a drain on economic resources and an obstacle to sustainable development, lies at the heart of the problem of neo-liberalism. The demands of labour for higher wages, better housing, improved working conditions and more social benefits are met within neo-liberalism by the response that they violate 'macro-economic constraints' — the country cannot afford it, workers will be pricing themselves out of a job. I do not deny the existence of real economic constraints to which any policy maker has to pay heed, nor do I wish to say that neo-liberalism contains no truth, no validity, but what is at issue is the understanding of these constraints within the neo-liberal orthodoxy.

The social demands of labour are not just a drain on resources. They are part of the dynamic of capital accumulation, a driving force which impels capital out of stagnation to move from backward forms of absolute surplus value to modern forms of relative surplus value, from a low productivity low wage economy to a high productivity high wage economy. This transition, which many economists and social scientists on the left in South Africa are speaking and writing about, cannot be separated from the political, trade union and community struggles of labour for higher wages and a better quality of life.[7]

What is involved here is not just a question of government policy but a question also of the strength of labour and democracy generally, something which is deeply affected by how the government behaves and the rights it grants. The strength of labour does not have to be a problem for economic growth, as neo-liberalism typically assumes; it can also be its motor of change and modernization. In South Africa such a perspective on the production side coincides with the necessity of enlarging the domestic consumer market, the importance of which is magnified by the likelihood that South African manufactured exports will be squeezed out of the European Union market.

In arguing this, I repeat that I am not suggesting that state policy is free of fiscal constraints or that a future government does not need to take these constraints into account. But my argument points to a decisive economic alternative to neo-liberalism, one which revives some of the older perspectives of social democracy and which sees the freedom and vitality of civil society as an integral factor in economic growth.[8]

The salience of social democracy rather than neo-liberalism is often not properly understood or addressed — partly because it is associated with discredited strategies of capitalist rationalization (for instance in the United Kingdom), and partly because it is dismissed by the 'orthodox' left as compromising and necessarily doomed. The literature on the left and right is replete with analyses of 'the crisis of social democracy', which naturalize its decline as the inevitable effect of present-day capitalism and divorce it from any 'subjective' political factors. In fact, some form of social democracy has continued to be the key means of reconciling the economic 'realities' of the market with the political 'realities' of democratic redistribution.[9]

SOCIAL DEMOCRACY IN SOUTH AFRICA

The social base of this alternative social democratic perspective in South Africa lies predominantly in the trade union movement and local

---

7. Major discussions of an alternative economic policy may be found in Moll 1991; Kaplinsky 1991; Kaplan 1990; Erwin 1990; Bond 1991a; Pillay 1992; and SACP 1992. See also Lee and Schlemmer 1991.
8. For discussions of civil society in South Africa, see Fine 1992; Narsoo 1991; and Mayekiso 1990.
9. This has been arguably true in countries like Greece, Spain, Peru and Jamaica.

community associations, which together form the labour movement in 'civil society'. Many local struggles have long existed both over wages and conditions of work (in the widest sense) and over the allocation of state resources within society.

To take one example, there are currently a number of local campaigns being waged in opposition to the growing corruption associated with private housing development, especially between private developers and local authorities. This corruption represents an increasingly significant drain of public resources into a few private hands; its termination and the institution of an effective system of regulation over the allocation of public monies are crucial components of establishing a social democratic housing policy. At present the only bodies seriously attempting to control this drain of economic resources are local civic associations, supported by unions.

These local structures seem often to be politically aware of what workers in factories and communities need and skilfully capable of struggling to secure these needs. They are, however, hampered by the current growth in political and private violence and by the consequent disintegration of civil society in South Africa. And their own ability to construct a political alternative from below is precarious. The question, then, is what is to be done to build on these local initiatives in order to avoid their isolation and advance their potentiality?

I would suggest that a social democratic alternative would point to two closely related supplements to what currently exists.[10] The first is the establishment of a legal regulatory framework to which local community associations can readily appeal for effective redress of their grievances, as in the prevention of corrupt practices by the local state or by private business people. The second is the establishment in some manner or form of a political party or of political parties of labour to mediate between civil society and the state by representing the interests and needs of labour at the level of the general administration of society.

Such a party or parties of labour are an essential condition for the enactment and enforcement of laws regulating capital and the state, for the guaranteeing of rights of association in civil society, for the generalization of particular interests in civil society into a coherent and humane political whole, and for the generation of redistributive economic policies. The development of a party or parties of labour would serve as a

---

10 . I see this agenda as a perhaps dangerous supplement to the discussions on 'corporatism' in post-apartheid South Africa. See Bird and Schreiner 1992; Holdt 1991; Nupen 1992; and Vally 1992. For a historical elucidation of this notion of social democracy in the South African context, see Fine and Davis 1991.

necessary political counterweight to the predominance of business interests and their neo-liberal ways of thinking in conventional politics and
the inevitable admission of these interests and ways of thinking into the
national liberation organizations.

REFERENCES

ANC (1990) *Discussion Document on Economic Policy*, Harare
—— (1991) *Draft Resolution on Economic Policy*, Harare
—— (1992) *Ready to Govern: ANC Policy Guidelines for a Democratic South Africa*,
    Policy Unit of the ANC
ANC/COSATU (1990) 'Recommendations on Post-Apartheid Economic Policy',
    Transformation, no 12
Bird, A and Schreiner, G (1992) 'At the Crossroads: Toward Tripartite Corpor-
    atism or Democratic Socialism?', *South African Labour Bulletin*, vol 16, no 6
Bond, P (1991a) *Commanding Heights and Community Control: New Economics for a
    New South Africa*, Ravan, Johannesburg
—— (1991b) 'The ANC's Economic Manifesto: Can it Satisfy the Majority's
    Needs?', *Work in Progress*, no 75, June
Cammack, D (1990) *The Rand at War, 1899–1902: The Witwatersrand and the Anglo–
    Boer War*, London, James Currey
Cassim, F (1988) 'Growth, Crisis and Change in the South African Economy', in
    Suckling and White, qv
Colclough, C and Manor, J (1991) *States or Markets? Neo-Liberalism and the
    Development Policy Debate*, Oxford, Clarendon
Diamond, L, Linz, J and Lipset, S (eds) (1989) *Democracy in Developing Countries:
    Latin America*, London, Adamantine Press
Erwin, A (1990) 'Comments on the Harare Recommendations', *Transformation*,
    no 12
—— (1990a) 'South Africa's Post-Apartheid Economy', *South African Labour
    Bulletin*, vol 14, no 66
Fine, R (1992) 'Civil Society Theory and the Politics of Transition in South
    Africa', *Review of African Political Economy*, no 55
Fine, R and Davis, D (1991) *Beyond Apartheid: Labour and Liberation in South
    Africa*, London, Pluto, and Johannesburg, Ravan
Gelb, S (ed) (1991) *South Africa's Economic Crisis*, David Philip, Cape Town
Harris, L (1990) 'The Economic Strategy and Policies of the African National
    Congress', in McGregor (ed), qv
Held, D (ed) (1993) *Prospects for Democracy*, Cambridge, Polity Press
Holdt, K von (1991) 'Toward Transforming South African Industry: A Recon-
    struction Accord between Unions and the ANC?', *South African Labour
    Bulletin*, vol 15, no 6
Innes, D, Kentridge, M and Perold, H (eds) (1992) *Power and Project: Politics,
    Labour and Business in South Africa*, Cape Town, Oxford University Press
Kaplan, D (1990) 'Recommendations on Post-Apartheid Economic Policy', *Trans-
    formation*, no 12
Kaplinsky, R (1991) 'A Growth Path of a Post-Apartheid South Africa',
    Transformation, no 16
Lee, R and Schlemmer, L (eds) (1991) *Transition to Democracy Policy Perspectives*,
    Oxford University Press, Cape Town

Lowenthal, A (ed) (1991) *Exporting Democracy: The United States and Latin America*, Baltimore, John Hopkins University Press

Loxley, J (1989) *Structural Adjustment in Africa*, Basingstoke, Macmillan

Mayekiso, M (1990) 'Building Civil Society', *South African Review*, vol 6, no 1

McGregor, A (ed) (1990) *Economic Alternatives*, Johannesburg, Juta

Moll, P (1991) *The Great Economic Debate*, Johannesburg, Skotaville

Moll, T (1988) 'The Limits of the Possible: Macro-Economic Policy and Income Redistribution in Latin America and South Africa', in Suckling and White, qv

Narsoo, M (1991) 'Civil Society: A Contested Terrain', *Work in Progress*, no 76, July

Nattrass, N (1992a) *Profits and Wages: The South African Economic Challenge*, Penguin, London

——— (1992b) 'The ANC's Economic Policy: A Critical Perspective', in Schrire, qv

Nupen, C (1992) 'Class Conflict and Social Partnership', in Innes (et al), qv

O'Donnell, G, Schmitter, P and Whitehead, L (eds) (1986) *Transitions from Authoritarian Rule: Prospects for Democracy*, Baltimore, John Hopkins University Press

Pillay, P (1990) 'Reconstruction in Post-Apartheid South Africa: The Potential of the Social Market Economy', in Schrire, qv

Schrire, R (ed) (1992) *Critical Choices for South Africa: An Agenda for the 1990s*, Cape Town, Oxford University Press

SACP (South African Communist Party) (1992) 'Stepping Stones to Socialism: How Socialists See South Africa's Economic Reconstruction', *The African Communist*, no 129, 2nd quarter

Suckling, J and White, L (1988) *After Apartheid: Renewal of the South African Economy*, London, James Currey

Tarp, F (1992) *Stabilisation and Structural Adjustment: The Crisis of Sub-Saharan Africa*, London, Routledge

Vally, B (1992) *A Social Contract — the Way Forward? A Critical Evaluation*, Johannesburg, Phambili Books

Whitehead, L (1993) 'The Alternatives to Liberal Democracy: A Latin American Perspective', in Held, qv

Chapter Four

The Employment Problem in Post-Apartheid South Africa

Leo Katzen

Poverty reduction is likely to be a central aim of economic policy in post-apartheid South Africa. Since unemployment is one of the major causes of poverty in South Africa, as elsewhere, a strategy to promote labour absorption will be one important element in this policy.

Apart from cyclical ups and downs, the long-run trend of labour absorption has been one of steady deterioration in the South African economy over the last three decades. In the 1960s non-agricultural employment grew at an annual average rate of 4.2 per cent per annum — well in excess of population growth and reflecting the rapid real income growth of about 6 per cent per annum in that decade. In the 1970s, in spite of a few years of high GDP growth due to buoyant primary product prices (the price of gold in particular) average annual real GDP growth fell to 3.9 per cent with only 2.7 per cent per annum growth in non-agricultural employment. This was barely equal to the increase in population. In the 1980s the situation deteriorated sharply with GDP averaging only 1.4 per cent growth per annum and employment 1 per cent — well below the increase in population. More recently, with negative GDP growth, the employment situation has continued to worsen.

There are, however, no accurate figures about black unemployment as official unemployment statistics cover only a limited number of registered black unemployed. To remedy this deficiency, the government set up a Current Population Survey (CPS) to measure unemployment among blacks, coloureds and Indians by a system of sample surveys. At first the CPS grossly underestimated black unemployment. Following a new sampling procedure in 1986 based on the 1985 census, it was thought that a more accurate method of measuring black unemployment had been arrived at. Estimates of black unemployment rose to well over one million. These estimates remained high for the rest of the 1980s, but in 1990, following estimates of an unaccountable decrease in unemployment when all the evidence pointed to an increase, the CPS for blacks was dropped. One of its serious weaknesses was that it excluded the four 'independent' homelands where a large proportion of the South African labour force resides. Unofficial estimates of unemployment range widely from 18 per cent of the economically active labour force (about 2 million in 1990) to 29 per cent (3.2 million) as calculated by the Bureau of Economic Research at Stellenbosch University. While reasonably accurate statistics exist for employment in the formal sectors of the economy, estimates of full or part-time employment in the semi-subsistence African rural areas and informal urban sector are subject to wide margins of error.

A major structural change in the economy in recent years, since the abolition of influx control, has been an accelerated migration to the urban areas. To what extent is this largely a shift from under- or unemployment in rural areas to its urban counterpart? What we do know is that formal sector employment has been growing very slowly. Only about one in ten of the new entrants into the labour force find work in the formal sector. Of critical importance, therefore, to the question of labour absorption and unemployment is the scale of the urban informal sector.

Casual empiricism suggests that this sector has grown rapidly in the major urban areas in recent years. It has been helped by the removal of most of the petty restrictions that have hampered it in the past. An obvious example of the significance of deregulation has been the huge expansion of mini-bus transport, owned and operated very largely by small-scale African entrepreneurs.

In determining the size of this sector there are a number of formidable problems. First of all there is the problem of definition. The view of the informal economy may differ according to the academic approach of the investigators, ie the view adopted by economists may differ from that of sociologists. If the classification of an activity as 'informal' is based on the technology used, then much of the 'formal economy' could well be classified as 'informal'. If, as is commonly the case, the informal economy is simply the sum total of unrecorded economic activities, this will include illegal activities such as drug-dealing and prostitution which may mislead or complicate policy decisions.

Methods of measuring informal activity also vary widely and give very different results. If one follows Kantor (1989), who has a monetary approach using excess demand for currency in relation to demand deposits as a proxy for unrecorded activity, a figure of 40 per cent of GDP is arrived at for the size of this sector. On the other hand Kirsten

(1988), using a labour market approach in which income and population data are derived from an aggregate of micro studies, comes up with a much smaller estimate of 6.5 per cent of GDP as the extent of unrecorded activity.

No attempt will be made here to adjudicate between the different methods of measuring informal activity. It is obvious, however, that differences in the contribution to GDP will also be reflected in the numbers employed in this sector.

So far the various studies of informal activity in South Africa have not arrived at estimates of the aggregate numbers involved. Abedian and Desmidt (1990), in their survey of the subject, do, however, make a calculation for what they term the Potential African Informal Labour Force. This is derived from the following factors:

- Potentially economically active population (ie those between 15 and 64 years of age);
- Those in formal employment;
- Students; and
- A participation rate.

The figure they estimate for 1988, which is the latest year for which they make calculations, is 2.6 million — almost double the 1970 figure. This figure represents their estimates of the African labour force which is either employed in informal activity or is unemployed and actively seeking employment in either the formal or informal sectors. It should be remembered from the experience of developing countries, that even where people are employed in the informal activity they may still seek employment in the formal sector when earnings in the latter exceed the former as is usually the case.

All this is rather unsatisfactory if accuracy is sought for our measure of unemployment. We do, however, know that the numbers are probably large and growing.

The unemployment problem has been aggravated not only by low growth but also by a sharp increase in capital intensity over time. If you compare South Africa with other middle income countries with GDP per capita levels that are similar to hers, like Brazil, South Korea and Malaysia, then the average economy-wide capital–labour ratio in South Africa was two or three times as high as these countries by the early 1980s. It is the case that when we look at an earlier period, like the early 1960s, the capital–labour ratio in South Africa is also substantially above that of these other countries due to the dominance of mining and other branches of heavy industry in the structure of the country's economy. But this trend towards capital intensity continues to grow rapidly in subsequent decades (Levy 1992). The evidence for high capital intensity is supported by comparative statistics on the incremental capital–output ratios in manufacturing industry. Again in the period 1971–79 the average incremental capital–output ratio in South Africa is estimated at 30.9 compared with 8 for Korea and 12.7 for Malaysia. This rises sharply in South Africa in the decade 1979–89 to 79.8 with little change in Korea and Malaysia to 9.4 and 15.2 respectively.

There are very big differences in capital–labour ratios across different sub-sectors of manufacturing industry. The capital–labour ratios in sectors like base metals, chemicals and paper is much higher than in clothing, footwear and furniture. The overall increase in capital intensity is, therefore, partly due to the relative increase in these capital-intensive sectors. Between 1951 and 1988 the share in the capital stock of manufacturing of the sub-sector's industrial chemicals, other chemical products, basic iron and steel and paper, rose from 24 per cent to 53.4 per cent. In the period 1971–76 the share of basic iron and steel in increments to the capital stock was 55.8 per cent. While again the share of industrial chemicals and other chemical products on their own were a massive 64.1 per cent of the addition to the capital stock in 1976–83. This in spite of the fact that chemicals, for example, have a comparatively poor productivity record compared with clothing, footwear, wood products and furniture.

A steady shift towards heavy industry is a normal accompaniment of economic development. But this process has been accentuated and accelerated in South Africa due to strategic decisions related to sanctions or the fear of sanctions. This applies in particular to industries concerned with the conversion of coal, and more recently gas, to oil. The state has had a big share in the ownership or control of these sectors and, therefore, decisions related to them have only been partly commercial. But in this context the broader and more long-standing policy of protection of manufacturing industry and import substitution comes into focus.

It can also be said that capital-intensive methods of production were looked upon favourably by the apartheid system, as they reduced the demand for unskilled black labour and therefore slowed down the rate of urbanization. With the end of sanctions and apartheid, it is no longer necessary to favour sectors or techniques of production that contribute to autarky or reduce the demand for labour.

While changes in the two lumpy sectors, steel and chemicals, have had a disproportionate impact on the trend towards rising aggregate capital-intensity — steel up till 1976 and chemicals between 1976 and 1983 — changes in factor proportions within sectors is also of some importance.

This involves changes in choice of technique in response to movements in the markets for labour and capital.

The effect on choice of technique of rising real wages and increasing African labour militancy since 1973, is more easily illustrated in the case of the South African coal-mining industry than in manufacturing. Unlike the gold-mining industry, where there have been long-standing technical limitations to mechanization, the coal-mining industry, by the early 1970s, had a wide range of technologies available to it that had been developed in advanced countries like the UK and USA with high wage costs. With the rise in real wages in the mining industry from 1973, combined with growing labour militancy and frequent interruptions in the supply of labour, the coal-mining industry rapidly began to move over from manual and semi-mechanized techniques of production to much more highly mechanized methods of underground mining and, where possible, very capital-intensive open-cost mining.

These conditions on the supply side happened to coincide with a big increase in demand for exporting low-ash steam coal after the big rise in oil prices in 1973. In an investigation by this author of the industry made in 1977, it was interesting to find that managerial decisions about choice of technique were based on expected as well as current factor prices. Given the long gestation period of mining investment, decisions to go for greater mechanization were being made even when these were not justified by current factor prices but in anticipation of future real wage increases. Other factors such as reliability of labour supply, product demand and price and scale of production also had to be taken into account.

Since the 1970s, South Africa has steadily become a relatively high wage-cost economy. It is interesting to compare the situation in South Africa with that in Taiwan (Osborn 1992). Whereas between 1975 and 1990 unit costs in manufacturing doubled in Taiwan they went up 600 per cent in South Africa. Wages in both economies went up by about the same amount over this period but whereas in South Africa labour productivity remained unchanged, in Taiwan it went up two and a half times. Wage increases in Taiwan have tended to follow productivity increases. In South Africa they have gone up for other reasons.

It would seem that an essential ingredient of industrial strategy favouring labour absorption will be the need to bring pressure to relate real wage increases to productivity increases. Fortunately there are indications that this message has begun to come over in sectors like gold mining, which is in great difficulties in being squeezed between low prices and rising costs. Trade unions are now more collaborative in moderating wage demands to economic circumstances.

Another important factor that raises costs and hence initiates against competitiveness and export orientation, is the level of tariff protection and import controls in South Africa. At times the latter has been more important than tariffs as a form of protection although in recent years there has been a shift away from quantitative restrictions towards tariffs in line with GATT (General Agreement on Tariffs and Trade) recommendations. But the effect of this has been to raise protection and in particular Effective Rates of Protection (ie rates of nominal protection on value added), to high levels in some sectors and on some products. While in aggregate nominal rates of protection are quite moderate at about 22 per cent, there are sharp variations between sectors with Effective Rates of Protection of over 150 per cent in about 30 per cent of manufacturing sub-sectors. These levels of protection enable firms to tolerate and absorb high wage costs and also encourage greater capital intensity.

South Africa is an open economy highly involved in international trade, with trade accounting for some 25 per cent of GDP. Her exports, though, are predominantly minerals — mainly gold, coal, platinum and diamonds — and relatively lightly processed agricultural products. Manufactured goods exports amounted to only 12.7 per cent of total exports in 1988 in South Africa, compared with 30 per cent for Korea and 41 per cent for Malaysia.

While in the past South Africa has had a comparative advantage in its traditional primary product exports, there is some evidence that the terms of trade are turning against some, if not all, of these products. Gold-mining, in particular, has been suffering for some years now from such low prices that several marginal mines have been closed or are threatened with early closure. It makes sense, therefore, to encourage manufactured exports to replace some of the hard-hit primary exports. Nor need increased exports come only from capital-intensive sectors like iron and steel, chemicals and paper. There seems to be export propensity in some of the least capital-intensive sectors, like garments and textiles. Because of good management, design flair and the dexterity of workers in the Western Cape, the garment industry has considerable export potential. In part it could be recovering markets it had in the early 1980s but lost because of sanctions.

The cost of creating export jobs is exaggerated if we take into account the lost sectors I have mentioned. It should also be said that the investment demand should not impose such a big burden on domestic savings as it has of late in so far as South Africa once again gains access to foreign sources of investment on reasonable terms. South Africa has at present an unusually low level of foreign debt for a country at its level of development.

I am not suggesting any sudden and drastic change in trade policy. An *ad hoc* and pragmatic approach will have to be adopted for tariff reduction. There is the danger that large and sudden tariff falls will result in the eclipse of some firms, so that there will be some loss of income and employment welfare to be set against any gain in price and consumer welfare. On the other hand, if tariff reduction reduces the cost of inputs of export industries, then the expansion of these industries will hopefully compensate for falls elsewhere. One is reminded of the old battle between the gold-mining industry, faced with a fixed price for its product in the late 1920s, and the new policy of protecting manufacturing industry after 1925. Tariff policy will have to be combined with export promotion. The overall approach should be outward orientated rather than import substituting from now on.

A crucial element in a labour absorbing industrial strategy is to meet the skilled labour shortage by investment in education and job training. Besides restraint in the increase in wages already referred to, improvement in labour productivity is also vital in keeping wage costs down. This requires a better educated and trained labour force. Again lessons in this connection can be learned from the NICs (newly industrializing developing countries) in the east.

South Africa has several advantages on its side: a well-developed industrial infrastructure, a stable macro-economic fiscal system, low international indebtedness, a vigorous and capable entrepreneurial stratum and well-trained managers and considerable natural resources. What will be needed is a climate to revive investor confidence, both domestic and foreign, and policies that point and encourage in directions that have scope for growth.

REFERENCES

Abedian, I and Desmidt, M (1990) 'The Informal Economy in South Africa', *The South African Journal of Economics*, vol 58, no 4

Kantor, B (1989) 'Estimating the Size Of Unrecorded Economic Activity in South Africa', *Journal for Studies in Economics and Econometrics*, vol 13, no 1

Kirsten, M (1988) 'A Quantitative Perspective on the Informal Sector in Southern Africa', *Development Southern Africa*, vol 5, no 2

Levy, B (1992) 'How can South African Manufacturing Efficiently Create Employment? An Analysis of the Impact of Trade and Industrial Policy', *World Bank, Informal Discussion papers on Aspects of the Economy of South Africa*

Osborn, E (1992) 'Industrialisation, Liberalisation and Export Promotion', *Nedbank Quarterly Guide to the Economy*, November

Chapter Five

Energy and Sustainable Development in Southern Africa

Phil O'Keefe and John Kirkby

The purpose of this chapter is to provide a description of the development context in southern Africa. It draws heavily on the ongoing work of the Southern African Development Community (SADC), the South African Energy Policy and Research Training Project at Cape Town, and the work on mineral benefication (ie downstream value added activity in the mining sector) being coordinated by Paul Jourdan for the Industrial Strategy Project. We look at the current debates informing institutional change in SADC, the energy context of an expanded SADC that will include South Africa, the determinants of future energy demand and the likely outcome of changes in the development future of the region.

CURRENT DEBATES

In the light of imminent democratic changes in South Africa and the implications of these changes for existing SADC member states, there have been significant discussions over the last two years about the future of SADC. Multilateral and bilateral aid agencies have been clearly indicating to SADC members that their future external support rests on SADC being commercially, rather than politically, focused. Although, in part, this is a reference back to the original Southern African Development Coordination Conference (SADCC) declaration, which emphasized a lessening of dependence on South Africa, it is largely driven by a realization that public funds must be used to generate private capital investment in the region. This 'real politik' produced a declaration, 'Towards the Southern African Development Community — A Declaration by the Heads of State on Government of South African States', which was signed in Windhoek, Namibia, on 17 August 1992.

Of course, behind these discussions were several subplots. The most significant was the re-emphasis on peace and stability, especially in the lusophone countries, but even as we write, these are difficult promises to deliver both because of the lack of control over the white South African Defence Force (SADF) and the problems of demobilization in Mozambique and Angola. There were other minor subplots, notably the reluctance of Zimbabwe to embrace South Africa in a regional role, not least because it challenged the pre-eminent position of Zimbabwe in SADC. And, of course, there were the perennial questions of whether Tanzania would leave and if Zaire could join SADC.

The Zaire issue is interesting, for our own analysis, because Zaire could be a major source of power to the southern African region, especially if there is a significant drive to cleaner generation technology, which favours hydropower.

ENERGY IN AN EXPANDED SADC

Regional cooperation in energy can help minimize the costs of supplying energy, enhance the reliability and security of the supply, ensure that efficient energy performance is maintained and avert adverse environmental impacts. Regional cooperation in electricity supply and use transmission will contribute to the growth in trade whilst simultaneously building a platform for an integrated electricity system in southern Africa.

The key to regional cooperation will be the political will to opt for regional supply options on the basis of least cost, instead of pursuing the goal of national energy self-efficiency. From a technical viewpoint, rather than increase the risk of insecurity, energy interdependence enhances fuel security. As political stability increases, particularly with the incorporation of South Africa into the SADC community, there will be an opportunity for building regional interdependence.

Energy is required for subsistence needs and for economic development. Energy for subsistence needs is largely met from woodfuel, particularly in rural areas; energy for economic development is associated with commercial fuels, namely electricity, liquid fuels, natural gas, coal and coal derivatives. As all countries are committed to increasing the welfare of their citizens and developing significant levels of industrialization, the pre-eminent sector in which regional interdependence can occur is the dominant objective of individual governments.

Electricity is a dominant focus because of its convenience, the range of end uses it supports and its comparatively low price when compared with the real costs of other energy. While electricity cannot substitute other commercial energy forms for specialized application, for example transport, it serves as a catalyst for modern urbanization and industrialization.

Raising capital for energy projects, particularly electricity projects, is difficult because of the long gestation periods involved in bringing supplies on stream. As a consequence, energy planners have tended to overestimate and then over-provide for future energy supplies so that, within the region, the essential critical task is now to deploy existing energy supplies rather than build new capacity. Such a task requires the development of a regional grid and will offer exporting countries a substantial foreign-exchange opportunity.

There are significant energy resources within the region; substantial coal resources exist in southern Africa, accounting for over 95 per cent of Africa's proven reserves. With the exception of Angola, the region does not, however, have significant proven reserves of urban gas, although substantial deposits of natural gas have been discovered off the eastern and southern African coast. At a regional level, particularly if Zaire is included, there are significant hydropower opportunities which remain under-developed. Biomass resources vary significantly across the region and, in semi-arid areas and around towns, there are significant local shortages of fuelwood.

South Africa dominates energy consumption, having almost four times the energy consumption of all SADC countries. This clearly demonstrates the existing linkage between energy and development and indicates that if existing SADC members pursue a similar development path, energy consumption will rise dramatically. Existing energy consumption should not be taken as an accurate reflection of demand. The shortage of foreign currency in SADC member states limits the purchase of fuel and technology and prevents the electricity supply utility expanding its networks to reach potential customers. Demand is also influenced by pricing where substantial subsidies exist in the provision of commercial fuels to existing urban households.

Although the situation in South Africa and in the SADC member countries varies enormously, wood fuel is a cause for concern throughout the region. In SADC 75 per cent of the energy supply is biomass, but this resource is under increasing pressure because of the expansion of land agriculture. It is a difficult problem to solve because it requires local management of resources in an integrated land-use programme. SADC's energy sector has, however, taken an international lead with its work on wood-fuel provision.

In Angola and Mozambique, the particular concern is to restore the energy supply infrastructure destroyed during the years of political instability. In both countries, as in Zaire and Zimbabwe, a sound energy supply infrastructure provides opportunities for energy exports. In Zimbabwe, the critical problem is in the management of the electricity sub-sector, where government interference has led to the under-performance of this nationalized utility; years of indecision over investment have led to a supply crisis which must be addressed if Zimbabwe is to remain a significant industrial producer. In South Africa, the central issue is electrification of the townships and rural areas, coupled with environmental concerns over the operation of existing thermal and nuclear power plants.

There is significant regional cooperation in the energy sector coordinated by the SADC Technical and Advisory Unit (TAU) in Luanda, Angola. As with other SADC activities, the energy sector has been dependent on donors for project support. Increasingly, however, it is seeking an active role in portfolio management and is searching for ways of negotiating deals in the private sector with the support of multilateral and bilateral agencies. In terms of the number and value of projects, the electricity sub-sector has dominated energy activities; this is quite simply because the potential for regional cooperation is greatest with electricity interconnections. There is a need for a significant emphasis on building grid interconnections in future electricity sub-sector planning. The technical advantages of grid interconnections are improved reliability and frequency stability, while simultaneously maintaining lower spinning reserves in each national system. Economic gains are harder to measure, although the current spate of power outages is clearly at a significant cost to the economy of Zimbabwe. Efficiency savings, because of a least-cost approach and higher technical specifications, are likely to be substantial. SADC should substantially revise its electricity planning to include Zaire and South Africa, as well as Namibian/Angolan and Mozambique/Botswana/Zimbabwe and South Africa connections.

In the oil sector, Angola has repeatedly offered oil at a differential price to SADC member countries to cement regional trade. Substantial regional projects have existed with the rehabilitation the TAZAMA (the Tanzanian–Zambian pipeline company) pipeline, and regional security has been provided for the Beira–Mutari pipeline. Although regional procurement policies have been considered, substantial institutional arrangements will have to be made if savings are to be realized.

There are joint petroleum exploration programmes but there has not been significant cooperation in natural gas. The entry of South Africa into SADC will allow the expertise of GASCOR (the South African gas utility) to be utilized throughout the region. In a similar manner, there has been little regional cooperation in coal, a situation which is likely to continue when South Africa joins SADC because of the dominance of South Africa in coal mining.

It is useful to distinguish soft and hard interventions in energy integration in the SADC region. Soft interventions which can be readily operationalized include (a) integrated regional planning with particular reference to electricity, (b) the sharing of efficiency and environmental standards to ensure fair competition and a least-cost solution for individual member states and (c) the sharing of experience in addressing the local management of woody biomass resources. In addition, there are substantial opportunities for sharing technical knowledge and training across all energy sub-sectors.

The hard options concern the actual building and deployment of energy supplies, in particular, and these decisions are hard because they involve substantial amounts of capital and recurrent expenditure. Both international and regional experience of cooperation to date shows that the electricity sub-sector offers a substantial opportunity in the enhanced SADC region especially when the expertise of ESCOM becomes available.

If the SADC energy sector is to drive forward it must pursue these hard projects and ensure that they are commercially viable. It is only by having the SADC energy sector operate in such a commercial context that energy security and regional integration can be guaranteed.

Energy, of course, cannot be discussed without mentioning environment. The environment of SADC member countries and South Africa is undergoing substantial change. As economic development occurs, local people are moving from husbandry resources to mastering resources, a substantial change in the people–environment relationship that parallels industrialization and urbanization. Such change has given rise to political concern at international, regional, national and local levels, although, as yet, there is little political resolution of environmental problems.

Central to these concerns are the depletion of non-renewable resources such as hydrocarbons, the destruction of conditionally renewable resources such as water and soil and the eroded capacity of the environment to act as a sink of pollution. In the SADC region, particularly if South Africa is included in wider membership, the most significant resource shortfall is the provision of water. As individual nations states share river basins there is a need for urgent negotiation over riparian rights. Future capital investment in water resource development will require rigorous environmental analysis to ensure that supply meets demand, that regional scarcity is avoided and that fossil aquifers are not substantially depleted. Such a regional approach to water resource management — which is the only way to avoid scarcity — will require careful cost analysis and the establishment of a water pricing policy that reflects the scarcity.

Significant environmental issues underlie the energy sector where the dominant mode of regional integration is likely to be the expansion of an international grid system. Such a strategy would provide electricity most cheaply to new subscribers and would offer the opportunity for least-cost investment that accommodated a level of real environmental cost.

It is important that this issue is taken seriously because future international trading will probably require evidence of environmental best practice and energy inputs will be closely monitored for their international impact, carbon emission and regional pollution — acid rain as well as local despoliation.

Although there are significant levels of land degradation in the region, especially in the more marginal, communal land, the environmental problems cannot be adequately addressed until the inequities of land distribution are addressed. Ironically, given such an equity, it is surprising that only a relatively small portion of land is currently devoted to agriculture. The constraints on an expansion of sustainable agriculture are, however, the ecological and climatic constraints of much of the region. Land degradation can only be addressed at local level and the purpose of addressing this issue on a regional scale is to search for models of best practice in areas with similar ecological, socio-economic and demographic characteristics. Parallel to the land-use issue in rural areas is the issue of urban poverty and pollution, particularly but not only in South Africa. This has a direct impact on people's health and there is need for the development of strong environmental health programmes to combat this growing problem.

Significant areas of land in the region are given over to wildlife conservation. Wildlife makes a substantial contribution to national economics through wildlife viewing, safari hunting and game cropping. Existing SADC member countries can strengthen their wildlife industries by examining South Africa's own wildlife industry, for wildlife industries offer a significant opportunity for foreign-exchange earnings.

At the present moment, there is significant institutional under-capacity in the environment sector. Multilateral, bilateral and private funds must be sought that ensure that at a national and regional level, global and regional environmental standards can be adhered to without limiting development opportunity. Such institutional development requires significant support for policy formulation, research and training, particularly as, with industrial development, there will be substantial opportunity for the regional provision of toxic waste facilities. Above all, it is important to accept that there has to be a level of political choice with regard to environmental resources. Increasingly, commercial considerations will have to underlie conservation initiatives; unless conservation pays its own way, it will be a drain on decreasing resources available to the public purse for other developments.

THE DETERMINANTS OF FUTURE ENERGY DEMAND

Energy is needed for everyday activity in SADC as it is elsewhere. From power stations to open fires, energy provides services. But in southern Africa, energy problems are pervasive — blackouts, oil shortages and deforestation all contribute to this. The physical shortcomings of the energy systems are exacerbated by lack of investment. People in many areas simply cannot meet their energy needs.

Energy arrived on SADC's development agenda with the 1979 oil price rise. The first rise, in 1973, had little impact because export commodities simply paid for oil imports. In the mid-1970, however, export commodity prices fell dramatically. SADC economies, which unlike developed economies had not adjusted, were thus poorly placed to resist the pressure of the second oil price rise. The local economies, as a consequence of these changing price structures and of cheap loans, gradually increased their level of indebtedness in such a way that they are now suffering from 'compulsory' IMF readjustment policies.

Southern Africa's energy system is characterized by a number of factors.

1. It has a relatively low commercial energy consumption
2. This is accompanied by a high percentage use of fuelwood. Wood meets 70 per cent of SADC's energy requirements.
3. The SADC economies faces a high dependency on oil as a commercial fuel; for many countries oil and capital equipment represents 50 per cent of the import bill and thus hard currency is used for energy requirements. The one exception is Angola, though most of its oil revenue goes to fuel the ongoing war.
4. Energy efficiency tends to be low, wasting existing scarce resources.
5. There is increasing demand from the rapidly expanding urban centres for a large-scale energy delivery system.
6. There is a high dependence on the north, both for the development of the energy sector and for research and prospecting.

Energy and development remain inextricably intertwined. This is demonstrated by the close relationship between energy consumption and GNP, although there are gains to be made by increasing efficiency which would help uncouple this relationship. It is not feasible for southern Africa to rerun Europe's energy development path, not least because of the environmental impact of such a carbon based — and therefore global warming — scenario. How this will be resolved is unclear.

South Africa does, and simultaneously does not, follow a similar pattern to the SADC countries. At a household level, in South Africa lack of access to usable and affordable energy is an important aspect of urban and rural poverty. Lack of access to electricity, which is arguably the most convenient source of energy for household consumption, is perhaps the clearest indication of the link between energy and poverty in South Africa. Whilst there is currently a substantial surplus generating capacity on the national grid, and South Africa produces more than 50 per cent of the electricity generated in the entire African continent, electricity is only provided to the homes of about one third of the population. The majority of the population who live in unelectrified rural and urban areas are dependent on more expensive and less convenient energy sources such as wood, paraffin, gas and coal.

Fuelwood is the traditional energy source for most of South Africa's rural population. Some households in peri-urban areas also use fuelwood. In total, fuelwood contributes about 6 per cent of primary national energy consumption and is used by over half of South Africa's population for heating and cooking. It is clear from a number of studies that fuelwood is becoming an increasingly scarce resource in many rural areas. This has significant impact on the natural environment in terms of deforestation, soil erosion and the loss of natural habitats. The effect on rural people themselves is also severe: in many areas the distances that must be covered, mostly by women, to collect fuelwood have increased, and some households have been forced to purchase other fuels that they can ill afford. In unelectrified urban areas, households make use of gas, paraffin (especially in coastal areas where it is cheaper) and coal (particularly near the Transvaal and Natal coalfields). Expenditure on energy accounts for a significant (between 7 and 22 per cent) proportion of total household expenditure in informal areas and townships.

While mining, industry, most of commercial agriculture and middle and upper income residences in the towns have been electrified, roughly two thirds of the population remains without the benefits of electricity. These poorer households experience conditions not dissimilar to other developing countries and rely on biomass or transitional fuels such as paraffin (kerosene), LPG (liquefied petroleum gas), coal, candles and batteries.

In the past, South Africa imported all its crude oil requirements but following the oil price increases of the 1970s and the imposition of a global oil embargo, decisions were made to expand the production of synthetic liquid fuels from SASOL oil-from-coal production plants and a new Mossgas oil-from-natural gas plant. Approximately one third of petrol and diesel needs are met from these plants.

The state has also heavily invested in energy. In 1984, South Africa's first, and only, nuclear power station was commissioned at Koeberg, 30 kilometres north of Cape Town. The Atomic Energy Corporation receives large annual parliamentary grants and has developed a limited local production capacity for uranium enrichment and fuel-rod fabrication.

Until recently, very little attention has been given to the energy needs of the urban and rural poor. The state has begun to develop a strategy for this sector which includes investigating electricity supply options for remote areas and a biomass initiative. ESCOM (the national electricity corporation) has also announced an ambitious plan to bring electricity to 900,000 homes, as well as assistance to local authorities for the electrification of a further 1.7 million households over five years. But the political demand is for a more accelerated programme.

South Africa therefore exhibits a similar profile for household end-use demand as other SADC members, but it simultaneously has huge reserves of coal and, currently, an overproduction of electricity. The huge resources of coal are increasingly questioned as a suitable electricity source given the regional availability of hydropower; the current overproduction of electricity is a short-term phenomenon given the promises that already exist to commit power reserves to large mining and mineral benefication projects. South Africa's energy future will largely be determined by its development future. South Africa's development future will, in time, drive the regional development and energy future.

LIKELY OUTCOME OF CHANGES IN THE DEVELOPMENT FUTURE OF THE REGION

With democracy in South Africa, regional integration will expand. South Africa's economy therefore will largely dominate regional trends. To date, however, Africa's economy has been significantly misrepresented; deliberately for ideological reasons and unintentionally because of a statistical aberration. South Africa has been characterized as an economy that has developed significant manufacturing capacity over the last 25 years while mining has remained relatively constant and in some sub-sectors declined. It served cold-war rhetoric and apartheid ideology to maintain this myth but it was largely a statistical quirk — mineral benefication was counted as the manufacturing not the minerals sector. Virtually all growth in 'manufacturing' for 25 years can be accounted for by the increase in mineral benefication.

South Africa's development future will likely build on this primacy of the mining sector which contributes over one third of current GDP. It will as a net exporter — unlike manufacturing — contribute substantially to the maintenance of foreign exchange reserves and to supporting the rand as a convertible currency. The advantages of South Africa's existing economy are essentially fivefold, namely:

1. an extensive mineral resource endowment;
2. a key metropolitan role in a regional market;
3. an internationally competitive resource extraction capital goods industry;
4. low cost energy; and
5. developed infrastructure.

To build on these advantages South Africa is likely to accelerate mineral benefication and develop an export market for its resource extraction capital goods industry. It will increase its manufacturing of low-value added goods for the regional market. It will also lead out with a demand-driven policy for a resource-based infrastructure development effort emphasizing transport, electricity, water, health and education.

What will these developments mean? In practical terms, they will probably mean an accelerated search for cheap, clean electricity — a move towards hydropower that will rapidly pull Mozambique, Angola, Zambia and Zaire into a South African controlled transmission system. And beyond electricity, South Africa will continue the regional search for sustainable water supplies. There is a danger in such a strategy. South Africa's regional intervention could precipitate a collapse of emergent resource-based industry, particularly in Botswana and Zimbabwe. It could also lead to a slow transformation of the South African infrastructure, which would not keep pace with the expectations and political needs of the black townships.

These are not idle thoughts. Even as we write, multinational and national capital is negotiating with the ANC to set this resource-based future in place. It knows that the ANC will introduce anti-monopoly, anti-trust and mergers policies; it knows that the economy cannot continue to be dominated by a small part of the white minority; it knows that the private sector will have to be more efficient to preserve its competitiveness. But the same multinational and national capital also knows that it is needed for South and southern African development.

The ANC knows it will be difficult to continue government support for large capital energy projects such as SASOL (which extracts oil from coal) and nuclear power, but these are state bureaucracies and they will not be difficult to dismantle. The ANC knows it will be difficult to close coal extraction — except for export — but that is likely to be a consequence of the new global agenda as South Africa can access hydropower generation. Above all, the ANC knows that it has to access foreign exchange and that means a strategy of mineral benefication, but little new employment opportunity.

Chapter Six

Zimbabwe's Experience in Promoting 'Sustainable' Rural Development and the Implications for South Africa

Lionel Cliffe

In exploring how South Africa's stark agrarian inequalities can be addressed in a post-apartheid future, the only comparable experiences are those of other ex-settler colonies in Africa. If their efforts, their successes and failures in trying to reverse these patterns are ignored by the popular movement in South Africa and its leaders they will miss out in a crucial learning process, and may be condemned to follow a version of those limited and flawed reforms of other settler-dominated forms of agriculture.

In offering a résumé of Zimbabwe's struggles over land, this chapter is in no sense suggesting any aspect of policy there that can be used as a blueprint. Indeed, its overall conclusions are that Zimbabwe's efforts at land reform have been too limited; that the land redistribution which has occurred does indeed have positive aspects which are seldom acknowledged, as well as shortcomings; that vast problems of the sustainability of the environment in the 'reserves' of their farming systems, and most crucially of the people themselves have still to be properly addressed.

Southern Africa in fact abounds with learning opportunities foregone. FRELIMO's (Frente de Libertaçao de Mozambique) leaders' long acquaintance with Tanzania's experiments did not prevent them replicating the environmental, economic and political disaster of forcing people needlessly into a bureaucratically conceived and administered 'villagization' programme which was in fact reminiscent of the apartheid government's 'betterment' even though it was labelled 'socialist' (on Tanzania see Raikes 1975; on Mozambique, Raikes 1984).

In the same way Zimbabwe's national movement was apparently uninformed of the experience of another British settler colony, Kenya. They did in fact repeat to an uncanny extent Kenya's very limited reform of the inherited racial inequalities. In the first five years after independence Zimbabwe managed to distribute land of former white settler farms to 35,000 households, almost exactly the same number of beneficiaries as in Kenya between 1963–68 — a figure which hardly put any dent in the large number of near landless households. Both countries redistributed only 25 per cent of the land formerly monopolized by whites. In each country the initial beneficiaries were the landless and impoverished, but once this political 'steam had been let out of the kettle', to use Kenyatta's phrase, those better-off peasants (and officials) with resources and/or influence were the ones to get land.

The veteran Kenyan nationalist Oginga Odinga (1967) saw one reason for this limited reform when in his autobiography he recounted that during the constitutional talks, while the African delegates were locked in long wrangles about second chambers in the legislature and regional government, the real issue — over land — was being settled behind closed doors by the Kenya whites and British officials (Odinga 1967). In both countries the prospects for land reform were severely curtailed by property rights being entrenched in constitutions. This manner of settling the land issue left the white settlers with much of their holdings intact and, just as crucially, underwrote the legal rights of all property owners and the *value* levels of their property. It thus guaranteed the conditions inducing property owners to stay put in a retrenched and slightly reduced 'large-scale commercial farm (LSCF) sector'. It thereby provided the whole underpinning for the 'neo-colonial' solution (Leys 1975).

The Zimbabwe experience closely paralleled that of Kenya in another respect: policies which reversed the virtual monopoly to grow high-value crops, and on credit, technical inputs and skewed prices to maize grown by LSCFs led to 'agricultural success' amongst some of the better-off peasant producers in the environmentally more favoured of the reserves.

The same kind of scenario, varied in its detail so as to fit specific South African conditions to be sure, is being actively pursued by white interests in the Republic of South Africa (RSA) with backing from foreign diplomatic influences.

One issue that will need discussion is to attempt to resolve the contradictory views about Zimbabwe's experience. Among commonly held misconceptions about that record, two generalizations are not only widely accepted but the reiteration of these myths and their unquestioned absorption by Zimbabwe officials was a factor in the curtailment of reform programmes and will no doubt be resurrected in the South

African debate. First, with respect to resettlement, *The Economist* (22 May 1993) is typical in the way it can still trot out as an accepted truth, the view that: 'The [Zimbabwe] government's previous attempt at land reform, shortly after Independence, was not regarded as a success... White farmers argue that parcelling out commercial farmland in small plots will reduce productivity and so jeopardize the country's ability both to feed its people and to export valuable crops.' A similar conclusion is recently asserted by a usually balanced Zimbabwean scholar (J Moyo 1993). The land redistribution may have been limited but, such as is was, it was in fact highly successful economically. Moreover, the reforms of peasant agriculture have done much to diversify 'the country's ability to feed itself', so that it is no longer anything like so dependent on the LSCFs.

The Inherited Structure of Settler Agriculture in Zimbabwe and South Africa

To see how far comparisons can be made, the two countries' agrarian structure can be compared. The colonial state allocated half of all the productive land in Zimbabwe exclusively to whites; similar areas were allocated as 'native reserves', today antiseptically designated 'Communal Areas' (CAs), but still the same locations with only slightly improved conditions. The white commercial farming area of 12.5 million hectares was a much smaller area than that outside the reserves in South Africa (85.7 million hectares), but the average size of a farming unit was higher than that in RSA despite a marked concentration of ownership in the latter since 1960 (Marcus 1989). In both countries, white commercial agriculture had historically been by far the single largest employer; despite the mechanization of production and rationalization of production, over one million people are in permanent employment in agriculture in South Africa, with almost 0.75 million dependent on casual, seasonal work. At the peak of employment in the late 1970s in Zimbabwe, over 350,000 were employed, making commercial agriculture relatively an even more important sector for employment than in RSA, and also providing for more jobs proportionately to its much smaller area: a third of the jobs of South Africa but on one seventh of the land.

These racially exclusive LSCF sectors in the two countries shared other characteristics. The holdings include specialist, intensive crop-growing areas devoted to fruit, vines, tea, coffee and sugar, plus those producing grain, others producing food and industrial crops on a less intensive basis on the 'high veld', but also considerable semi-arid areas more suited to ranching. It is also crucial to realize that white commercial farming in both countries was not everywhere a success: there are examples of technologically complex and efficient production but also farms that are not well-managed, are under-utilized and generate little surplus. Both the technical advances of the efficient farming units and the survival of the inefficient were underwritten by huge government subsidies.

In Zimbabwe, the LSCF sector, now constituting some 4500 farms, average size just less than 3000 hectares, monopolized a huge territory, but also comprised much of the best land. The 22 million hectares of agricultural land is classified into five Natural Regions (NRs) of vastly different potential.[1] The CAs comprise some 800,000 peasant households and some 16.4 million hectares — averaging 20 hectares available per family, but this figure means little as the greater part is common land devoted to grazing, so the average size of household arable plots is as low as four to five hectares. There are now in addition the Resettlement Areas (RAs) (approximately three million hectares) and the Small-scale Commercial Farming (formerly 'African Purchase') Areas (1.4 million hectares). But access to the high potential land in NRI and II is highly skewed. One third of the LSCF sector is in these regions; less than one tenth of the CAs. In other words over 90 per cent of the land from which peasant households seek their food and other needs would only be regarded by commercial farmers as suitable for ranching.

Similarity between the two countries in the past extended to farming in the 'reserves'. Both had experienced periods of distinct growth in peasant production for the market around the turn of the century, before land pressures and government policies and subsidized prices for whites undermined this 'competition' to white agriculture. Insofar as production levels and farming systems in the CAs were 'static' and non-sustainable in recent decades, that was *induced* and not inherent. The resulting pressures on land and on households in Zimbabwe's CAs had indeed created crisis conditions by the 1950s. It is this objective imperative of a real 'land problem' in many heavily-populated areas that resonates with the kind of 'land and freedom' ideological thrust that Ranger (1985) identifies as a crucial element in the combined guerrilla/peasant consciousness: a demand for the restoration of 'lost lands' that fuelled the liberation war.

---

1 . NRI (specialized and diversified farming, including fruit and plantation crops); NRII (intensive farming of crops and livestock); NRIII (semi-intensive farming, marginal for crop production alone); NRIV (semi-extensive farming, in which even drought-resistant crops are unreliable and farming systems should be based on livestock); and NRV (extensive farming where cattle or game ranching is the only viable farming system).

Independent Zimbabwe's Efforts toward Agrarian Reform

Immediately after independence in 1980, the Zimbabwe government began a programme of 'Resettlement' under which it was to acquire land from the white commercial farmers on which African producers were then settled, plus efforts to increase production in CAs. In devising resettlement policy, a number of issues had to be confronted:

- *Land Acquisition*: How much land should be taken from whites and of what type? Should it be the most productive, or the least utilized, or certain kinds of farms, like the smaller, mixed farms that were priori- tized in Kenya? On what terms? With or without (full?) compensa- tion?
- *Patterns of Resettlement*: What forms of production would replace the settler farms or ranches? Should one maintain large-scale ones or sub- divide? Should it be through peasant, cooperative or state farming?

Even if the circumstances of RSA are so different or South Africa's popular movement is not impressed by its neighbour's experience as to warrant different answers to Zimbabwe, the same operational questions will have to be answered in South Africa. Of course, any answer should ideally be based on criteria and priorities which have been established by posing even more fundamental questions of strategy, questions as to what should be the basic aims behind any policy. White commercial interests, but also planners from the Zimbabwe government and the international agencies had a tendency to see the issue as optimizing production by 'appropriate land use' of regions of different potential. They might grant a (limited) concession to equity but this was always seen by definition as a 'trade-off' against 'growth', whereas both goals were served simultaneously by the agriculture reforms in the 1980s. But, an even more fundamental mistake was to define the problem as a *'land question'*, rather than seeing access to land as a *means* to solve the grave socio-economic problems which so many African people faced, notably by providing some additional source of livelihood to those whose access to land, employment or other earnings did not provide them with the basics.

In the event, some 2.5 million hectares of land were acquired in the period just after independence, much of it properties abandoned during the war of liberation, or already 'squatted' on by African peasants, plus farms that whites were ready to sell — often of marginal quality; what one Zimbabwe resettlement official called 'baboon country'. In this way popular pressures have driven the resettlement programme. Some 36,000 households, perhaps 250,000 people, were resettled on this land between

1980 and the end of 1985. This represents something like the original target declared at independence, but only a small proportion of the 162,000 families in the revised target announced in 1982. The pattern of resettlement was that, after a slow build-up of the necessary framework and procedures, some 15,000 were placed on the land in 1983 only for a virtual halt to be called after that. In fact during the 1985/6 fiscal year, a new target of 15,000 resettled families was set, equal to the highest in any one year, although never realized — and that figure was again announced as the annual target for the 1990s in a second phase of land redistribution.

It is perhaps instructive for South Africa to explore why the redistribution of white-owned land was so limited, but also why the process was characterized by the 'start-stop' of the 1980s. Among many reasons cited in a useful summary by S Moyo (1991), problems of land acquisition was often given as one factor. Acquisition was in fact constrained by the terms of the Constitution. Its 'bill of rights' entrenched the rights of existing property owners by clauses that could not be changed by any means for ten years, which stipulated that government could only acquire land which is underutilized, and only then by full and immediate compensation at market rates, payable in foreign exchange. The nationalists were finally induced to accept these restrictions at the Lancaster House Conference on Independence by a promise from the US government of $1500 million, which would have financed substantial land purchase even on these expensive terms. In the event the USA reneged on that promise; the British did in fact provide grants of £20 million towards the cost of resettlement, including that half which represented land purchase. No other donors, including a few that did fund other resettlement costs, would finance the Zimbabwe government buying back its own land. Policy therefore had to avoid compulsory purchase and rely on buying that land which it was offered for sale — a 'willing-buyer/willing-seller' basis — thereby paying the going rate but in local currency. But this means of acquisition meant there was little choice about which type or area of land to acquire — much of it marginal for arable, only 22 per cent in NRI and NRII but 41 per cent in NRIII (but thus still an improvement on the land of the overwhelming majority of CA dwellers).

Insofar as constitutional constraints on land acquisition explain the limits to resettlement, they in turn have to be explained. Among the factors cited for the compromise nature of the constitutional settlement are the limited radicalization of the liberation movements and their leaders (Saul 1979) and their cadres (Kriger 1988), and the 'peasant' consciousness of the movements' main social base in the countryside (Ranger 1985). But overarching was the nature of the balance of power that circumscribed Lancaster House: one where settler state forces were fought to a standstill rather than defeated — circumstances that dictated a compromise. By comparison, the liberation movement in South Africa can claim even more of a political stalemate and less of a victory especially in relation to the agricultural sector — there are no semi-liberated rural areas in RSA; relatively few farms have been deserted or squatted on. The strength of the diplomatic, aid-related and strategic pressures on the Zimbabwe state to abide by the compromise agreements it signed have also to be appreciated (S Moyo 1991), and similar external and internal pressures to restrain any radicalism will be felt in a future South Africa.

Arguably, however, difficulties of land acquisition (as a result of whatever set of factors) should not be seen as determinant. They do not explain the rapid curtailment of the programme after its lively expansion up to 1983, or the watering down of an original draft of the Land Acquisition Act of 1984, which would have offered some ingenious ways around the Constitutional limits, or the fact that the UK government provision of matching funds for resettlement were not used up until after 1990 because the Zimbabwe government economized on half of the budget provision. These trends could be seen as pointing to a 'lack of political will', but the use of that phrase simply restates the problem rather than explains it.

A more composite explanation of the limitations of agrarian reform and the cutbacks might suggest that the basic political circumstances of the transition did in fact dictate reformist rather than revolutionary strategies — a similar situation to that which all commentators, even on the left, recognize to be the emerging pattern in RSA. But within that range of reformist options, promising initiatives in fact emerged although, in the kind of circumstances mentioned in the above paragraph, all too often the less progressive or ambitious outcome emerged. Analysing one of these moments of opportunity, it has to be recognized that the high tide of resettlement in 1981–83 was in large measure a matter of official sanctioning and institutional backing for pre-emptive squatting by peasants (Herbst 1989) — and the lesson of the importance of popular mobilization for future outcomes in South Africa has been stressed (Levin and Wiener 1993; Bernstein 1994). However, that should not obscure the extent to which determined and energetic initiatives by progressives in the Zimbabwe government charged with planning these settlements of squatters contributed to making them successful as means of livelihood and units of production. Nor should it be underestimated how far and effectively resettlement policy was undermined through questioning in a Parliament Estimates Committee in 1983 and in the corridors of the technicist Ministry of Agriculture, by a coalition of right-wing Zimbabwean politicians (many of them acquiring commercial farms of their own along the way), the well-organized lobbying of the Commercial Farmers' Union, and international aid 'experts'. In this infighting in policy circles progressive elements were outflanked, partly as a result of three specious lines of argument not being significantly countered and becoming widely accepted. These arguments are once again being raised as Zimbabwe contemplates a possible second stage of land reform now that constitutional constraints have been removed — and their parallels are already being voiced in RSA. The first we have met — that resettlement has not worked — and its ignoring of the facts will be discussed below. The second is that resettlement will catastrophically undermine production, employment and foreign-exchange earning of the LSCF sector and in turn the food security of the nation and the overall economy (Kinsey 1983). This proposition is demonstrably untrue to the extent that land acquisition concentrates on the many commercial farms which are of low productivity and with land left idle. This prediction of short run economic doom will only be proved false if land acquisition in South Africa gives priority to that underutilized land. In such a way the inevitable compromise nature of the transition can be recognized and implemented in a more vigorous way than did Zimbabwe in the 1980s: a significant land redistribution to peasants is to a degree compatible with the retention of the interests of white agrarian capital; a degree of equity is compatible with short-run national economic balance. Unfortunately some of the tendencies at work in Zimbabwe in the 1990s seem bent on a path of ignoring this economic rationale by attempting a mixture of bureaucratic and short-run populist calculations to acquire land in designated blocks irrespective of their productivity.

The third orthodox argument which had a significant role, in so far as it was not countered, in undermining reform was a version of environmentalism. This 'conservationist' view (Cliffe 1988a) held that environmental degradation characterized African farming (see next section) and would inevitably be replicated in resettlement. The premise for this argument is that the LSCF was the optimum land-use system for much of southern Africa.

The contentions of the argument in the next paragraphs is that in economic terms, as far as it goes, it can be claimed a significant advance — which is not to say that the particular patterns of settlement, the 'models', could not be improved upon.

Most of the 50,000 households that had benefited by the early 1990s had been resettled under a pattern, referred to as 'Model A', whereby individual householders receive five or six hectares of arable land for cultivation plus access to common grazing areas for a small herd of cattle for ploughing and milk, which varied in size depending on the differing potential of the NR. Another few thousand have formed cooperatives which collectively received a large farm intact which they were expected to continue to

run as a single operating unit. Some of these have done so quite successfully, but many have found it hard to overcome the lack of practical as
opposed to rhetorical support from the government (see Hanlon 1986) plus
the difficulties of handling a large and sophisticated operation and at the
same time of organizing themselves into a relatively large cooperating
group without training or a step-by-step approach to familiarize them with
cooperative practices. Some isolated resettlements represent experiments
either of settlement of 'out-growers' around a core (company or state-
owned) estate or a system of using former ranching to provide extra remedial grazing on a rotational basis for neighbouring CA livestock owners.

Targets for resettlement specified a gradual build-up of production,
yields and incomes, as a result of the settlers putting increasing amounts of
their allocated land to use and as a result of management, extension and
credit. By and large these were achieved ahead of schedule, so that by 1986
the RAs with 6.5 per cent of the total land area were providing 5.8 per cent
of the national maize production, a similar proportion of groundnuts, 3.6
per cent of sorghum and 3.5 per cent of cotton. Yields tend to be higher
than for CAs in the same natural region but have still not reached the
average for LSCFs. However, the fact that over 2 million hectares of land in
NRs III–V were put to use under a different farming system means that
there is a more intensive arable use of this type of land, which was previously just used for ranching under the former commercial ownership.

The generally very impressive achievement of production targets and
especially incomes has, however, varied between schemes but has been
extremely skewed within them. Surveys by the government and by the
British official aid agency (GOZ 1986; ODA 1989) suggest that some 5 per
cent of resettled households do not cultivate all their allotted arable holding; about half do not apply any fertilizer and they most likely have low
yields and often higher costs (especially when they have to hire tillage);
many do not take up their allocated option for livestock numbers, very
largely because they had few or no livestock when they joined the scheme
and have not been able to acquire it subsequently. Many families in the
RAs remain very poor; almost 50 per cent have no cattle. Moreover, the
overall result is that some arable land is not cultivated and much of the
very extensive areas set aside for grazing have not been fully utilized (in
1987 only 57 per cent of the recommended carrying capacity overall). Thus,
contrary to the politically-promoted mythology the problem of 'sustainability' in the RAs is not one of 'environmental degradation', but of lack of
resources and under-utilization of land.

These patterns reflect the original criteria for selection of settlers — that
they should be the needy (with little or no land and without other means of
support). Now there is a strong lobby by rich peasants supported by

technicist officials to repeat Kenya's precedent and to offer land exclusively to 'well-trained black farmers' (*The Economist*, 22 May 1993) — a premise based on a faulty perception of the actual evidence in reports mentioned above: that it is lack of resources, specifically draught animals, not of know-how that explains why some of those resettled have not prospered. The simple answer would be to provide more credit for oxen so the poor can make full use of their land allocation, rather than to exclude them from the schemes.

Sustainable Development and the Communal Areas

The Zimbabwe government's measures since independence have generated successful improvements in production in peasant agriculture. From less than 10 per cent of marketed output of maize and cotton in 1979, the CAs were contributing almost 50 per cent of each crop by 1989. In part these production increases were a result of the peasant sector receiving a bigger (but still minority) share of credit, of fertilizers and often chemical inputs, of marketing and transport facilities, of extension advice. However, they had very definite limits in terms of class and location, being confined to areas in NRII and NRIII, and in those areas to the better-off minority of those peasant households with more land, labour and draught power (Cliffe 1988b; Wiener et al 1985). They did not solve the problems of poverty amongst the majority of rural households; they did not provide a model of sustainability — both limitations being brought home starkly by the severity of the human effects of the drought of 1990–92.

The problem of sustainability of the CAs has in fact been side-stepped since 1980; policies pursued have been a matter of supplying agricultural 'inputs' — undoubtedly welcome and partially productive. Apart from a few pilot projects, any structural changes in the farming system have been studiously avoided, although government remains committed to 'Communal Lands Reorganization'. There is no scarcity of prescriptions, however. The most influential remains what might be termed the 'conservationist orthodoxy'. A current example is a National Conservation Strategy (NCS) document presented to a conference in 1985 which 'sees the problem as acute': in agricultural areas 'soil erosion has become excessive and dangerous ... often critical,' the extensive grazing lands 'show advanced degradation,' especially those in the CAs, which are marked by 'advancing desertification ... [which will be] difficult to reverse.' The explanation that the Rhodesian-style conservationists offer for this situation is based on a Malthusian perspective of over-population leading to overuse and misuse of land — too intensive cultivation, without fallow periods of land that is often 'unsuitable' for crops, plus overgrazing of the natural pasture. This tendency is combined with the shortcomings of a peasant agrarian system in the CAs, where farming and herding practices and social patterns militate against sustainable agriculture. Specifically, cultivation is said to ignore contours, encroach on watercourses, which in turn generates silting, and generally to use land that is unsuitable because of slope, poor or fragile soils, or climatic marginality. There is some recognition nowadays that these practices are not simply due to ignorance, but they are then put down to a land shortage resulting from a generalized over-population rather than the highly skewed racial distribution of land. Beyond that, lack of sustainable arable practices are put down to the so-called 'communal' land tenure system; the theoretical right that family land can be allocated (which scarcely operates in practice given the necessity of permanent cultivation) supposedly breeds an insecurity which apparently inhibits CA farmers from making permanent improvements or worrying about soil conservation in the long run.

Degradation of grazing land, also the source of firewood, is seen as an even more serious problem, resulting from overstocking of available pasture; the NCS document's diagnosis is that 'in spite of good livestock management and veterinary practices, there is frequently a virtual lack of understanding of range management ... [and] a popular demand for more land and more livestock to satisfy socio-economic aspirations.' Again the cause is seen to be the indigenous social system, specifically the absence of any management of 'common' grazing land.

The prescriptions that flow from this diagnosis are predictable. The same technical prescriptions that Beinart (1984) argues were identified in South Africa decades ago: for arable husbandry 'ploughing should be along the contours and strips of veld should be left between the lands; *dongas* (gulleys) should be filled in and planted, vegetation left untouched around watercourses and vleis'; for livestock husbandry 'stock numbers should be limited; animals should be driven along the contour ... kraaling should be limited and dispersed watering places in fenced paddocks provided'.

To get over the structural problem of 'communal' land tenure supposedly inhibiting incentives for proper land use, what had been proposed in the past, under the 'Native' Land Husbandry Act of the 1950s, for instance, was for individual titles to be issued for existing cultivated land — which left a proportion of the people permanently landless. This supposed incentive of a market in land was coupled with regulations to enforce conservation. Nowadays, perhaps in the knowledge that land husbandry's reliance on compulsion and the resulting impoverishment were successfully resisted, no one openly advocates individual tenure. And thus Zimbabwe today has avoided what has been introduced recently in the 'Bantustans' of South Africa. Nevertheless the settler conservationists' belief that paternalist enforcement is necessary to overcome African peasant attitudes is reinforced by the authoritarian, statist knee-jerk reflexes of the new bureaucrats. Thus the strategy document calls for 'strict action against landholders who persistently ignore advice and allow their land to deteriorate.' One change in land tenure that is being mooted once again in the 1990s is not individualization but the state taking over freehold — which sounds very radical — but where leasehold would be extended as a 'permit to use' to which would attach conditions of 'proper use'. Thus the 'strict action' for those who 'ignore advice' would then be landlessness — draconian (and counter productive even in its own terms because it is a recipe for insecurity offering even less incentive to improve land), but also, thankfully, politically and administratively unimplementable so far — except in the RAs where new settlers have no guaranteed rights of access to land.

Thus proposals for 'improved land use' remain the same as in the 1950s: the top-down specifying of ideal sizes of arable holdings and cultivation patterns and of land-livestock ratios. This has been the basis for the Resettlement Schemes, and the NCS proposed this same approach for the CAs. But in the context of land shortage this always implies some dumping of 'surplus people' off any 'properly-managed' lands. The land may be conserved but the people's predicament is ignored.

If Zimbabwe, or a future South Africa, were to implement such prescriptions, many would argue that they represent too high a social cost even if they conserved the soil. But a rigorous scrutiny of the evidence behind these diagnoses brings home the very spurious basis on which these draconian proposals are made. After one of the very few works that has bothered to re-evaluate the data, Biot et al (1992) conclude that 'the evidence on the existence, cause and effects of erosion in the CAs has so many discrepancies as to be of little value in the debate over resettlement.' And, one might add, over communal land reorganization. They point out that the source for many predictions of soil losses of over 100 tons per hectare is one particular field trial, among others that were far less; that another method uses a model which forecasts soil losses from maize cultivation more than ten times those subsequently observed. Other research which has sought to chart the actual *process* of erosion by using aerial photographs since 1947, finds 'no real worsening of erosion in 40 years' (J Elliott, personal communication). The orthodox conservationists are thus being increasingly revealed as having no clothes and a suspect methodology, which lays bare their implicit racism and their hidden political agendas.

CONCLUSIONS

This chapter has sought to indicate some aspects of Zimbabwe's land redistribution and broader efforts at promoting sustainable and productive peasant agriculture which might be instructive as South Africans plan a post-apartheid future. Its basic argument is that Zimbabwe's experience would repay careful and systematic study. Some areas where Zimbabwe's experience would indicate the need for serious investigation, creative thinking and popular mobilization can be indicated.

Constitutional and legal battles over property rights
Too many concessions to white interests could seriously hamper reform in South Africa; political negotiations will need to look at the fine print carefully; focusing popular mobilization around land rights could strengthen the hand of nationalist negotiators.

Models and procedures for redistribution of land
Although limited in scale Zimbabwe has generated programmes for distributing large commercial farms and ranches to African smallholders, which have maintained and even enhanced overall production and employment and, arguably, could make RAs even more intensive. There are also experiments with cooperatives, which have been productive where there is a high level of commitment, but have often been too ambitious in required scale of organization and starved of inputs; with state farms, which have generally been expensive to set up and then only special crops are worth the expense; with out-grower schemes, which link smallholders to a commercial plantation; and with schemes in semi-arid areas where former ranches have been made available to extend grazing in CAs. The two examples of the last have scarcely justified the expense, but the demand for grazing is one of the strongest grassroots pressures and alternative forms might prove more economic and sustainable. Only careful study of these 'models' can reveal which ones, in what modified form, might be applicable to specific environments and situations in South Africa — otherwise South Africa will be reinventing the wheel.

Zimbabwe's experience also reveals 'dos' and 'don'ts' about the organizational structures required for land redistribution: in sum, a record of successfully building-in technical improvements and valuable infrastructure, even if perhaps too 'top-down' in its approach to settlers and land allocation rights, too ready to find reasons to blame settlers for any lack of economic or environmental success, and too eager to use this as an excuse for backing the better-off peasants at the expense of the poor. Zimbabwe's second stage of land reform might be facing a dearth of the multi-disciplinary mobilizing cadres as a result of the running down of the programme in the late 1980s. Certainly, South Africa will quickly have to identify what kinds of resettlement cadres it will use and begin training them, if it is not to have a similar bottleneck.

Restructuring and revitalization of the communal areas
Zimbabwe shows what can be achieved simply by removing restrictions on agricultural opportunities in the reserves and providing a minimum of chemical inputs, credit, extension advice and marketing facilities with the same fair, realistic and guaranteed prices that white agriculture has enjoyed in the past. However, it has so far shrunk from any more rigorous restructuring of land use, of land tenure and of the basic farming system in the CAs. In refusing so far to return to the prescriptions of private land titles of the 1950s, Zimbabwe has avoided worsening the massive problem of unemployment, which would have occurred from the inevitably resulting landlessness. In this respect the land titling in South Africa may mean that the Republic's starting point is closer to that of Kenya — but the pre- and post-independence registering of land titles has created many problems there (Hunt 1984).

Being more significant than any insights from specific methods and patterns, Zimbabwe's experience forces anyone concerned with South Africa's future rural development and reform to clarify certain basic thinking. In particular, three propositions, each of which challenge commonly held beliefs about the Zimbabwe experience, seem to need airing in the context of policy planning in South Africa:

1. Under the right circumstances and with careful planning, African smallholder production could replace some of the underutilized parts of white agriculture and thus combine equity with enhanced economic performance — and combining these goals is important for the compromise reform situation facing South Africa at this stage of its transition.
2. Environmental sustainability must also be maintained in any transition, but is not best attained by the application of the conservationist orthodoxy's' rigid rules of 'proper' land use, and by their being imposed rather than emerging through participatory networks.
3. The outcome of the transition with respect to land and agrarian reform will indeed be settled by popular forces, just as the continued pressure from 'squatters' in Zimbabwe (and still to this day in Kenya) keeps up some momentum for land redistribution, rather than through the drawing up of blueprints designed in a laboratory, as S

Moyo (1991), Levin and Wiener (1993) and others have argued. But this insight from Zimbabwe's experience should not absolve those who write and discuss these issues from doing the one thing for which they are paid — their homework. They should be ready to say what might and might not work, and to attempt to draw up plans — for wider discussion certainly — which give practical expression to popular demands. Most crucially, it has to be recognized that in the kind of transition occurring, one dimension of the struggle is going to be between alternative teams of planners and alternative modes of thinking about agrarian issues. Those who would like to see more progressive outcomes are, specifically, going to have to find counters to arguments that are already being advanced by the self-styled 'practical' and 'technical' planners, drawing on their own interpretation of Zimbabwe to argue that land redistribution does not work in economic and environmental terms.

REFERENCES

Beinart, W (1984) 'Soil Erosion, Conservationism and Ideas about Development: A Southern African Exploration, 1900–1960', *Journal of Southern African Studies*, vol 11, no 1

Bernstein, H (1994) 'South Africa: Agrarian Questions', *Southern Africa Reports*, vol 9, no 3

Biot, Y, Lambert, R and Perkin, S (1992) 'What's the Problem? An Essay on Land Degradation, Science and Development in Sub-Saharan Africa', *Discussion Paper 222*, School of Development Studies, University of East Anglia, Norwich

Cliffe, L (1988a) 'The Conservation Issue in Zimbabwe', *Review of African Political Economy*, no 42

—— (1988b) 'Zimbabwe's Agricultural "Success" and Food Security in Southern Africa', *Review of African Political Economy*, no 43

Colburn, F (ed) (1989) *Everyday Forms of Peasant Resistance*, New York, Sharpe

GOZ (Government of Zimbabwe) (1986) *First Annual Survey of Settler Households in Normal Intensive Model A Resettlement Schemes*, Harare, Ministry of Lands, Agriculture and Rural Resettlement

Hanlon, J (1986) 'Producer Co-operatives and the Government in Zimbabwe', mimeo, London

Herbst, J (1989) 'How the Weak Succeed: Tactics, Political Goods and Institutions in the Struggle over Land in Zimbabwe', in Colburn, qv

Hunt, D (1984) *The Impending Crisis in Kenya: The Case for Land Reform*, Aldershot, Gower

Kinsey, B (1983) 'Emerging Policy Issues in Zimbabwe's Land Resettlement Programmes, *Development Policy Review*, no 1

Kriger, N (1988) 'The Zimbabwean War of Liberation: Struggles within the Struggle', *Journal of Southern African Studies*, vol 12, no 1

Levin, R and Wiener, D (1993) 'The Agrarian Question of Politics in the "New" South Africa', *Review of African Political Economy*, no 57

Leys, C (1975) *Underdevelopment in Kenya*, London, Heinemann

Marcus, T (1989) *Modernising Super-exploitation: Restructuring South African Agriculture*, London, Zed Press

Moyo, J (1993) 'The Political Dimension of the Zimbabwe Land Acquisition Act (1992)', mimeo, Harare, Department of Political and Administrative Studies, University of Zimbabwe

Moyo, S (1991) 'The Zimbabweanisation of Southern Africa's Agrarian Question: Lessons or Domino Stratagems?', mimeo, Harare, Zimbabwe Institute of Development Studies

ODA (1989) 'Land Resettlement in Zimbabwe: A Preliminary Evaluation', Evaluation Report EV 434, London, Overseas Development Administration

Odinga, O (1967) *Not Yet Uhuru*, London, Heinemann

Raikes, P (1975) 'Ujamaa and Rural Socialism', *Review of African Political Economy*, no 3

—— (1984) 'Food Policy and Production in Mozambique since Independence, *Review of African Political Economy* no 29

Ranger, T (1985) *Peasant Consciousness and Guerrilla War in Zimbabwe*, London, James Currey

Saul, J (1979) 'Transforming the Struggle in Zimbabwe', in J Saul, *The State and Revolution in Eastern Africa*, London, Heinemann

Wiener, D, Moyo, S, Munslow, B and O'Keefe, P (1985) 'Land Use and Agricultural Productivity in Zimbabwe', *Journal of Modern African Studies*, vol 23, no 2

PART II:
THE STATE, NGOs AND
SOCIAL POLICY

Chapter Seven

Sustainable Development, Democracy and the Courts in a Democratic South Africa

François du Bois

The crumbling of the apartheid state is accompanied by the breakdown of the traditional South African identification of environmental concern with nature conservation. The National Environmental Awareness Campaign (NEAC), the 'greening' of the civics, and environmental policy statements by the African National Congress (ANC) and the Pan-Africanist Congress (PAC) have focused the sustainable development debate on the quality of the human environment, with a resource-rich and biologically diverse natural environment as part thereof (Hart 1992: 53–5, and Cock and Koch 1991). In the words of the NEAC's *1990 Position Paper*: 'We question those whose concern for the environment focuses on saving various species of animals from extinction or preserving small areas of land for game parks patronized mainly by whites whose financial status enables them to enjoy nature in its natural state.'

This transformation in the conception of sustainable development is not, of course, uniquely South African. Internationally, too, the stress increasingly falls on environmental sustainability as a component of the sustainability and quality of human life (Lélé 1991; Bartelmus 1986: 1–13). The relationship between poverty and environmental degradation has received growing attention, leading to recognition of the harsh environmental burdens economic development has imposed on impoverished communities (Hardoy and Satterthwaite 1984, and 1989) and their lack of the political clout needed to transform such development into environmental improvement (Hart 1992: 56).

It is precisely this link between political powerlessness and the imposition of environmental burdens that makes law relevant. To the extent that people can use the law to affect the environmental consequences of development, legal systems can function as mechanisms for public participation in environmental policy. This is particularly important in South Africa, where the formal structures of environmental policy-making provide very little opportunity for public input.[1] To what extent might post-apartheid law contribute to the democratization of environmental policy-making and the equitable sharing of environmental burdens?

That question has been placed on the agenda by both major participants in the CODESA (Congress for a Democratic South Africa) process: the recognition of environmental rights is as prominent in the South African government's proposals for a Charter of Fundamental Rights as it is in the ANC's Bill of Rights proposals.

This chapter is therefore aimed at addressing that question through an exploration of these proposals. An examination of the state of the law these proposals are intended to rectify, is followed by an analysis of the major recommendations for protecting environmental rights currently on the table. The third section of this chapter further explores an important feature common to the ANC's and South African government's proposals — improved access to environmental justice — by briefly examining the experience in countries which have taken this route.

ACCESS TO ENVIRONMENTAL JUSTICE IN PRE-DEMOCRATIC SOUTH AFRICA

Broadly speaking, there are two ways in which courts may feature as fora for public participation in environmental policy-making. They may, firstly, be called on to prevent, or order compensation for, the environmentally harmful activities of individuals and companies through the ordinary civil litigation process. Secondly, the procedure of judicial review may be used to ensure that the state acts in accordance with the requirements of sustainable development. As the proliferation of environmental statutes in South Africa and elsewhere indicates, however, the former method of environmental protection plays a steadily declining role. This part of the chapter will therefore focus on the legal gateways for ensuring that the state promotes a sustainable — and sustaining — environment.

---

1. For example, the Environment Conservation Act 73 of 1989 has been described as providing probably the most 'extensive opportunities for public comment and representations in respect of administrative decision-making' (Rabie 1992: 101), yet provides only for the publication of notices in the *Government Gazette* or *Official Gazette* with a view to eliciting public comment on proposed administrative measures.

South African law provides scant opportunities in this regard. In the absence of enforceable constitutional rights, the legislature is free to act as it pleases and the scope for judicial review is restricted to administrative acts. Within this limitation the rules which govern access to the courts (known as the *locus standi* requirement) are restrictive, and the grounds on which administrative acts may be challenged narrow. These restrictions provide the context in which proposals for post-apartheid reform have to be assessed, and must, therefore now be examined.

Access to the Courts

The major limitation on access to the courts under current South African law is that litigants must show that they are personally harmed by the administrative act they seek to challenge,[2] or that their own legal rights are in issue.[3] South African courts have consistently refused to allow people to sue the state administration simply on the ground that it is doing something contrary to law and that it is in the public interest that it should be stopped.[4] This principle is applied so strictly that even 'surrogate standing' is virtually unknown to South African law: the courts have allowed a concerned individual or organization to approach them on behalf of another only where the life or liberty of that other was in danger.[5]

The requirement of personal harm and legal rights has, moreover, been interpreted restrictively. Firstly, it has been held that it is not enough to suffer harm; the person who suffered that harm will only be able to sue the state if that harm violated a legally enforceable right.[6] This has important consequences for environmental litigation, because environmental interests have not been clearly defined and formulated in

---

2 . *Bagnall v The Colonial Government* 1907 (24) SC 470; *Director of Education, Transvaal v McCagie* 1918 AD 616; *Milani v South African Medical and Dental Council* 1990 (1) SA 899 (T).

3 . *Dalrymple v Colonial Treasurer* 1910 TS 372; *Bamford v Minister of Community Development and State Auxiliary Services* 1981 (3) SA 1054 (C). This is the case even where someone seeks to enforce a statute enacted in the public interest: *Roodepoort–Maraisburg Town Council v Eastern Properties (Prop) Ltd* 1933 AD 87; *Madrassa Anjuman Islamia v Johannesburg Municipality* 1917 AD 718.

4 . See *Bagnall v The Colonial Government*, above n 2; *Dalrymple v The Colonial Treasurer*, above n 3; *Von Moltke v Costa Areosa (Pty) Ltd* 1975 (1) SA 255 (C).

5 . See *Parents Committee of Namibia v Nujoma* 1990 (1) SA 873 (A)

6 . *Bagnall v The Colonial Government*, above n 2; *Dalrymple v The Colonial Treasurer*, above n 3; *Roodepoort–Maraisburg Town Council v Eastern Properties (Prop) Ltd*, above n 3; *Milani v SA Medical and Dental Council*, above; *Aucamp v Nel NO* 1991 (1) SA 220 (O).

South African law as 'rights'.[7] Whereas environmental degradation often affects 'merely' the quality of life, only financial and physical harm (to someone's body or property), and possibly a threat to health,[8] will clearly constitute the violation of a legally enforceable right.

These restrictions on access to the courts mean that it is not possible in South African law to challenge administrative activities simply on the ground that they harm the public interest in environmental sustainability. Only (some) private interests in environmentally sensitive policies can be protected. Indeed, in as much as these requirements are more likely to be met by those who harm the environment than by those experiencing the consequences of such harm — the owner of a factory or waste-dump has no difficulty in showing that environmental regulations affect his particular financial and property interests — these rules are weighted in favour of those wishing to frustrate environmentally sensitive administrative policies. Small wonder that one of the few instances of successful judicial review proceedings in environmental matters[9] concerned a landowner's objection against the imposition of a planning condition designed to safeguard the slopes of Table Mountain as a public amenity.

The requirement of violation of a legally recognized right also limits the opportunities for environmental NGOs (non-governmental organizations) to go to court. It means that the fact that the specific purpose of an NGO is to promote environmental protection will not be sufficient to enable it to obtain a court hearing. Indeed, this requirement has been so restrictively interpreted as to mean that an organization may not even come to court as representative of the interests of its members, but must show that its own interests, as distinct from those of its members, have been infringed.[10]

The Scope of the Courts' Powers

The grounds on which administrative acts may be challenged in South African law are likewise ill-suited to the promotion of environmental

---

7. In *Von Moltke v Costa Areosa (Pty) Ltd*, above n 4, standing was denied to an applicant alleging that his natural surroundings were being destroyed, but the court did not specifically consider whether he had a right to the enjoyment of natural surroundings.
8. Recognized as sufficient in *Dell v Town Council of Cape Town* 1879 (9) Buch 2.
9. *Administrator, Cape v Associated Buildings Ltd* 1957 (2) SA 317 (A).
10. *Ahmadiyya Anjuman Ihaati–Islam Lahore (South Africa) v Muslim Judicial Council (Cape)* 1983 (4) SA 855 (C); *South African Optometric Association v Frame Distributors (Pty) Ltd* 1985 (3) SA 100 (O); *Natal Fresh Produce Growers Association v Agroserve (Pty) Ltd* 1990 (4) SA 749 (N).

sustainability through the courts. They limit the courts' powers in such a way as to make it virtually impossible to challenge the environmental soundness of government measures.

The scope for challenging the validity of administrative acts is mainly restricted by the rule that courts may not normally decide on the merits of an administrative act, for example on whether it was in the public interest or not. Only where legislation specifically empowers a court to do so, can it hear an appeal against an administrative decision which would enable it to consider whether that decision was correct. In the absence of such legislation South African courts only have the power to 'review' administrative acts for legality, that is, to determine whether the acts in question were covered by legislative authorization (Baxter 1984).

Since South African environmental legislation makes no provision for appeals concerning the merits of administrative actions (Rabie et al 1992: 138), judicial review proceedings provide the only avenue for attacking environmentally unsound administrative acts. For that avenue to lead anywhere, however, a legislative obligation to act in accordance with environmental considerations is essential. Yet even the Environment Conservation Act 73 of 1989, which authorizes the Minister of Environment Affairs to determine an environmental policy, binding on the state, is ambiguous as to its enforcement (Rabie 1992: 105). The result is that there is virtually no scope for challenging administrative acts on the basis of their environmental soundness.

It is also in principle possible under South African law to request a court to enforce a statute so as to force the administration to carry out duties imposed on it by the statute (Baxter 1984). The wide range of environmental statutes in South Africa makes this a potentially important avenue for using the courts to promote environmentally sustainable development. However, the restrictions imposed by the courts on the enforcement of statutory duties and the way in which South African environmental legislation has been drafted, combine to limit the usefulness of this legal remedy.

The basic restriction is that the court can only order an administrative body to carry out the precise duty prescribed in the legislation. This means that if the duty leaves some discretion to the administration, if it requires an administrative body to exercise judgement, then a South African court will only order the administrative body *to consider* the matter. The court will not prescribe how that judgement has to be exercised; it will not prescribe the actual decision the administration has to take.[11]

This renders the remedy under discussion virtually meaningless in the context of environmental legislation, for this type of legislation character-istically leaves much to the discretion of the state administration. The Environment Conservation Act 73 of 1989, for example, leaves almost the entire fields of noise control and waste management to be regulated by administrative discretion (Rabie 1992: 112–13).

Current South African law is therefore singularly ill-suited to the democratization of environmental policy-making through the judicial process. It is difficult to gain access to the courts, and access would, at any rate, often be of little use. What is more, there is a single cause for these two difficulties: the absence of a clearly established right to a sustainable environment. It is because South African law does not recognize such a right, that the rules of standing allow little scope for using the law to improve public access to environmental policy, and that the grounds for challenging administrative acts fail to impose an effec-tive obligation on the state to promote environmental sustainability.

NEW OPPORTUNITIES IN THE FUTURE?

In view of the foregoing it should come as no surprise that the current debate about a Bill of Rights for South Africa has produced a number of proposals for recognizing constitutional environmental rights. If enacted, any of those proposals would certainly transform current South African law by bringing legislation too under the purview of judicial review. Depending on how such a right is formulated in a new South African Constitution, it may also greatly expand the scope for access to environ-mental justice. I now wish to examine and compare the two most important of these proposals, paying particular attention to whether they would expand the opportunities for mobilizing legal resources for environmental protection.

Proposals by the ANC

The ANC's Bill of Rights for a Democratic South Africa (ANC 1992)[12] deals in Article 12 with 'Land and the Environment'. Paragraph 13 of that Article provides:

---

11 . *Bonnievale Wine and Brandy Co Ltd* v Gordonia Liquor Licensing Board 1953 (3) SA 500 (K); *Moll v Paarl Civil Commissioner and Another* 14 SC 463.

12 . *Preliminary Revised Text* May 1992. The provision is virtually identical to that contained in Article 12 of the 1990 *Working Draft for Consultation*.

All men and women shall have the right to a healthy and ecologically balanced environment and the duty to defend it.

Paragraph 14 seeks to spell out some implications of this right. It provides:

In order to secure this right, the State, acting through appropriate agencies and organs shall conserve, protect and improve the environment, and in particular:

a) *prevent and control pollution of the air and waters and erosion and degradation of the soil;*

b) *have regard in local, regional and national planning to the maintenance or creation of balanced ecological and biological areas and to the prevention or minimising of harmful effects on the environment;*

c) *promote the rational use of natural resources, safeguarding their capacity for renewal and ecological stability;*

d) *ensure that long-term damage is not done to the environment by industrial or other forms of waste;*

e) *maintain, create and develop natural reserves, parks and recreational areas and classify and protect other sites and landscapes so as to ensure the preservation and protection of areas of outstanding cultural, historic and natural interest.*

Paragraph 15 specifies that environmental legislation shall promote public participation. It provides:

Legislation shall provide for co-operation between the State, non-governmental organizations, local communities and individuals in seeking to improve the environment and encourage ecologically sensible habits in daily life.

Paragraph 16 provides for access to environmental justice:

The law shall provide for appropriate penalties and reparation in the case of any damage caused to the environment, and permit the interdiction by any interested person or by any agency established for the purpose of protecting the environment, of any public or private activity or undertaking which manifestly and unreasonably causes or threatens to cause irreparable damage to the environment.

Access to courts is addressed explicitly only in Paragraph 16, which provides for wider access than is currently the case *provided that* the order requested from the court is one prohibiting an activity. It would therefore give greater access to the courts only in respect of certain judicial remedies. However, as explained above, someone's capacity to go to court depends under current rules on whether a legally recognized right has been infringed, and much of the difficulty surrounding access to environmental justice at present derives from the absence of a clear right to the environment. Paragraph 13 is therefore also important, since its recognition of a right to a healthy and ecologically balanced environment would expand the scope for arguments that rights have been infringed by environmentally unsustainable activities. Taken together, these two paragraphs of the ANC's proposal would significantly increase the opportunities for gaining access to the courts in the pursuit of environmental sustainability.

Both paragraphs, it must be noted, nevertheless circumscribe the circumstances in which courts can make orders, thereby limiting the potential impact of enhanced access. Paragraph 13 would only authorize court orders in the case of environmental health hazards and disturbance of the ecological balance; paragraph 16 would only allow the prohibition of an act which *'manifestly and unreasonably* causes or threatens to cause *irreparable damage* to the environment.' (emphasis added.)

These paragraphs would cover litigation against the state as well as litigation involving only individuals and non-state bodies. Paragraphs 14 and 15, however, apply to the state alone and would, if enacted in a Bill of Rights, greatly alter the scope for enforcing environmental sensitivity on the state administration. By recognizing a duty on the state to 'conserve, protect and improve the environment' in various specified ways, paragraph 14 would fill the gaps noted above in current South African administrative law. Any administrative decision with an environmental impact could be questioned in court on the ground of 'legality' if it failed to 'conserve, protect [or] improve the environment.'

Proposals by the South African Government

The South African government has also recently proposed a *Charter of Fundamental Rights for South Africa* (Republic of South Africa 1993). Article 32 therof suggests the adoption of the following provision:

> *Every person shall have the right not to be exposed to an environment which is dangerous or seriously detrimental to the health or well-being of man, and the right to conservation and protection of the environment.*

However, Article 2 of this document imposes the following qualification on its operation:

No provision of this Charter shall be construed so as to create or regulate legal relations other that (sic) *those between the state and a person...*

The government's explanatory note to Article 32 indicates the thinking behind this provision: the 'vertical application of this right will ensure that this right can only be enforced against the State, which will prevent a witch-hunt against private entrepreneurs'(Republic of South Africa 1993: 20).

This points to a crucial difference between the proposals published by the ANC and the South African government respectively: the former is explicitly formulated so as to enable litigation against private polluters, the latter so as to block this avenue of access to environmental justice.[13]

A further contrast in the formulation of these two proposals is the absence in the South African government's document of any express duties on the state such as those contained in paragraph 14 of the ANC's proposal. This is important, even though logically every right is accompanied by a duty. It is important because while the existence of a right gives rise to a duty not to violate that right, it does not necessarily give rise to a legal duty to act positively so as to achieve that right. Indeed, some believe that the imposition of positive duties on the state would be inappropriate[14] — a view shared by the South African courts which have in the past been loath to enforce duties imposed on the state by statute. Everything will depend on the approach a future South African court adopts with regard to these matters, but it can be said that the absence from the South African government's proposals of positive duties on the state to achieve environmental sustainability means that in this respect too, it holds out less promise than the ANC's proposal for using the courts to achieve this goal.

The South African government's proposals also fail to deal with the question of access to the courts. As explained above, the ANC's proposal expressly seeks to widen this in respect of activities that are manifestly and unreasonably causing irreparable harm to the environment. The absence of a similar provision in the government's proposal is significant,

---

13. Paragraph 13 of the ANC's proposed Article 12 explicitly imposes an environmental duty on *every person* and paragraph 16 provides for court orders against 'any public *or private* activity or undertaking.'
14. The South African government expresses this view in the 'Introductory remarks' to its proposals. It is also shared by the South African Law Commission — see below.

because the draft Bill of Rights submitted to the government by the South African Law Commission (1989) did contain a provision seeking to expand the range of people capable of enforcing the Bill of Rights. It is not, however, a fatal flaw. The established South African principle, outlined in the previous section, is that the capacity to approach a court depends on the violation of a right. The South African government's proposal to recognize a right to the environment as belonging to 'every person' should therefore in itself prove sufficient to expand the opportunities for gaining access to the courts. However, as in the case of the ANC's draft, the failure to deal with this matter explicitly would be bound to bring about uncertainty and thereby inhibit effective access to environmental justice.

LESSONS FROM ELSEWHERE[15]

It is crucial to bear in mind that the discussion of future trends has so far been deliberately confined to an examination of particular texts in the context of current South African law. The practical effect of any of these texts would, of course, in large measure depend on judicial interpretation. The judiciary in a post-apartheid South Africa might be very different from what it was under apartheid and might seek to mould the law so as to be more responsive to the interests of social justice.

A post-apartheid judiciary may find itself drawn to the significant expansion of access to environmental justice achieved by judges all over the Commonwealth during the past decade or so. Like South Africa, these countries inherited their 'standing' rules from English common law and therefore proceeded from the same starting point as will confront a post-apartheid judiciary in South Africa.

In England itself, and in Australia, statutory reformulations[16] of the standing requirement provided the pegs on which judges could hang decisions rejecting 'outdated technical rules of *locus standi*' similar to the current South African rules outlined above, and to introduce more liberal

---

15. My discussion of Commonwealth developments apart from India draws heavily on an unpublished paper by my colleague Professor James Read (1993).
16. In England this development was sparked off by the enactment in 1978 of Order 53 which introduced the requirement that an applicant for the judicial review of administrative actions must have 'sufficient interest in the matter' — see *IRC v National Federation of Self-Employed and Small Business Ltd* [1981] All ER 93, particularly Lord Diplock's speech at 107. In Australia the Administrative Decisions (Judicial Review) Act 1977, allowing 'a person who is aggrieved' (including 'person whose interests are adversely affected') to bring proceedings, played a similar role — see *Tooheys Ltd v Minister for Business and Consumer Affairs* (1981) 36 ALR 64.

access rules. In Australia, for example, it was held that, 'The necessary interest [required for *locus standi* under the Administrative decisions (Judicial Review) Act 1977] need not be a legal, proprietary, financial or other tangible interest. Neither need it be peculiar to the particular person.'[17] Through these developments the door has been opened to litigation by NGOs like the Child Poverty Action Group in England,[18] and unions, conservation groups[19] and members of Aboriginal communities[20] in Australia.

In Canada, on the other hand, the reformulation of standing requirements was stimulated by the Constitution, although it has percolated throughout the legal system (Read 1993: 9). The important impact that the mere existence of judicial concern for upholding the Constitution can have on access to justice is evident from the leading case of *Thorson v Attorney-General of Canada*.[21] There Laskin J indicated that the appropriate definition of the standing requirement depended on 'whether a question of constitutionality should be immunized from judicial review by denying standing to anyone to challenge the impugned statute.' The rule subsequently adopted by the Canadian Supreme Court was that:

> to establish status as a plaintiff in a suit seeking a declaration that legislation is invalid, if there is a serious issue as to its invalidity, a person need only to show that he is affected by it directly or that he has a genuine interest as a citizen in the validity of the legislation and that there is no other reasonable and effective manner in which the issue may be brought before the Court.[22]

In Nigeria, however, the courts found that the Constitution could also restrict their ability to give effect to the view that 'it is better to allow a party to go to court and to be heard than to refuse him access to our courts.'[23] In *Thomas v Olufosoye*,[24] for example, it was held that the

---

17 . *United States Tobacco Co v Minister of Consumer Affairs* (1988) 83 ALR 79 at 86.
18 . *R v Secretary of State for Social Services, ex parte Greater London Council and Child Poverty Action Group, The Times,* 16 August 1984.
19 . See the list of ten such cases contained in *Ogle v Stickland* (1987) 71 ALR 41.
20 . *Onus v Alcoa of Australia Ltd* (1981) 36 ALR 425.
21 . *Thorson v Attorney general of Canada* [1975] 1 SCR 138, 43 DLR (3d) 1. This impression is reinforced by *Australian Conservation Foundation Inc v Commonwealth* (1980) 28 ALR 257 where a majority in the Australian High Court, denying the applicant standing on the ground that the relevant had created no private rights, pointed out that constitutional cases raised different issues.
22 . *Minister of Justice v Borowski* [1981] 2 SCR 575, 130 DLR (3d) 588, per Martland J at 606.
23 . Per Fatahi-Williams CJN in *Senator Adesanya* [1981] (Read 1993: 12).

constitutional provision empowering judges to determine questions of 'civil rights and obligations' meant that plaintiffs had to show how their rights and obligations were affected in order to be entitled to a hearing. Consequently Obaseki JSC pointed out that: 'As the law stands, there is no room for the adoption of the modern views on *locus standi* being followed by England and Australia.'

It is equally important to note that the widening of the rules determining access to the courts has not enabled everyone wishing to litigate an issue to obtain standing. Thus it was held in Australia that 'intellectual or emotional concern about the environment' does not confer standing;[25] in England that a society formed especially for the protection of a historical site did not by virtue of its purpose obtain a right of standing its members did not possess as individuals;[26] and in Canada that the Canadian Abortion Rights Action League lacked the 'genuine interest' needed to enable it to contest the validity of legislation regulating abortions.[27] Various reasons have been given for continuing to exclude certain applicants, among them the need to preserve judicial resources[28] and that 'endless litigation' would 'result in a dramatic change in our democratic system of government.'[29] Common to all these jurisdictions has been the concern to exclude 'mere busybodies' and restrict access to those 'directly affected'.[30]

This concern, and the fear that too liberal standing rules would affect the constitutional relationship between courts and other branches of government, both indicate some unease on the part of Commonwealth courts in being confronted by law suits raising issues of public interest in which the applicants hold no personal stake. Underlying this is, I believe, the sentiment that it would be wrong in a democracy for the courts to replace the legislature as focal point for political debate. Courts are, after all, neither representative nor guaranteed to have access to all points of view, whereas legislatures are, at least in theory, representative.

Inasmuch as this suggests that expanded access to courts in environmental matters is not an unqualified good, it should be taken seriously in

24 . [1986] 1 All NLR 215.
25 . *Yates Security Services v Keating* (1990) 98 ALR 68 at 76.
26 . *R v Secretary of State for the Environment, ex parte Rose Theatre Trust Co* [1990] 1 All ER 754.
27 . *CARAL Inc v Attorney General of Nova Scotia* (1989) 63 DLR (4th) 680.
28 . *Canadian Council of Churches v Canada* (1992) 88 DLR (4th) 193 at 204 per Cory J. This argument was discounted by Lockhat and Wilcox JJ in *Ogle*, above n 19.
29 . *CARAL Inc*, above per Nunn J.
30 . *Minister of Finance v Finley* [1986] 2 SCR 607, 33 DLR (4th) 321; Australian Law Commission *Standing in Public Interest Litigation* (1988).

post-apartheid law. For in a democratic South Africa the capacity to mobilize legal resources effectively, which coincides largely with wealth, education and social status, will be enjoyed by the minority, by those with the least political power. Hence the incentive to use environmental rights to transfer the environmental burdens of development onto disadvantaged members of society, will coincide with the capacity for doing so. Conversely, the largest proportion of the voting public will be least able to use the law effectively. Since socio-economic position also affects perceptions of environmental priorities, this means that liberalized standing rules may in a post-apartheid South Africa serve to enable the white-middle class to frustrate the development priorities of a democratically elected legislature.

This possibility brings home the hazards of following the lead of legal systems in economically developed, and socially more egalitarian, countries. For it is intimately connected with the fact that the liberalization of *locus standi* in England, Australia and Canada was designed to increase access to the courts across the board, rather than specifically to enable the courts to pursue social justice. It is because these developments divorce the question of whether someone should have access to the courts from the interest she thereby seeks to promote, that they would create the possibility in South Africa of 'green rights' being turned into 'white rights'.

This contrasts rather starkly with the development of 'public interest law' or 'social action law'[31] in India, which was deliberately designed to assist the economically or socially weaker sections of society (Baxi 1987: 34–6). Basing themselves on constitutional provisions guaranteeing fundamental rights, the Indian courts have not only relaxed the rules of standing, but also developed procedural mechanisms aimed at making it easier for people without financial or educational resources to use the courts to enforce their rights.

This development started off with the liberalization of the standing requirements, but did not end there. In the leading Supreme Court decision of *Gupta v Union of India* it was held that:

> where a legal wrong or legal injury is caused to a person or to a determinate class of persons by reason of violation of any constitutional or legal right or any burden is imposed in contravention of any constitutional or legal provisions or without authority of law or any such legal wrong or legal injury or legal burden is threatened, and *such person is by reason of poverty, helplessness or*

---

31 . This is the term preferred by Upendra Baxi (1987).

socially or economically disadvantaged position unable to approach the Court for relief, any member of the public can maintain an action for an appropriate direction, order or writ.[32]

One of the most notable features of this case is that the liberalization of standing was justified by reference to the transformation of the law into a tool of social, rather than individual justice. Individual rights, Bhagwati J said, were 'practically meaningless in today's setting unless accompanied by social rights necessary to make them effective and really accessible to all.'[33]

A crucial facet of this development is that the purpose underlying the liberalization of standing rules — the transformation of law into an instrument for social justice — also led to other changes in legal procedures facilitating access to justice. Thus the courts accepted that in public interest matters letters, telegrams and even articles in newspapers should be treated as equivalent to the formal documents that normally have to be filed to start legal proceedings (Baxi 1987: 39–41).[34] And, as importantly, public interest plaintiffs have in some cases been relieved of the cost and burden of gathering and presenting evidence. State-financed commissions, consisting of social activists, teachers and researchers, as well as court officials and judges of lower courts have been used to gather the evidence necessary for courts to settle disputes of fact (Baxi 1987: 44).

In these ways the Indian courts have removed some of the financial, educational and institutional obstacles in the way of socially and economically deprived people seeking to gain access to environmental justice. Unlike their counterparts in the rest of the Commonwealth, the Indian judiciary sought not merely to expand access to the courts, but to expand access to justice.

The liberalization of standing rules has also, of course, opened the doors to those seeking to advance their own sectional interests. For example, in *Chhetritya Pradushan Mukti Gangarsh v State of Uttar Pradesh*[35] the petitioners were denied the opportunity by the Indian Supreme Court to use public interest litigation to further a 'long history of enmity and animosity' on the ground that the advantages of this procedure should be confined to a 'person interested genuinely in the protection of the society on behalf of the ... community.'

---

32 . AIR 1982 SC 149 at 188. Emphasis added.
33 . Above, note 33 at 191.
34 . See also *Peoples' Union for Democratic Rights & Peoples' Union for Civil Liberties v Minister of Home Affairs* [1986] CLR (Const) 546.
35 . AIR 1990 SC 2060.

This case illustrates that even under the Indian system the courts still seek to control the capacity to sue.[36] But it also shows that the considerations used in exercising this control are the exact opposite from those which operate in England, Australia and Canada. In India the criterion applied to determine who gains access to the advantages public interest litigation provides is the pursuit of social justice, rather than the existence of a personal interest on the part of the litigant.

This makes the Indian experience pivotal to those seeking to enhance access to environmental justice in post-apartheid South Africa. It provides an example of the techniques one could — probably has to — use if one were to provide the opportunity for pursuing environmental sustainability through the courts without simultaneously enabling those who benefited from apartheid to use the courts to impose the environmental burdens of development on those who suffered from apartheid.

However, the Indian experience also points to two important institutional requirements for achieving a legal system accessible to social action litigation. The first of these is the importance of the judicial personnel. It is widely acknowledged that the development of public interest litigation is largely due to the determination of two judges, Bhagwati and Krishna Iyer, who were prepared to step beyond the confines of precedent.[37] The second is the necessity of 'legal pegs' on which judges can hang arguments justifying such a development. Article 32 of the Indian Constitution, specifying that the Supreme Court can be moved for the enforcement of a fundamental right by any 'appropriate proceeding' and empowering the Supreme Court to 'issue any order or direction', was pivotal in this development (Craig and Deshpande 1989: 363–6).[38] The Indian experience, like that of England, Australia, Canada and Nigeria, highlights the need even the most 'activist' judges have for textual authority.

CONCLUSION

It is no surprise that the environmental burdens economic development has imposed on those kept voteless and poor by the apartheid state are

---

36 . 'If courts do not restrict the free flow of such cases ... the traditional litigation will suffer. ...' observed Khalid J in *Pandey v State of West Bengal* [1988] LRC.

37 . See especially Baxi (1987), who describes Indian Social Action Litigation as 'judge-led and judge-induced.'

38 . Likewise, the existence of similarly widely-worded provisions concerning the powers of state High Courts were crucial in enabling them to follow the lead of the Supreme Court.

becoming increasingly prominent. The transformation of the environmental debate in South Africa is part and parcel of the decay of the apartheid state itself.

This link between environmental concern and the structure of the state highlights the need to pay attention to the promotion of sustainable development in the constitutional preparations for a democratic South Africa. Current South African law leaves much to be desired in this respect. So too do the most important proposals for enacting environmental rights in a new South African Constitution, albeit to a lesser extent. Yet the experience of Commonwealth countries, where judges refashioned rules, much like those presently in force in South Africa, to provide wider access to courts, indicates that law can provide a mechanism for public participation in environmental policy. Indian developments in particular, characterized by a convergence of wider access and expanded notions of justice, and arising from a convergence of socio-political problems with a constitutional framework guaranteeing fundamental rights — a combination that will also characterize post-apartheid South Africa — suggest a way forward. In illustrating the importance of careful constitutional drafting these developments also direct attention to the urgency of embarking on this path while a democratic South Africa is still under construction.

REFERENCES

ANC (1992) *A Bill of Rights for a New South Africa: A Preliminary Revised Text*, May

Bartelmus, P (1986) *Environment and Development*, London, Allen and Unwin

Baxi, U (1987) 'Taking Suffering Seriously: Social Action Litigation in the Supreme Court of India', in Timchelvan and Coomaraswany, qv

Baxter, (1984) *Administrative Law*, Cape Town, Juta

Cock, J and Koch, E (1991) *Going Green: People, Politics and the Environment in South Africa*, Cape Town, Oxford University Press

Craig, P and Deshpande, R (1989) 'Rights, Autonomy and Process: Public Interest Litigation in India', *Oxford Journal of Legal Studies*, vol 9

Fuggle, R and Rabie, M A (1992) *Environmental Management in South Africa*, Cape Town, Juta

Hardoy, J and Satterthwaite, D (1984) 'Third World Cities and the Environment of Poverty', *Geoforum*, vol 15

—— (1989) *Squatter Citizen: Life in the Urban Third World*, London, Earthscan

Hart, T (1992) 'Socio-Political Factors', in Fuggle and Rabie, qv

Lélé, P (1991) 'Sustainable Development: A Critical Review', *World Development*, vol 19

Rabie, M A (1992) 'Environment Conservation Act', in Fuggle and Rabie, qv

Rabie, M A et al (1992) 'Implementation of Environmental Law', in Fuggle and Rabie, qv

Read, J (1993) 'Public Interest Litigation: Commonwealth Responses', paper prepared for the 1993 conference of the Commonwealth Legal Association

Republic of South Africa (1993) *Government's Proposals on a Charter of Fundamental Rights*, 2 February 1993
South African Law Commission (1989) *Project 25 Interim Report on Group and Human Rights*, Pretoria
Timchelvan, N and Coomaraswany, R (1987) *The Role of the Judiciary in Plural Societies*, Pinter, London

Chapter Eight

The Bank, the State and Development: Local Government in Maseru

Chris Peters

This chapter will look at a project to implement democratically elected, devolved local government in Maseru, the capital of Lesotho (Maseru City Council — MCC) in March 1989.[1] MCC was a major component of the Urban Sector Reorientation Project (Urban II) (USRP) funded by the World Bank through a loan and grant (World Bank 1988). MCC was to be overseen and accountable to the Ministry of Interior, Chieftainship and Rural Affairs (MICARD). MCC was viewed as providing the model for local government in other urban conurbations in Lesotho.

Through an examination of this project, and the role the World Bank and the Government of Lesotho (GOL) played in its planning and implementation, such concepts as devolvement, participation and sustainability will be considered; it is hoped that this will place the particular problems regarding the implementation and running of local government in Maseru into a broader perspective.

POLITICAL ECONOMY OF LESOTHO

During the late nineteenth and early twentieth centuries, Lesotho (then Basutoland) was the major supplier of winter wheat to the gold and diamond fields in South Africa; this was later banned by the UK administration and Basotho migrant labour became the primary export 'commodity'. It remains so today, though migrant labour as an export is declining. In 1986/7, 46.8 per cent of the source of all household income was through migrant labour, of which 44.7 per cent was miners' remit-

---

1. The relevant exchange rates that apply to this chapter are: 1 loti (plural malotis) = 1 Rand, 4.5 Rand = £1 = $1.7.

tances (Cobbe 1991: 20). Dependence on migrant labour, membership of the Southern African Customs Union (SACU), and aid are the mainstays of Lesotho's economic existence. Apartheid has ironically benefited investment in Lesotho, giving a major boost to South African investment by offering the prospect of production and/or 'finishing', particularly in textiles, in an adjacent country to South Africa which was exempt from sanctions. Further foreign investment, mainly from the Pacific Rim, arrived during the 1980s. A cheap loose labour pool, tax holidays and evasion of tariff agreements — such as the Multi-Fibres Agreement — helped attract this investment.

In consequence of its geographic position and nominally independent status, Lesotho has been the target of much foreign political representation (such as embassies and diplomatic missions). Aid to Lesotho is now in decline. Disbursements have dwindled from $699 million in 1988, to $118 million in 1991, 26 per cent of its GDP (World Bank 1991a: 242). There were 72 organizations active in development work of some variety or other in Lesotho between 1974 and 1984 (Ferguson 1990: 5–7).

After some 28 years of international development assistance, Lesotho has produced very little in the way of an alternative and sustainable economic base, nor any form of lasting representational government.

However, interest from foreign governments and aid agencies has declined since the end of apartheid and the full resumption of diplomatic links with South Africa. The Lesotho Highlands Water Project (LHWP), the biggest civil engineering project in Africa at present, costing some $1.4 billion, is heavily South African, European Union — and World Bank — funded and will alone ensure a continued interest in the region from these agencies for many years to come.

Maseru

A former army post, lying east of the Caledon River border with South Africa, Maseru is now the capital city of Lesotho. It now covers 138 kilometres. The total active labour force — 65,200 in 1986 — is projected to increase to 103,451 by 1995 (World Bank 1987). The size of the so-called 'informal sector' is not known precisely, but is rapidly expanding (MCC 1990). Unemployment is estimated at 15 per cent for men and 30 per cent for women (MDP (Maseru Development Plan) Working Paper 2). However, these above figures can be held as no more than rough estimates.

Rural–urban migration accounts for increasing uncontrolled peri-urban settlement; the majority of this migration is permanent, with diminishing or no ties to a rural base. This heavy migration to Maseru may well be viewed by migrants as a second-best option to migration to

South Africa (Wellings 1983: 1, 23). The population is estimated to reach 140–200,000 by 1995; the city is reckoned to be increasing in population by as much as 7 per cent per annum.[2] Some 25 per cent of domestic investment is in Maseru. Studies in emerging peri-urban areas by Wilkinson and Wright (quoted in Leduka 1991: 16) estimate that over 70 per cent of migrants to Maseru are landless.

Lack of infrastructure and minimal enforcement of existing planning legislation exacerbate the chaotic spread of piecemeal housing with few, if any, basic services, especially in the peri-urban areas. Piped water is supplied by central government via the Water and Sewage Authority (WASA) and is claimed to cover 80 per cent of all urban areas (BOS 1986). Coverage is, in reality, sketchy. The use of standpipes invariably provides the only source of water where private articulation is either scarce or non-existent. Payment for this water is disputed, with GOL 'insisting' that water costs — roughly R200,000 per annum — are met by MCC. Water is viewed by much of the community as the key political and social issue in Maseru. The drought of 1992/3 provided the opportunity for the closure of many standpipes. WASA has officially adopted a policy of phasing out all standpipes by 1995 (personal communication 1993).

Land rights, administered through MICARD by the Department of Lands, Surveys and Physical Planning (LSPP) since the Land Act of 1979, are still a much-disputed arena. Land, previously held 'in trust' for the nation by the king, and allotted through chiefs and headmen prior to 1979, was hence to be under the administration of GOL, through MICARD. In practice, however, chiefs continue to sell land privately, much of this activity being undertaken in connivance with GOL.

Rented terraces of rooms owned by absentee landlords are rapidly expanding and, in some areas, becoming the dominant means of housing. Recent estimates cite a density of 4.4 people per room (BOS 1986) in Maseru as a whole.

There is 50 per cent water-borne sewage in the old reserve, the business district and other 'pocket' areas. The existing sewage system, laid in 1958, is old and inadequate. In inner-city slums (for example Sea Point) and mixed peri-urban areas (for example Upper Thamae), use of pit latrines accounts for 44 per cent of human waste disposal, with 12 per cent of that total being met by Ventilated Improved Pit Latrines (VIPs).

---

2 . Three scenarios are represented: low 3.5 per cent, medium 3.5–7.0 per cent and high 7.0 per cent (MDP 1990: Working paper 6A). The base year used was 1986: 109,200 (preliminary 1986 Population Census Results, Bureau of Statistics GOL 1990).

Some 400 night soil buckets were phased out by MCC in 1992/3. Conservancy/septic tanks are present in many areas, particularly in the new housing areas such as Maseru East and Mabote (MDP 1990: Working Paper 10).

Rubbish disposal is restricted to a few middle-class and outlying industrial areas. Roads are badly under-maintained; GOL only has direct responsibility for gazetted roads, which are few in number. Roughly 290 kilometres of road within the city are ungazetted, of which 70 per cent have dirt or gravel surfaces. These are the direct responsibility of MCC.

THE 'NEED' FOR DEVOLVED GOVERNMENT

That decentralization and devolvement have been viewed as key ingredients for successful and sustainable development need not be reiterated. However, the fact that they have, quite consistently, failed to live up to their promise in Africa, and elsewhere, should not be forgotten.[3] The focus of development is, however, increasingly viewing empowerment, community participation, and the 'bottom-up' approach to power and decision-making at a grassroots level (Davidson and Munslow 1990; Riley 1992: 549; Friedman 1992) as a prerequisite for successful project implementation.

But, if the solution to more equitable and sustainable development is, indeed, the necessity to realize such 'empowerment', the systemic problems of decentralization, devolvement, the state and the role played by development agencies remain largely unsolved.

The World Bank has been involved in urban projects within Maseru since 1980 (Wellings 1983: 6). Maseru's present physical structure, however, reveals the degree of failure of these largely piecemeal projects. Urban planning has remained minimal, as has the enforcement of relevant building legislation.

Pressure to implement a devolved local authority originated as early as 1983 from the World Bank (Leduka 1991). By 1989 MCC was the

3. See Smith (1985: Chapter 10) for a full discussion and critique of the benefits that decentralization is perceived as providing for successful development. These benefits are: effectiveness in planning to meet local needs, including the needs of the poor; improved access to administrative agencies and opportunities for grassroots participation; improved speed and flexibility in decision making; and the role that decentralization plays in enhancing national unity. Devolved local government may be defined as a further stage in the process of decentralization. It is legally entitled to raise its own funding —usually through a local property tax (rates) — and to elect (democratically or via chiefs or government appointees) a local council responsible for its policy and financial administration.

inheritor of a complex, over-bureaucratized and yet largely unstructured city, with a rapidly-developing peri-urban area and inner-city slums which lacked even a modicum of basic service coverage. In this, MCC's problems have much in common with every urban council within the African continent and elsewhere.

DECENTRALIZED GOVERNMENT IN MASERU

The Town Office

The potential of an uncontrollable urban explosion in Maseru has long been recognized (Wellings 1983: 22–3). In 1970, this prompted GOL to restructure the district commissioner's office as a decentralized town office with a town clerk. The office was charged with implementing services (rubbish collection, road maintenance, stray animal collection, public health, public paths and gardens). It was financed by rates-plus-service-charges, together with additional GOL funding, and was staffed by GOL civil servants (Rating Act 1980). In 1983, the Urban Government Act (UGA) officially codified its existence.

The geographic service area covered by the town office (as detailed above) reflected the town's colonial antecedents, concentrating on the old reserve, central Maseru and the central business district, and new isolated businesses and urban pockets. Rate eligibility, however, had a reasonably wide spread across 4130 properties — government, non-government, domestic and commercial/industrial (MDP 1990). Thus, the key economic factor, the legal requirement to pay a property rate, was already in place. However, inherited arrears from the town office amounted to 70–80 per cent of rates due: some 3.4 million malotis (MCC 1990).

Objectives of the USRP Project Regarding MCC

MCC was set up to fulfil, in brief, the following objectives:

- to establish a devolved form of local authority based on the British model (post-1973 reforms);
- power to raise a property tax — rate — of 0.25 per cent residential and 1.5 per cent commercial rateable value;
- power to demand grant-in-lieu of rates from central government and an additional 1 million malotis per annum for the first five years of the project;
- legal responsibility for the implementation of services governed by a series of schedules;

- to hold local elections for 15 councillors to represent the newly demarcated 15 wards, and for three principal chiefs to hold ex-officio councillor office. Local 'grassroots' participation to be through a forum of chiefs, for which 15 urban ward district councils would be set up with ten elected members and the ward councillor as chairperson.
- to act as an urban planning coordinator for parastatals, local business, NGOs and central government;
- to act as central administrator for other related projects, such as housing plots and a designated development area (Maseru South);
- to express its legal authority through a number of 'bylaws';
- to assume the legal authority and responsibilities of town planning and control of building regulations.

The Maseru Development Plan

Concurrent with the founding of MCC was the publication of the Maseru Development Plan (MDP 1990), a detailed five, ten, fifteen and twenty-year development plan for Maseru attempting to integrate the expansion of the city. Unofficial estimates put the implementation costs of such a project at $100 million, plus $20 million per annum in recurrent costs. The sources of funding for the plan were not identified. MCC was to be a key player in the implementation of the MDP.

THE MASERU CITY COUNCIL

Participation

The complete lack of any grassroots participation in the setting up of MCC underlined the contradiction of offering local elections in a country where political parties were officially banned under the military regime's Order Number 4 of 1986.

In an attempt to promote participation through voter education, detailed plans were drawn up by MCC's Public Relations Department for a three-month multi-media campaign. Focused on the press and radio, such issues as voting, standing for election, and basic knowledge of local government practices like collecting rates or providing services, were covered. These plans for consciousness-raising about local representative democracy were repressed by GOL.

Pitsos (traditional public meetings), to be held in each ward, and forums for local businesses, including representatives of market traders associations and the 'informal' sector, were similarly banned. As a result, people of all classes tended to see MCC's creation as relevant to their lives in only one respect: the town office, which had never efficiently collected the local rate or prosecuted defaulters, was to be superseded by a new and seemingly more powerful 'government' authority. Local property tax was being extended to cover the entire city, involving all property owners in a legal obligation to part with money to no obvious end.

The Elections

Some 35.47 per cent of those who registered to vote actually voted — comprising about 4 per cent of the total population of Maseru (MCC 1990), but a surprisingly high number in view of the circumstances under which the elections were held.[4] To circumvent Order Number 4, only politically non-aligned individuals were allowed to stand. Notwithstanding this restriction, 11 members of the 15-strong newly elected council revealed themselves after the election to be Basotho Congress Party (BCP) members. The government now faced a new dilemma: a banned political party was holding legitimate control over the new local authority.

The BCP council members used their position to cause as much political disruption as possible, seeking to develop their own power base by establishing patron–client relationships and promoting BCP sympathizers within the executive. The impeachment of the chief executive as a representative of central government was a primary aim.

In November 1990, the council was suspended by GOL and the chief executive assumed total legislative and executive control of MCC under the direction of MICARD. A Commission of Inquiry was set up, overseen by two civil servants. It eventually dismissed the mayor, deputy mayor and two councillors, recommended that the Urban Government Act of 1983 be revised, and prescribed closer monitoring of MCC by MICARD (GOL 1990). The remaining councillors were reinstated in March 1991.

Revenue

It soon became apparent that, with inherited rate arrears of R3.4 million from the town office, and a commitment to the World Bank to collect 70 per cent of rates due, a severe problem was emerging. Apart from a history of non-collection, as already mentioned, collection was further hampered by inadequate information and incomplete valuation rolls,

---

4. This percentage is roughly on a par with local elections in the 'developed' world.

whose accuracy was vital if successful court actions could be pursued. Eventually a system of batching 50 arrears per month was introduced and a private attorney engaged to process them.

The current law regarding rate defaulting demands sequestration of the debtors' entire property. However, in practice, no rate defaulter had, as far as could be ascertained, ever been brought before the court, and enforcement of such sequestration had never been applied. The private attorney was eventually dismissed and the matter of rate defaulter prosecution passed to the office of the attorney general. The sequestration legislation remains unchanged.

Further problems occurred with the Lesotho National Development Corporation (LNDC), the largest parastatal and largest rate debtor. LNDC claimed exemption from its rateable arrears of some R2.3 million. LNDC's assertion that 'publicly sourced funds' were not rateable was at odds with the fact that LNDC itself collected rates from its own business tenants. It took until 31 May 1991 for an agreement to pay R1.4 million to be reached, though LNDC still contest interest on arrears.

GOL's grant-in-lieu of rates for 1990/1 was received, but that for 1989/90 remains outstanding. A working budget of some R6 million, even if achieved, meant that any extension of basic services outside the currently-serviced areas is severely limited. Plans for the development of Maseru South — another component of the USRP — were largely covered by World Bank funding, though the realization of this funding was co-dependent on meeting the target of a 70 per cent rate collection.

Over 4000 domestic properties were worth so little that their rate collection proved uneconomic. The process of surveying rateable values of existing plots in new rateable areas, and of finding out who the leaseholders were, proved laborious and, in some cases, even dangerous for MCC/LSPP staff. This underlined the virtual failure of implementing the Land Act of 1979.

Not only was the current level of rating proving impracticable to collect, but projected rate increases as stipulated by the USRP agreement with the World Bank to increase revenue would mean that a commercial ratepayer paying R3000 in 1991 would pay R9000 by 1995/6: a 300 per cent increase.

SERVICES

MCC was authorized to chair committees on a regular basis with parastatals involved in the provision of services such as water, sewage collection and electricity, and relevant NGOs such as the Urban Sanitation Improvement Team (USIT). This was to help coordinate city-wide works and improvements. However, the parastatals followed their own agendas and the multilateral synchronization of planning and work never materialized; the committees never met on a regular basis. MCC still remains without the legal gazetting of its powers to act as building authority for the city.

Service Sourcing and Empowerment

By 1990, with an awareness of the severe limitations on its resources, MCC identified crucial services (health, sanitation, waste disposal and roads) and sought to extend them where it could through the formation of 'task forces'. A 'Clean-up' task force was initially set up to examine rubbish disposal, health and sanitation; a second was formed for roads.

The 'Clean-Up' task force provided MCC with the opportunity to pool resources with schools, businesses, charities, NGOs and parastatals, to extend rubbish disposal and disseminate information on rubbish disposal to the general public.

Further committees were formed which sought private finance for road maintenance. Clearing and recycling of abandoned cars was also started with a local scrap metal dealer removing wrecks for no charge. Organized removal of empty drinks cans proved more difficult to achieve, though can collection and paper recycling offer the only opportunities that certain sections of the community have of earning a small wage. Scavenging on the only municipal refuse dump is a major source of recyclable scrap and was supervized by MCC.

Waste collection was expanded on an experimental basis in four pilot areas, ranging from small fenced communal rubbish enclosures to plastic bag collection and metal waste containers. These operations may be taken over by private contractors in future; the capital investment and recurrent costs of sustaining viable and growing public service utilities would be astronomical unless further subcontracting is entered into, but even this cannot be adequately funded on current budget forecasts and the continuing growth of unplanned peri-urban areas.

Road maintenance was subcontracted on a limited scale to local private contractors but, with some 290 kilometres of non-gazetted roads to maintain, this subcontracting will probably involve contracting from South Africa in future.

Will this policy of part-privatization, perhaps operating on a service charge basis, deny the poor the most basic of services? This remains, at best, a moot point.

Devolving the 'responsibility' of a ward to its occupants, and giving it the power to respond to market opportunities, does offer a variation on the informal/formal scenario, perhaps to a degree that empowers wards to form their own cartels for price fixing of service supplies or running their own garbage disposal services.

A feature of peri-urban Maseru, as well as the established impoverished inner-city areas, is the growing frailty of community cohesion and traditional forms of authority, and the lack of adequate foci from which to build alternatives. Urban ward development committees (UWDCs), are held in deep suspicion by many people, and have no executive power; they may therefore be seen as just another powerless committee.

But UWDCs working with the task forces did allow a degree of limited community action to be realized. That community funds had built up in certain wards prior to UWDCs reflects a sense of community welfare. Investment of such funds in a central account would allow interest to accrue to the benefit of the community. The two community halls run by MCC also provided a focus for entertainment, choirs, religious and civil events and, at least, went towards balancing recurrent costs if not the capital investment.

However, community participation in service provision was on neither GOL's nor the World Bank's agenda. Thus, promising experiments in devolving the provision of services down to communities, at least over some aspects of service provision, were hampered by a general lack of interest or commitment from GOL and its parastatals.

Stren (1988: 242–3) argues that the devolution of service provision to the informal sector is a key element in keeping costs and wages low and forms an appropriate vehicle for service provision at a number of different levels and ranges. By keeping service provision informal, but based on economies of scale, Stren further argues (1988: 243) that the inherent class divisions which are expressed through access to public services — through a service charge — would be seriously undermined.

Certainly water selling is now a thriving and growing informal sector activity in Maseru, but the charges — 50 cents per 20 litres — should be set against the prices currently charged by WASA: R1.25 per kilolitre (WASA 1992: 29 July, p 3). Bus and taxi services have always been provided by the private sector (both informal and formal) and the public have no say in charges (or routing).

Adopting a practice applied successfully in South Africa, formal sector businesses were targeted to buy advertising space on street rubbish bins. This proved successful in Maseru — the cost of the bins and their erection being wholly paid for by businesses — whilst MCC took on an extra 15 daily-paid staff to cope with the increased number of bins.

Over 200 bins are now in place, and subsidy through advertising has been extended to street signs and bus shelters. However, the rubbish bins have been limited mainly to the old reserve and the central business district — in poorer areas, the bins were either destroyed or stolen (mainly for the brewing of beer).

Personnel Resource Management

Problems stemming from ritualism, clientelism and patriarchy, inherent in central government, were present in MCC. There was also a persistent lack of skilled personnel, particularly in accounts, engineering and administration. Many Basotho who have successfully finished training in a profession seek work in South Africa or other sub-Saharan African countries. In accounting, suitably qualified personnel simply did not exist within the country to the required level of expertise. Relatively low salaries compared with the private sector further exacerbated the situation.

In-house training could only take skills-upgrading to a certain level. The 'informal' suspension on USRP, imposed by the Bank in 1990, due to the project's perceived failure to meet its financial targets, blocked the acquisition of a computer network, which further slowed down clerical and accounting staff.

DISCUSSION

I have given here at best only a thumbnail sketch of certain basic factors in a project that, from its outset, was faced with a number of complex problems, most of them reflecting the piecemeal and conflictual history of local development in Maseru, and the role of state bureaucracy in managing those affairs. In seeming recognition of these factors, the World Bank has rightly stressed the 'many complex issues [that] have to be resolved if local government is to be strengthened in the developing world' (World Bank 1983: 48).

But, how is this 'strengthening' to be achieved? For the World Bank, the current answer still largely lies in its promotion of political duality and the 'liberation' of markets from the state at all levels; the imposition of untrammelled 'choice' within a liberal democratic environment. This analysis addresses neither the cultural and historical particularities that had produced and sustained Lesotho, and still govern its economic and political development at a national, urban and regional level, nor the problems that current developments in a post-apartheid South Africa pose for the continued existence of so dependent a front-line state as Lesotho.

This scenario begs the question: for whose benefit are such projects implemented, and why? Two years into the MCC project, a member of the Department of Geography at the National University of Lesotho, reviewing the MCC project, suggested (Leduka 1991: 34) that: 'It cannot ... be presumptuous to conclude that the MCC was simply a reciprocal gesture on the part of the government towards the World Bank as a major sponsor of both urban projects and the MCC itself. This is again shown by the proposed establishment of similar institutional structures in [other] towns.' In my view, both the World Bank and GOL, as the major protagonists in a crucial and necessary exercise in implementing a local democracy, are ultimately furthering a patron–client relationship that perceived the complex (and particular) issues involved in the MCC project as of secondary importance to the 'reciprocal gesture' that such an undertaking encapsulated.

In this view, GOL accepted the World Bank's agenda because it had no other choice. However, the fact that participation in this project meant that GOL could itself devolve the insoluble problems of local planning, service provision, rate collection and enforcement to a devolved agent (MCC), must not have lacked a degree of attraction.

Maseru, as a conceptual framework for implementing a local authority, was deliberately constructed by the World Bank to fit the available technocratic and political criteria which such 'development' requires. Thus, the sustainability of such a project, and its efficacy in solving the complex social and political problems it was supposedly 'designed' to address, were simply ignored, or, at best, taken as given — there was no effective dissenting voice to argue otherwise.

That the World Bank apparently viewed these problems as the exclusive domain of largely expatriate city planners, engineers and accountants, should surprise no one. As far as I am aware, there was no community input into any of these complex issues. There was no social science input into the project formulation.

The attempt in Maseru to implement a devolved form of local authority is but one example in a long line of expensive 'solutions' that are doomed to remain, at best, a gesture of intent rather than a viable proposition for even a modicum of self-sufficiency and sustainability. Similarly, the assumption that people would welcome and exercise pluralist democratic 'rights' in electing a city council reflected a superficial awareness of the implications of local government's role in extracting revenue from a largely poor population: if it meant more taxes, people did not want MCC.

The number of votes cast in the council elections of November 1992 showed a dramatic drop in the exercise of local representative democracy from the March 1989 elections — just 1.5 per cent of the population of Maseru voted (MCC 1992). What is further revealed by this figure is the increasing irrelevance of local government, as expressed by MCC, to the people of Maseru — of all classes.

How the BCP, the first elected government in Lesotho for 23 years, will address the problems of urban life in Maseru and other conurbations awaits to be seen. Traditionally, the BCP has its roots in grassroots participatory democracy. With total victory in the elections of 29 March 1993 — it took all 65 seats in the lower house — it has a strong popular mandate with which to govern. However, MCC remains likely to remain the sole exercise in devolved, democratic local government in Lesotho. The BCP is presently considering a form of decentralized administration for the regions, not devolved democratic local government (personal correspondence from MICARD). The other regional conurbations continue to decline in population, whilst Maseru continues to grow (MDP 1990: Working Paper 6a). Elections of new UWDCs appear to have had little popular impact on their wards (personal communication from MCC staff).

That the BCP will have to address the problems of Lesotho's political and economic dependency on international aid, which is now in decline, is an unpalatable fact, as is the country's dependency on South Africa. How the new South Africa will treat its tiny neighbour is open to question: is union along the lines of the EU at all practicable? (Cobbe 1991). Thus, the linkages and dependencies continue, as does the 'fiction' of the 'independent' state of Lesotho.

How devolved government in South Africa will fair in a 'new' South Africa, given the chaotic situation that apartheid has bequeathed to the new government when it comes to power, is a subject of much debate (for example, Gildenhuys 1991), but so far there has been little concrete policy to redress the situation.

Devolvement is an acknowledged ANC goal to promote more equitable distribution of resources, opportunities for employment and access to information and participatory decision making; this is a fine concept, but how does it translate into practical terms? (See ANC 1992.) This question becomes particularly pertinent when placed in the context of South Africa's own economic and social problems and the strong regionalist tendencies by certain ethnic groups which much of the present violence underlines.

Similar problems are reflected in South Africa's relationship to the 'homelands', which may be viewed as sharing some of the problems that beset Lesotho in style of government and in lack of basic infrastructures, resources and planned urban environments. They are also entirely dependent on South Africa for their economic survival.

Whether the World Bank is undergoing a fundamental policy change and will begin to implement its 1991 report on urban policy remains to be seen. The report does present an apparent change in the bank's conceptual framework, and acknowledges the complex linkages between local and central government. The relationship between macro and micro policies on the economic and social viability of urban life is also stressed. Whether Michael Cohen's plea for a return to urban research and 'adequate urban understanding' will be heeded, or can be politically implemented, remains a moot point.[5]

Certainly, regarding urban development and the devolution of power to a politicized populace in South Africa, the World Bank appears set to treat South Africa as another technocratic and ideological exercise (see, for example, Bond and Swilling 1992). It may well be argued that South Africa does not want or need the bank. However, it would appear that the bank not only wants South Africa, but will insist on its own terms (Bond and Swilling 1992).

THE BORDER CONTEXT

The predicament of MCC, whilst reflecting much that is applicable only to Lesotho, also reflects much that may be observed in varying degrees in other local authorities in Africa and elsewhere. The current dilemmas that face local authorities, whether devolved, or, in varying degrees, decentralized from central government, are not only problematic for the developing world but increasingly affect all forms of local self-government on a global scale. The problems of too little revenue versus greatly expanding demands for services, of dependency on government grants and of financing capital expenditure through loans must be firmly placed within the context of an increasing degree of political antagonism and metropolitan interference.

This increasing need for centralized control over regional affairs, whether expressed through the market place and government, or

---

5 . World Bank 1991b; Cohen 1992: 21. The latest *aide-mémoire* from the World Bank, of 12 May 1993, on MCC, though primarily concerned with rate collection and related financial concerns, does admit that, 'The design of the project was constrained by the absence of an existing city council that would establish priorities and objectives — circumstances resulting largely from the fact that part of the project's objective was to set up a city council. Thus, a council is now in place that did not have a part in the shaping of the current operation — a situation that might explain the difficulties being experienced with implementation.' Apart from this concession, MCC appears to remain, in the eyes of this particular mission, at least, an exercise in technocracy and revenue collection. The project was due to go into formal suspension in July 1993.

bureaucracy and 'the state', is symptomatic of a much deeper social and economic malaise. The public sector and its 'rights' within a society to provide even basic services for the 'public good', including administering contracts from the private sector, and its ability to regulate an errant market, is in conceptual (and therefore implemental) disarray at every level. The 'survival of the fittest' mentality sits uneasily with the embedded notion of the public servant dispassionately administering his or her 'public' duties.

Devolution may, as Riley (1992) suggests, be the only way to achieve stability and increase participation in politics in Africa (and elsewhere); but new ways are needed to realize this democratic potential and, in this instance, its practical application in such areas as the supply of basic service and amenities.

If part of the answer to successful devolution does lie with a movement away from bureaucracy and an increase in NGO and community based action, linked to new forms of administration, then how is this to be achieved? How is it to be financed? What shifts in our own cultural, political and economic thinking are required?[6]

This short chapter has outlined some possible solutions, but has equally shown, within Maseru (and hopefully a broader context) not only the problems — political, economic and cultural — that exist, but the paucity of ideas the north has to offer the south, and why it offers them.

The implementation of cost-effective alternative strategies for basic service provision requires real innovation and communication. What is needed is a synthesis of approaches that relate to people's lives and to their cultural perceptions of 'the city', a synthesis that is linked to local — and central — government and which seeks to express more than the 'political will' of 'the people'.

There is much written but little new thinking on topics that demand urgent consideration if we are to progress from the current conceptual cul-de-sac that accepts that a large part of the world's population is 'surplus' to economic requirements — dog eat dog in a man's world — and that such a concept is humanity's 'natural' lot. The written work that challenges accepted paradigms is, currently, largely condemned to remain within an academic ghetto and to have little impact on 'mainstream' development thinking or its implementation.

Until alternatives are on the agenda of those who ultimately decide the economic (and therefore political) rationale behind such projects, the

---

6. For a discussion on 'the relation of organization and democratic government' in the 1990s and beyond, see Mars 1993.

World Bank and other agencies will continue to steam-roller 'suitable' reforms and development — continue to treat the symptoms and not the malaise — at great benefit to themselves, and governmental and class elites, but not to the vast majority of ordinary people for whom such 'development' is supposedly meant to help and 'empower'.

This situation can only get worse unless fundamental changes in attitude are recognized and put into practice. For the World Bank — and other policy makers — to acknowledge publicly that their own house is, conceptually, in an economic and social mess, would be a brave first step in that direction.

REFERENCES

ANC (1992) *Ready to Govern: ANC Policy Guidelines for a Democratic South Africa*, May

Bond, P and Swilling, M (1992) 'World Bank Financing for Urban Development — Issues and Options for South Africa', presentation to the Joint Technical Committee, Central Witwatersrand Metropolitan Chamber, 16 July

BOS (Bureau of Statistics) (1986) *Statistical Yearbook*, Maseru, Lesotho, Government Printers

Cobbe, J (1991) 'Lesotho: What will Happen After Apartheid Goes?', *Africa Today*, 1st quarter

Cohen, M (1992) 'The Challenge for Developing Countries', in Harris, qv

Cook, P and Kirkpatrick, C (eds) (1988) *Privatisation in Less Developed Countries*, London, Harvester

Davidson, B and Munslow, B (1990) 'The Crisis of the Nation-State in Africa', *Review of African Political Economy*, no 49

Ferguson, J (1990) 'The Anti-Politics Machine — Development, Depoliticisation, and Bureaucratic Power in Lesotho', *Journal of Modern African Studies*, vol 28, no 4

Friedman, J (1992) *Empowerment: The Politics of Alternative Development*, Oxford, Blackwell

Gildenhuys, J S H (1991) 'A Comparative Study of Alternative Options for Local Government and Management in South Africa', *Politikon*, vol 18, no 1, January

GOL (1990) *Report of the Commission into the Affairs of Maseru City Council*, Maseru, Lesotho, Government Printers

Harris, N (ed) (1992) *Cities in the 1990s*, London, UCL Press

Leduka, R C (1991) 'Aspects of Urban Management in Lesotho: The Case for the City of Maseru', Department of Geography, National University of Lesotho. Paper presented to the RUPSEA conference on Urban Management in Southern and Eastern Africa, Lilongwe, Malawi

Mars, T F (1993) 'Public Sector Organisation: Where Next?', *IDS Bulletin*, vol 33, no 4

MCC (Maseru City Council) (1989) *Report from the City Treasurer to the Management Committee*, Maseru, Government Printers

—— (1990) *Department of Health and Environment, Working Paper*, Maseru, Government Printers

—— (1992) 'Report of the Chief Executive of the Election of 1992', unpublished

MDP (1990) *Maseru Development Plan, Volume 2*, Maseru, LSPP, Working Papers 1, 2, 6a, 7, 8, 9, 10

Riley, S (1992) 'Democratic Pressure or Political Adjustment: Democratic Politics and Political Choice in Africa', *Third World Quarterly*, vol 13, no 3

Smith, B C (1985) *Decentralisation: The Territorial Dimensions of the State*, George Allen & Unwin, London

Stren, R E (1988) 'Urban Services in Africa: Public Management or Privatisation?', in Cook and Kirkpatrick, qv

WASA (1992) *Public Standpipe Usage for Community Leaders*, Ministry of Water, Energy and Mining, WASA, MICARD and MCC, July

Wellings, P (1983) *A Case of Mistaken Identity: The Squatters of Lesotho*, Development Studies Unit, University of Natal, Durban, Working Paper, Number 4

World Bank (1983) *Policies for Strengthening Local Government in Developing Countries*, Staff Working Paper No 582, Washington, World Bank

—— (1987) *Country Report, Lesotho*, Washington, The World Bank

—— (1988) *Urban Sector Reorientation Project (Urban II)*, Washington, The World Bank

—— (1991a) *The Challenge of Development: World Development Report*, Oxford, Oxford University Press

—— (1991b) *Urban Policy and Economic Development: An Agenda for the 1990s, World Bank Policy Paper*, Oxford, Oxford University Press

—— (1992) *World Development Report*, Oxford, Oxford University Press

—— (1993) *Aide-Mémoire on USRP/MCC*, Washington, The World Bank, May

Chapter Nine

NGOs, Institutional Development and Sustainable Development in Post-Apartheid South Africa

Charles Abugre

The NGO scene in South Africa is unique in several respects. Perhaps the most obvious is its sheer complexity. The term non-governmental organization (NGO) has a very broad application in South Africa far and beyond its traditional usage.[1] In South Africa the term applies to a complex web of civil organizations, quasi-government bodies like the Independent Development Trust (IDT), organizations affiliated to liberation movements such as the Kagiso Trust and even multilateral agencies. Some sections of South African opinion classify even the European Union (EU) and the World Bank and bilaterally funded projects as NGOs once they are not executed directly by government ministries. Civil organizations in South Africa range from neighbourhood structures to sophisticated national networks, sub-networks and alliances, as well as numerous service and research organizations providing essential services to communities or mediating between them and the state or financial resources.

Another important characteristic of South Africa in general is the difficulty of perceiving civil organizations outside the political arena, in the same way as it is difficult to understand community leadership outside political affiliations. In the first place, most civil organizations grew out

---

1. An NGO usually broadly applies to two kinds of organizations — institutionalized self-help organizations at the grassroots level and their affiliations, and professional organizations that provide a range of services to the grassroots groups. The latter are variously referred to as service or intermediary organizations, or non-governmental development organizations (NGDOs) to distinguish them from political organizations or popular movements, for example organized labour.

of resistance to apartheid, either overtly through boycotts and mass protest actions, or covertly through making organized claims on the state and self-help activities. They have fought for democracy, equal opportunities, a better life and against racial and other oppression, inequality, dispossession and degradation of their natural resources.

Such community-based organizations (or CBOs in NGO parlance) include various neighbourhood bodies, boycott committees, organizations of hostel dwellers, community crisis committees and land claims committees. A large number, mostly unregistered bodies, fight for services, mobilizing labour and resources to provide them, supporting one another in petty trade and informal credit and savings systems. Others organize to fight eviction, to fight for democratic rights and to raise consciousness. The community resource or legal advice centres are major focal points for these groupings. CBOs may or may not have national and regional affiliations and networks, but almost certainly have some political identity or the other. The South African National Civic Organization, for example, was formed in 1992 more or less as a federation of federations, but is considered as an ANC structure. Women's organizations take several forms. The major liberation movements have women's leagues. The ANC Women's League has initiated various regional groupings to assist with the CODESA process. The Domestic Workers' Union is organizing a large sector of women whilst various alliances of women's organizations are playing various strategic political roles.

A notable characteristic of many CBOs at the present time is that they are changing rapidly in form and purpose. This is of course a microcosm of the events and processes of change taking place in South Africa in general. Political and social change currently proceed at such a pace that analysis and projections may easily be rendered obsolete shortly afterwards. For example, the civics, organized loosely around community affiliations to resist apartheid, have had to take on new purposes, new forms of resistance or influence, or dissolve. Those that survive are transforming into community self-help groups seeking to mobilize resources and channel them into economic and social development, learning new forms of establishing claims on the state or new ways of channelling organizational energies.

The phenomenon of institutionalized service organizations is, as in the rest of Africa, relatively recent. Most of them emerged only in the 1980s, mainly as sanctuaries for committed activist professionals and labour leaders, covert avenues for channelling the political struggle, as channels for donor money or as means by which white liberals could express their support and 'alliance' with the oppressed. Many planners, lawyers, academics and environmentalists initiated intermediary organizations designed to support or complement the struggles at the grassroots levels.

There is now literally an explosion of service organizations, performing three broad groups of functions — enabling communities and organized bodies to make effective claims on the state or resisting apartheid's legacy, training and research, and relief and development. They may be issue-specific organizations, for example environment, they may be coalitions and committees, for example the Urban Forum or the Drought Forum, or they may be integrated development organizations. Service/intermediary organizations tend to be staffed with highly qualified people, mostly white. Most are still urban-based organizations though some of the urban-based organizations have operational bases in the homelands. There are also a few township or homeland based NGOs, which usually do not have the same access to resources and expertise as the white, urban-based ones, and therefore tend to be marginal. There is, of course, a regional differentiation in the distribution of NGOs, the heaviest concentration being in the largest cities and richest regions.

Compared to other African countries (perhaps with the exception of Kenya, Senegal and Zimbabwe), South Africa has a relatively developed NGO sector concentrating on research and policy questions. To varying degrees, these organizations are engaged in supporting grassroots groups, people's organizations and even intermediary NGOs in various training and research needs. Affiliates of the NLC (National Land Commission) are engaged with communities in the struggle for land rights, shelter rights and land-use. They are documenting, with communities, historical claims and together making presentations and demands to the state for land restitution and reparation. They are fighting recent government land-reform policies that seek to entrench the status quo of land-holdings through privatization and transfer of state lands to corrupt Bantustans.

The Foundation for Contemporary Research (FCR) has set up an African trans-urban programme, an applied research project working with community-based organization in four sub-Saharan African cities. These are Nairobi, Kinshasha, Lagos and Abidjan. They plan to research migration linkages, entrepreneurship and trade, market linkages and the diffusion of skills and resources in urban areas across Africa. The FCR welcomes contacts with northern Africa and through the Port Sudan programme could be an important linkage point.

The Education, Resource and Information Project in the Western Cape provides organizational, leadership and skill training. It cooperates with the SPP (Surplus People Project) to design and carry out training related to land issues. It also cooperates with the FCR in developing training programmes designed to address local government issues. The Group for Environmental Monitoring is also mainly a research, information and pressure group on land and environmental resource management. There are several other research NGOs all over the country, including those linked to the labour movements or to the universities. The Women's Information Training Institute at Wilgespruit, the Grail in Johannesburg and the Women's College in Cape Town provide skill and research training to women.

Another interesting phenomenon, also uncommon elsewhere in Africa, is the level of interaction and even collaborative action involving NGOs and the business sector. Several development coordinating committees or forums bring together business representatives, labour and many civil organizations, including NGOs. Private businesses are co-financing development and environmental programmes. Operation Hunger, one of South Africa's oldest indigenous NGOs, mobilizes most of its funding from the white business sector and the public at large, applying creative fund-raising techniques. Many NGOs and CBOs also benefit from government funds, channelled through quasi-government organizations such as the IDT and the Development Bank of South Africa (DBSA). These experiences present opportunities and challenges unavailable even to many European NGOs. Few European NGOs are able to engage the business sector in joint action beyond charitable donations, or for lobbying purposes.

Development forums are one of the most striking advances in the run-up to a multiracial South Africa, and usually bring together a broad range of stake holders, including businesses, political parties, labour and NGOs. A host of economic development forums have sprung up in recent times. There is a national forum that seeks to bring representatives of various stake holders at the national level together to discuss the economic situation and plans to deal with it. Regional development forums have also sprung up with a shared aim of promoting coordinated action and attracting investment. The dynamics of each forum differ from the other. The Border-Kei Regional Development Forum is one of the 'embryonic' ones. The PWV (Pretoria–Witwatersrand–Vereeniging) area development forum is considered as adopting a cautious approach, whilst Durban's Operation Jumpstart programme may be the most ambitious so far. Development forums have also been formed in rural areas and in villages.

The impetus of these forums is various. In the PWV area it came out of the Wits Metropolitan Chamber's economic working group. Operation Jumpstart came out of a report on the economic situation commissioned by Tongaat Hulett, one of the biggest businesses and landowners in

Durban. The driving force of the Western Cape Regional Development Forum was the Association for the Promotion of the Western Cape's Economic Growth (Wesgro). Wesgro is a joint municipality and business initiative. Its main objective is to promote growth and employment.

Unlike the rest of Africa, foreign operational NGOs are few, mostly environmental, for example the World Wide Fund for Nature, concerned mainly with species protection, or Ford Foundation, mostly involved in human rights issues. There is now, however, a swarm of foreign NGOs settling on South Africa, some opening operational offices, others seeking 'partners'. This development is not without trepidation. The prospect of an 'invasion' of aid agencies is not entirely an exciting one if the lessons of many developing countries are anything to go by. The EU-funded R70 million Umthombo Programme for Rural Integrated Development (the so-called U-Pride) in North Eastern Natal is a case that seems to re-enforce suspicion and caution against foreign multilateral funded projects (Nell and Shapiro 1992: 20–2). U-Pride is said to be overly dominated by the EU. The EU is accused of pushing its agenda in a top-down manner, its staff arrogant and directive.[2] Another reason for feeling apprehensive about foreign NGOs is the apparent non-transparency of their agenda and the non-reciprocal nature of the conditionality and criteria for monitoring and evaluation they demand.

CONCEPTUALIZING SUSTAINABLE DEVELOPMENT IN THE SOUTH AFRICAN CONTEXT

However defined, sustainable development involves a complex interaction among at least three environments; the sociopolitical, the economic and the ecological. At the centre of these interactions is humankind. The essence of sustainable development is the fragility of the balance that must be obtained and maintained if human progress is to be secured

---

2 . U-Pride seems to reflect some of the worst attributes of foreign aid; coercive, deterministic, controlling and manipulative. U-Pride is alleged to have adopted and incorporated the vision and the strategies of the North Eastern Natal Development Committee, a grouping of CBOs and NGOs in the area, which had been working towards an integrated approach to rural development promotion based on participatory approaches long before U-Pride. It then allegedly pressurized other organizations to join and to act according to the EU's pace and timetable, insisted on a direct relationship between these NGOs and the EU and more or less forced an association between the NGOs and the DBSA indirectly through U-Pride's association with the DBSA. It is criticized, among other things, for being a mechanism through which the EU imposes its programmes and projects on communities, for its cumbersome monitoring and reporting requirements and, for its distrust of illiterate local people and groups.

over time without damaging the prospects of a better life for future generations. The three environments, or systems, are on the one hand conditionalities for sustainable development and on the other, limitations imposed upon one another and upon human actions or inactions. Whether the limits imposed on development are defined in environmental or economic terms,[3] in the South African situation the socio-political and historical constraints — the contradictions of 40 years of apartheid — are perhaps the most binding on sustainable development, however defined. The most blatant testimony of this contradiction and unsustainability of apartheid is the collapse of the edifice itself, leaving in its ruins explosive social, political and economic disorder on the one hand and multiple, often conflicting, expectations on the other.

The skyscraper economy erected on apartheid's edifice depended on the maintenance of a large reserve of dehumanized and expendable labour, injected once in a while, as required, into the white economy as an adjustment mechanism. It required the forceful uprooting of whole communities, the dispossession of their lands and dumping nearly a third of the population on barren, desolate land to scrape a living, policed by murderous and dictatorial lackeys. Under apartheid and its legacy, environmental destruction is inextricably linked with social and political repression. It required the most brutal of methods to maintain apartheid for so long. The crumbling of the system shows that even oppression has its limits.

Under apartheid and its legacy, the concept of a community takes on a new form as people hitherto unknown to one another reconstruct alliances and bonds to overcome apartheid's seeds of discord sewn in multiple ways. New mechanisms of trust, self-confidence and self-esteem have to be established. Even the concept of a household takes on a new form for families and children torn apart and estranged from one another for years. Scraping a living on such marginal or desolate lands only accelerates degradation, whilst the excessive subsidies for white farmers and manufacturers leads to inefficient and, therefore, environmentally wasteful and harmful use and disposal of natural resources. The first victims of dangerous waste are those who handle it, the workers, and those communities considered expendable enough for the waste

---

3. For environmentalists the principal constraint on development is the depletion of environmental resources and the production and disposal of dangerous waste. The condition for sustainable development is therefore one in which no human action or inaction leads to irreversible damage of the eco-system. In economic terms, sustainable 'growth' is conditional on a stable growth in productivity leading to a reduction in mass poverty and vulnerability, without endangering macro-economic stability.

to be dumped in their back yards — the non-white communities and the poor in general. They are the ones who are incapable of recycling it and who are unable to pay for the medical and other costs of its effects. The worst affected victims of degraded soils are the people who depend on those soils for their very survival.

Sustainable development in the South African context is a justice issue and 'justice requires changing the system which exploits, redirecting resources and incentives and redistributing wealth and opportunities and helping the hitherto oppressed to build self-esteem and confidence.'[4] Therefore, in whatever way one looks at it, achieving sustainable development is first a political balancing act, entirely dependent on the process of change taking place and only second on the mechanics of policy. It will take a lot to balance what is with what should be; to narrow the gap between what should be done and what can be done, as well as between what is expected and what can be.

SUSTAINABLE DEVELOPMENT CHALLENGES FOR NGOS

We have argued that the constraints on environmental resources are basically sociopolitical, arising from the apartheid system, and that therefore a just political solution (one that also leads to an equitable system of governance and access to and redistribution of resources) will enhance sustainable development. Secondly, apartheid has substantially disrupted community life and the social fabric of the majority of the South African people. A new sense of community needs to be built, one based on tolerance, self-help and collective action. The key to this sense of belonging and comradeship is trust and a common purpose. Apartheid has substantially affected the self-esteem of millions of people, black and white. Self-esteem is essential for rediscovering one's creativity and drive. Creativity is also a function of accessibility to skills (technical or organizational) and information.

To a large extent NGOs are contributing to building a foundation for sustained change. NGOs developing from a tradition of labour and civic organization are learning to take on board the challenges of shifting from protest to creating and harnessing opportunities. Sectoral-activity oriented groups, like agricultural oriented groups, are learning to incorporate institution-building objectives into technical information transfer

---

4. Bonil Jack of the ANC Lands Department. Quoted from a speech made at a seminar in Pietermaritzburg on the theme: 'What Does it Mean to [be] Green in South Africa?', August 1992.

programmes. Middle-class white groups have to struggle to gain acceptance whilst black groups must learn to harness the expertise of the white society for their own agenda. These are lessons that are still being learnt.

Also crucial with regard to alleviating poverty is the relationship that will develop between the state and NGOs. Will it be mutually supportive, or will NGOs remain on the margins picking up the pieces? Will government policy ease the rules and mechanisms by which the poor can take advantage of opportunities in the formal sector? Many CBOs and NGOs face multiple challenges; they lack resources and have to cope with the momentum and unpredictability of change in such a way as to enhance the relationships between CBOs and service-providing organizations. At the centre of these challenges are broad institutional questions. Institutional development (ID) will play a central part in enhancing both coping mechanisms and the resilience to be active agents of change.

INSTITUTIONAL STRENGTHENING FOR SUSTAIN-ABLE DEVELOPMENT

ID is one of those buzz words in development jargon that means different things. It is sometimes understood as being synonymous with strengthening organizations, ie organizational development (OD). There are distinctions between the two. An institution refers to 'norms and behaviour that persist over time and which serve to influence society.'[5] Institutions exert themselves on society through the values and norms they espouse (for example self-reliance, empowerment and social justice) and through their rules (the dos, don'ts and hows). These norms and rules may or may not be promoted (manifest themselves) through an organization. An organization is a 'social unit which is purposefully structured, and is role-bound' and designed to achieve a specific goal or goals.

An organization becomes institutionalized when it acquires a social value and stability and if its purpose and influence goes far beyond the organization itself. Needless to say, not all organizations are institutionalized (for example an estate agency), nor do all institutions (for example marriage, the market or money) have to be organizations. An institutionalized organization:

---

5. The definitions of institutional and organizational development are drawn from Fowler et al (1992).

- has a structure, a vision, a purpose and a set of values;
- interacts with and influences (hopefully is also influenced by) the values and lives of communities and social structures in general;
- has acquired permanency and stability and intends to retain them.

OD refers to the process of strengthening the internal workings of the organization in order to achieve efficiency and effectiveness. It refers to the channels of information flows, the decision-making structure, the monitoring and evaluation mechanisms including financial and other reporting. These elements are meant to enable the organization to achieve stated objectives and to function within its mandate.

ID on the other hand refers to changes occurring, or intended to occur, within and outside the organization that influences patterns and behaviour in the wider society. These changes may include:

- those occurring within the organization that influence the way it interacts with society. For example, how it operates, ie how it takes, conveys, implements, monitors and evaluates decisions and activities; how it administers itself; its information and communication systems; its accountability mechanisms; and its sensing mechanisms, ie the way the organization gathers and monitors mood, reactions, effects and impacts within and outside itself.
- the forms and patterns of relations between an organization, the communities it supports and the state;
- the purpose, vision and values.

Put simply, ID is OD plus vision and scope of interaction with the broader society with the aim of influencing the behaviour of the society. ID clearly has political and social goals far and beyond efficiency concerns.

WHY IS ID NECESSARY FOR SUSTAINABLE DEVELOPMENT?

The strength of NGOs should lie, among others things, in the relevance of (and effectiveness in achieving) their goals, in their responsiveness to needs and in their ability to mobilize resources to maintain their services. Relevance is measured against the needs and perceptions of the communities being supported. Needs and perceptions change over time. Effectiveness and responsiveness are in part functions of organizational efficiency and effectiveness (at all levels) but also the level of response (participation) of the communities. An organization's efficiency or effectiveness cannot be divorced from the system of needs assessment and forms of intervention employed. The success in fund-raising is in part a function of the public's or donor's perception of the relevance and effectiveness of OD, the creativity of the organization's fund-raising methods and environmental factors, including the political interest of donors.

The growth of interest in participatory development approaches is based on evidence that top-down or deterministic approaches to development promotion have had marginal impact on poverty alleviation in general, and on project impact and sustainability in particular. Consequently, it is believed that development promotion through effective participation enhances project success (quality) but also a sense of ownership, continuity and growth (of the organization and the resources and confidence of the people it supports). Participatory methods aim to improve self-confidence, local innovation and adaptation, to enhance local capabilities and to increase diversity and complexity (see Pretty and Chambers 1992). The core goals are growth, sustainability (of the organization or its activities) and greater self-reliance and self-esteem. Participation is also a means to new forms of partnership, dialogue and sharing between the organization and the people it supports. This must lead to changes occurring not only among the people but also within the organization, created by new demands made upon the organization or new lessons learnt from the people. Participation cannot be limited merely to the relationship between the organization and the people. Participatory methods must also permeate the organization.

To ensure that grassroots participation leads to sustained and sustainable change, three conditions are essential:

- participatory methods and approaches;
- a participatory learning environment; and
- a participatory institutional (including organizational) environment.

Methods and Approaches

Participatory approaches relate to the methods of interaction between the organization and the community/group, or interaction within the organization itself. It refers to the way information is acquired, conveyed, analysed and applied in both directions. It also includes the means by which effects and impacts of the interaction, or changes in general, are monitored and evaluated *ex post facto* and the way the lessons are put to use. Participatory methods are essential not only for enhancing learning but also for ensuring that information is generated interactively and is based in part on local knowledge.

The Learning Environment

A participatory learning environment is one in which learning is inter-active. In other words, grassroots people learn from the organization (values, expertise) at the same time as they feed new knowledge, ideas and values into it, thereby playing a part in shaping it. Within the organization, it applies to an environment in which the staff are encouraged to learn from the management and technical experts, whilst at the same time management decisions and expert knowledge are derived solely from interaction with staff at all levels. Resource material is made accessible and the management is not afraid to allow staff to gain independence of thought and vision. The same applies to organization/community relationships. Whether referring to the organization's relationship with the community, or to relations within the organization, a participatory environment is essential for creativity, initiative, commitment and joint ownership.

The Character of the Institution

Institutional support is essential if creative and innovative people are 'to gain freedom' to act and share with others and if participatory innovations in general are to spread. An institution managed in a congenial participatory fashion is more likely to encourage innovation and the testing of new ideas than a top-down top-heavy one in which the staff are frightened to death of going slightly out of line. Such an organization easily slips into routine activities with staff feeling limited to specified chores. It is likely to be rigid and self-satisfied.

A participatory institution also calls for a system of communication and decision-making that spreads responsibility more broadly and allows for the expression of a diversity of skills. Such an institutional environment discourages over-reliance on one individual, or small clique of people, upon whom all decisions lie and whose absence could sound the death knell of the organization. A participatory institution must also, in essence, believe and trust in people and therefore be committed to enhancing their self-esteem and independence.

The Interaction of the Three Environments

These three conditions (participatory methods and approaches, a participatory learning environment and a conducive institution) interact and overlap. A creative and participatory learning environment on its own will be marginal and short lived if it is not part of the institution's overall practices and cannot be shared beyond the organization. Similarly, institutional support for participatory processes will remain rhetorical if the environment does not permit it to be practised. Equally, methods are only as good as the environment to which they are applied and the commitment by the institution and its staff and management to apply them in full and to abide by the consequences of their application.

The point this analysis seeks to make is that it is insufficient to worry about participatory methods of interacting with people without equally ensuring a participatory institution and an enabling learning environment. A recognition of the need for grassroots participation must equally be a recognition for building a participatory institution and an enabling and supportive learning environment within the organization and between the organization and the people.

THE SCOPE FOR PARTICIPATORY DEVELOPMENT PROMOTION IN SOUTH AFRICA

One important result of the decades of struggle against oppression is that the level of organization and mobilization at the grassroots level in most parts of South Africa is high. Because no community is untouched by apartheid, there is no complete organizational vacuum anywhere. Some communities may be mobile, as people migrate in search of jobs, but there is often some organizational framework. As observed earlier, there is a growing research capability within the NGO sector. Intense networking is taking place among NGOs within and across sectoral or regional interests. This unique situation implies that whether one chooses to work directly at community level or through intermediary organizations, there are local organizations to contend with, no matter how loosely structured they may be. Any support for capacity building for organizational and institutional development would, if provided by external donors and NGOs, contribute immensely to the sustainable development processes internally initiated.

Similarly, there is generally a high level of democratic consciousness and a desire for participatory and democratic practice. The desire to construct a participatory environment is part of the wider goal of the long-standing political struggle. There is a clamour for participatory methods of doing things, whether it is training, project formulation or project implementation.

Charles Abugre

ORGANIZATIONAL STRENGTHENING FOR INSTITUTIONAL AND SUSTAINABLE DEVELOPMENT: THE ROLE OF FOREIGN NGOS

The challenges facing South African NGOs are immense, the biggest being the challenge of building a new society out of the smouldering lava of apartheid. The scale of confidence rejuvenation, trust-building and reconciliation that is required is almost without precedent in Africa. Given the unique role of NGOs in the struggle, the expectation of their role is equally high. The South African NGO, whether professional or CBO, is under more pressure than usual to construct new ways of relating and performing. These are the areas, however, that most South African NGOs can offer as experiences well learnt to the rest of the continent.

In spite of these experiences, several CBOs have various limitations. Among these are poor implementation skills, lack of trust, an absence of dispute resolution mechanisms, resource constraints, fluidity of membership as people migrate in search of livelihood, difficulty transforming protest organizations into development promotion, and a failure to formulate strategies and skills for negotiating with external interests.

New accountability mechanisms will also have to be learnt. As South African NGOs join the rest of the aid community, forms of accountability hitherto accepted by donors on the plea of a 'special situation' will increasingly be unacceptable. Already there are signs that some NGOs are finding the new sets of conditionalities for aid hard to bear and accountability requirements rather overbearing. Basic training may be required in such areas as project proposal writing, reporting, monitoring and evaluation systems and negotiating skills.

The consternation over the influx of foreign aid agencies and donor NGOs would need some resolution. There is concern about multiple intrusion and the dictation of conflicting agendas and methods of work as conditionalities for funds. To some extent, these will be inevitable and perhaps unavoidable. Yet, there must be ways of coordinating the activities and demands of donors in general. Experience shows that the best regulatory framework is voluntary. Where that is not possible, it may be desirable for the receivers of funds and conditionalities to initiate frameworks for joint bargaining or forums for the harmonization, as far as that is possible, of evaluation procedures. There is no reason, however, why donor NGOs should not initiate their own mechanisms for reducing distortions and unnecessary contradictions in the conditionality for funds.

Whereas the isolation of South Africa from the rest of the world has enabled South African NGOs to develop creative methods of working with the poor and dispossessed, the isolation has at the same time denied them access to information and methodologies developed elsewhere. Organizational forms that have been tried and failed elsewhere may be tried without the benefit of experiences from elsewhere. Exchange visits and information to (from) other parts of the world, but more importantly to (from) the rest of Africa, could help in these areas but also in building self-esteem and self-confidence. Donor NGOs also working in other parts of the continent could usefully facilitate these exchanges.

Internal networking is one of the unique strengths of South African NGOs. These networks perform vital functions, including coordinating isolated experiences, developing policy, coordinating political pressure and providing political protection for struggling groups. Maintaining these vital functions requires core funding. This, however, is difficult to obtain from donors, who prefer projects with quantifiable or visible qualitative outputs. Providing this type of support is perhaps the most relevant role foreign NGOs can play in South Africa. Participation of donor NGOs at this level may also help keep them away from too much meddling in communities in a direct and distorting way.

REFERENCES

Fowler, A et al (1992) *Institutional Development and NGOs in Africa*, Navib
Nell and Shapiro (1992) 'A Study of the Natal Region of South Africa', prepared for Navib, July/August, pp 20–2
Pretty, J and Chambers, R (1992) *Turning the New Leaf: New Professionalism, Institutions and Policies for Agriculture*, London, International Institute for Environment and Development

Chapter Ten

South Africa's Future Health Care Policy: Selective or Comprehensive Primary Health Care?

John Macdonald

The provision of equitable health care should be guided by the aspirations of our people as enshrined in the Freedom Charter and by principles which reflect the Primary Health Care approach adopted by the World Health Organization and the United Nations Children's Fund at Alma Ata in 1978.

(ANC 1992)

This endorsement of the principles of comprehensive primary health care (PHC) by the African National Congress (ANC) seems clear: the new South Africa should adopt an approach to health care, radically different from the one it will replace, following the policies outlined by the Alma Ata conference of 1978. The rest of the document makes it clear that it is the strong version of PHC (Wisner 1988) that is being proposed here and not any weak or diluted version of Alma Ata as encouraged by some selective approaches, a point to which we will return. The characteristics of strong PHC are policies founded on the principles of equity, people's participation and intersectoral collaboration (Macdonald 1993). Both the ANC document already referred to and the policy statements emerging from the South African Health and Social Services Organization (SAHSSO)/National Progressive Primary Health Care Network (NPPHCN) Health Policy Conference of December 1992 indicate a firm commitment to these principles.

Throughout the southern Africa region and in many other countries of the world the PHC approach has been widely discussed and variously implemented. It offers a more rational health-care system worldwide.

The implementation of strong PHC calls for considerable support from the state and from the medical establishment; it calls for change. There is a momentum for change in the current South African climate, a momentum which extends to the area of health care. Part of the international interest in emergent South African health policies stems from the fact that it is reasonable to suppose that what will happen in a post-apartheid South Africa will have an impact well beyond its own national boundaries. At this time of great change I feel we all to a greater or lesser degree hold a stake in this matter. What happens in South Africa affects us all.

Arguably, the conditioning factors, the factors which will determine the policy's success or failure are, in this situation as in others, the twin spheres of internal political will and the international medical model. Both spheres are spheres of power: social and professional; new policies will involve a shift in the distribution of power. I would suggest that in South Africa it is not yet clear if there is sufficiently strong political pressure to counteract the sphere of medical power, which is inherently conservative, in order to forge a rational health system to fit the population's needs; if this force is lacking then the pressures on a new South Africa to follow less innovative and therefore conservative and inequitable paths of health care will determine the future. I propose to touch on several of these factors: the comprehensive PHC approach, the obstacles in its path, and the strengths which could generate the energy to overcome these obstacles.

THE COMPREHENSIVE PHC APPROACH

Comprehensive PHC is not an extension of the health services into remote areas using poorly-paid workers to reach the parts of the community institutional care in towns cannot reach. It is an international movement, launched in the 1970s, which questions the appropriateness of a narrowly-based medical approach to health services (providing for the treatment/curative needs of the few) and which reorients the system towards the health needs of the whole community, including its preventive needs. In the broad lines of the PHC approach, as laid out at the Alma Ata conference in 1978, it is possible to see the framework of a new health-care model of universal significance. PHC is presented by the conference as a health system integrated into the development plans and programmes of a nation. It forms an integral part both of the country's health system, of which it is the central function and main focus, and of the overall social and economic development of the community (WHO/UNICEF 1978: vi).

It is unlikely that the countries that signed the document in 1978 realized the full significance of what they were endorsing. It will take still more years before we realize the full significance of what it means to make PHC the central function and main focus of the health system and the consequences of this for daily practice. Many Third World countries have tried to take this definition of PHC seriously. It is surely valid to ask all South African health workers if they see PHC, at least potentially, as forming the central function and main focus of their health system. In many countries, at least in the early days, it was often thought that PHC had to do with some rather minor activities at the periphery of the health services. Is this the case in South Africa as well?

Moreover, it useful and important to have the links between development and health (and consequently between underdevelopment and ill-health) brought to our attention in such a straightforward manner as in the above words of Alma Ata. Health workers, according to the PHC approach, are development workers and development workers can also be health workers.

This development approach to health, the comprehensive PHC approach, is the one endorsed by the ANC policy guidelines quoted above. They are quite clear on this:

> For people to be healthy it is necessary that families earn enough money to live decent lives, and work under safe conditions. People need decent housing, adequate and safe water, and sufficient nourishing food. ... People also need a comprehensive health service that promotes good health, prevents illness, provides care and rehabilitative services to the ill and to people with disabilities.
>
> (ANC 1992)

Other commentators within South Africa echo the same message: 'Clearly the health of a community is not just a reflection of the ability of a hospital to cure the population. It has to be a self-sustaining balance of facilities within a health-promoting economic and social environment.' (Robb 1992)

Of course, as we have said, PHC includes primary medical care, but is not synonymous with it. The vision of health care enshrined in the Alma Ata conference stresses the promotion of health and the prevention of disease, but it includes, of course, the treatment of conditions of ill-health: 'PHC addresses the main health problems in the community, providing promotive, preventive, curative and rehabilitative services.' (WHO/UNICEF 1978: Alma Ata Declaration VI (2))

PHC is often understood in terms of campaigns or programmes within medical services, or to mean health projects run by non-government agencies on the periphery of the medical system. This is not the meaning of PHC as put forward by Alma Ata. The conference envisaged PHC as a radical reinterpretation of health services. For the conference, Health For All represented a commitment to greater justice and equity in health resource allocation; this involves a denunciation of existing inequalities and, at least implicitly, the resolve to redress such imbalances. This commitment to equity is one of the essential pillars of the PHC approach. Another is the adherence to the principle of the right of people to be involved in significant decisions concerning their health services, the participation dimension of PHC, now increasingly referred to as community involvement in health. The third pillar of the PHC philosophy is the acceptance of the need for the medical profession to collaborate with other sectors that make significant contributions to the health of populations. This is referred to as intersectoral collaboration. These three 'developments', as Tarimo and Creese (1990) call them, are the basis of the PHC approach. They represent an enormous challenge to medical thinking and practice. Until Alma Ata, these three dimensions had been barely discussed in the health sector; now they are on the international health agenda and are at least more difficult to ignore than they had been in the past. They represent both the ideals of a new approach and a major challenge to existing policies and practice. The medical world can dispute the usefulness, appropriateness and feasibility of the PHC approach, but these three pillars erected by the conference demand an examination of issues that cannot easily be dismissed.

We have a vision here of PHC which does not allow it to be marginalized as some activity on the periphery: PHC involves directing national health services to community health needs. Unfortunately, however, national health services have rarely been planned according to such a rational assessment of the community's needs and appropriate solutions. PHC also involves a conscious effort to see health as an integral part of the nation's development; health planning and development planning must go together.

Secondary and tertiary health care cannot be said to be part of primary health care, but they must form part of a health-care system that focuses on the needs of the community in the spirit of PHC. All must be integrated into a rational entity. This is the spirit of the Alma Ata declaration; it deserves a further look for the perspectives it offers on an alternative approach to health services.

Much of the health care on offer to the Third World and poorer segments of Western society is inaccessible. The curative hospital-based model of health care is almost invariably urban-biased and so, almost by definition, access is denied to many people. Even physical proximity, however, does not mean ease of access, since economic constraints bar many from the use of such institutions, a situation which seems to apply to many South Africans. Lack of access is a characteristic of the health services in many countries. Alma Ata challenges such a situation: 'PHC is essential health care ... made universally accessible ... at a cost the community and the country can afford and is the first level of contact of individuals, the family and community with the national health system, bringing health care as close as possible to where people live and work.' (WHO/UNICEF 1978: Alma Ata declaration, VI)

The comprehensive view of PHC presented by Alma Ata stresses the need to go beyond a medico-technical approach to ill health; the macroscopic (as opposed to 'microscopic') vision of health and ill-health sees health-enhancing actions outside medicine as a legitimate concern of PHC (Macdonald 1993). The 'comprehensive' in comprehensive PHC indicates that this approach is concerned with health for all and in addition understands health as part of development.

Alma Ata, without any doubt, presented a strong version of PHC, a comprehensive view, insisting on the role of sectors such as agriculture, water and sanitation and education; it is the task of health workers to collaborate with these sectors since they make a major contribution to health and an appropriate health-care system along PHC lines must be operationalized as part of the overall social and economic development of the community. Documents following on from the conference have continued to stress this collaboration (see, for example, WHO 1986a, b, c and 1988). The comprehensive approach presented at Alma Ata placed considerable importance on people's involvement in the health planning process; participation, in this view, is not an optional luxury but a crucial dimension of health services. An editorial in *Tropical Doctor* goes so far as to say that the choice is now between health care delivered to populations or *participatory* health care, which sees the involvement of the community as being essential for effective health programmes (Lankester 1991: 1–2).

Likewise, the comprehensive approach to health matters brings justice and equity to the discussion table and into the planning process: health workers and programmes that try to implement a comprehensive approach find themselves being called upon to acknowledge the poverty and material deprivation dimension of disease; this often causes PHC supporters to become involved in anti-poverty programmes and in people's struggles for a more just distribution of resources.

Because PHC involves a reorientation of the whole system to support people's health needs, it acknowledges that health is not just a medical–technical problem, but has its origins in socio-economic conditions, with poverty often at the root of ill-health (Macdonald 1993). Consequently, PHC tackles prevention, health education and rehabilitation, as well as curative care, and looks for healthy alliances with other sectors like agriculture and education. It is not just primary medical care. As an approach it also takes seriously the idea of people's participation, allowing people as individuals and groups some role in decision-making about health services. This calls for serious reorientation of medical attitudes which are not commonly participatory. In South Africa, the ANC and other progressive bodies have given their endorsement to these principles:

> Health and lack of health are rooted in the economic and social fabric of any society. Socio-economic circumstances are more important than medical services in ensuring good health ... The primary health care approach is essentially that of community development. It aims to reduce inequalities in access to health services ... and integrates the many sectors of modern life such as education and housing. Further, it is based on full community participation.
>
> (ANC 1992)

SOME OBSTACLES TO THE IMPLEMENTATION OF A PHC POLICY IN SOUTH AFRICA

One can foresee serious problems facing those who try to incorporate the principles of PHC into South Africa's health policy. For one thing, black people have been denied access for so long to decent health services, which are symbolized by prestigious 'white' hospitals. PHC would involve a reorientation towards prevention and local community care and could seem like a cheap option to marginalized black populations. A massive popular educational programme would be necessary to address the understandable rage of the poor. In this sense, popular expectations could present an obstacle to the implementation of a comprehensive PHC policy in South Africa.

Thanks to the issues raised by the PHC approach and debate, which are already familiar to many health professionals in the country, it is becoming increasingly difficult for health planners to plan a simply *medical* rather than *health* service. Of course, there is no real dichotomy:

health care must always include medical care. But in the twentieth century there have been (and in many circumstances still are) distortions and contradictions, which have resulted in an over-emphasis on the role of medical technology focused on the treatment and possible cure of disease to the neglect of wider strategies of health-promoting and prevention activities. Health care has often meant medical care and sometimes even very limited medical care. Such an emphasis has become less and less tenable since the Alma Ata conference, one of the greatest contributions of which was to remind us of the *social* construction of ill-health and to call into question the medicalization of health. Nevertheless, there is such a thing as an international medical culture, focused on a de-contextualized view of ill-health and emphasizing physiological malfunctioning and its treatment to the virtual exclusion of social causality of ill-health and the implied social solutions (Macdonald 1993).

Others may have their finger more closely on the pulse of what the international agencies are doing in South Africa; I feel my modest contribution to the debate is to suggest that indications are that the marriage between international agencies and the medical model, embedded in the approach of returnee doctors, as well as in the expectations of those who have been deprived of proper health care, will produce a move towards inappropriate health care that will be hard to stop.

Some would say that to look at the medical model as a major obstacle is to miss the point. They would argue that the form a health system takes is determined by the political flavour of the government in question. An egalitarian regime will move towards a more egalitarian health-care system, a more conservative market-led government will move inexorably towards a 'health as a commodity' health-care system. There is clearly truth in this, but if the corollary is seen to be that all we have to do is struggle for a radical social transformation and the rest will follow, including a more PHC-oriented health-care system of the kind I have described, then I feel this is the cop-out option. Whatever shape the government takes, there is a risk that the inherent conservatism of the medical model will determine the nature and scope of the health-care system. This risk is as high in South Africa as elsewhere.

I want to suggest that there is such a thing as an international medical culture with the potential of dominating all health policies. Unless this is understood and acknowledged we will not move forward.

The Western medical model has been described as an engineering model (McKeown 1976; Engel 1976). The analogy of the body as a machine and the doctor as the medical scientist/engineer has proved useful to the development of certain aspects of medical care, especially in crisis interventions and in the treatment of acute clinical disorders. But the engineering analogy *is* only an analogy and the complexities of human health and ill-health in all societies, and not just in poorer countries, are such that health care and health services cannot be adequately contained within such a framework. There is a tendency to focus most effort and resources on the treatment/curative dimensions of health care. One of the greatest drawbacks of the medical culture that has grown up with the engineering model is the removal of the patient or the community from any situation of control in the encounter with the medical profession. Disease tends to be seen, by professional and layperson alike, as something objective, somehow in the individual or in the community, but separable from them, waiting to be identified and dealt with by the medical profession.

There has been considerable progress in the development of Western scientific medicine. Yet, even in the areas where we might have thought it reasonable to suppose a magic bullet would have been invented to knock out disease such as in the case of malaria, there has been lamentable failure. Malaria is on the increase despite millions spent on drugs.

The medico–technical progress which has taken place has often done little to alleviate much of the suffering and ill-health which exist in the societies of the Third World with their patterns of communicable diseases often rooted in poverty. The medical engineering model and the systems it informs also increasingly fail to deliver in Western societies where the common pattern of disease in the community at large is often one of psychosocial problems and diseases of an ageing population, conditions which are likewise not amenable to magic bullet types of solutions (Maglacas 1984).

It would be irrational to invest in medical science great expectations for the removal of this suffering, either of the diseases of poverty in the Third World, or of psychosocial and degenerative diseases in Western societies. Nevertheless, the allure of the myth that there is a medical answer to the problems of the world's health continues to be a most powerful one. South Africa will inevitably be drawn in this direction and the commitment to a comprehensive PHC programme will come into conflict with external as well as internal reactionary forces.

There are powerful voices promoting, not comprehensive PHC, but the *weak* version, selective PHC. This is no mere academic discussion. The debate concerning selective/comprehensive PHC can and does lead to crucial policy decisions being made which have a considerable impact on the form health services actually take, especially on the choice of who is to be served. The positions taken in South Africa will have profound effects on the nature and quality of future care, a point made by several discussants at a recent seminar on the matter in South Africa (Yach et al 1993). The debate concerning selective or comprehensive PHC, and the policy positions which result, can also be seen as illustrating the response of the medical professions to the challenges of the PHC approach.

In the light of what has been said already about PHC and the medical model, the selective version of PHC can be understood as a medical view of PHC, or a medicalization of the original PHC message. Given the medical model, and the way it has shaped health services in many countries, it was predictable that comprehensive PHC, as put forward by Alma Ata, would tend to find itself subsumed into a medical view of the world and have its impact and challenge inevitably diluted. This is just what has happened in many quarters. The holistic principles of PHC may be spelt out in Alma Ata: participation, working with other sectors in the development of communities, equity. But these policies are often implemented by health services and medically trained practitioners, already cast in the mould of medical care, the medical intervention model. The pouring of PHC principles into such a mould has the effect of diluting the impact; PHC becomes medicalized. There is an inbuilt tendency in systems informed by the medical model to reduce health interventions to medico–technical interventions and to reduce the role of people's participation in health, essential to the initial vision of PHC, to something that looks suspiciously like collective patient compliance. This medicalization of PHC is an aspect of the debate about the choice between selective and comprehensive versions of PHC which is often overlooked. Awareness of this tendency to medicalize and so undermine the PHC approach could go some way towards resisting this bias and so preserve some of the real force and impact of the comprehensive vision of PHC presented at Alma Ata.

Promoters of selective PHC, what Wisner (1988) calls the weak version, while applauding the aims of comprehensive PHC, argue that, since time and resources are limited, health workers must select and target for intervention the conditions of ill-health most amenable to low-cost technology. This line of thinking leads to a conclusions such as that of the Rockefeller Foundation's Bellagio conference, namely that 'until comprehensive primary health care (PHC) can be made available to all, effective services aimed at the few most important diseases (selective primary health care — SPHC) may be the best means of improving the health of the greatest number of people.' (Warren 1988: 891)

Some researchers (for example Banerji 1984) highlight the political dimensions of the move from strong to weak versions, suggesting that programmes with targeted interventions characterized by appropriate technico–medical interventions to be delivered to the public by health workers can help to obscure the need for political and social reform to remove structural barriers to health. Many health workers are not responsible for the overall approach of the systems or programmes in which they work and sometimes are too involved in the day-to-day tasks to realize some of the more general implications of the priority decisions being made. International agencies have considerable influence in determining the focus of much health work in developing countries. These agencies are often very interested in selective PHC, and have been the main proponents and funders of such programmes. Comprehensive PHC implies long-term developmental goals with aims sometimes as general as the increase in people's confidence in their ability to control some parts of their environment. This is unattractive to agencies who tend to opt for short-term achievable goals. Long-term development strategies stressing participation are in pursuit of goals which are not easy to measure and the promotion of participation and equity as strategies for achieving improved health status are often seen by the health profession as secondary or even disposable dimensions of health-care projects, having little place in the conventional view of dealing with disease.

The equity dimension of PHC may be embarrassing to international agencies and to certain members of the medical profession; by adopting the medico–technical view of 'selective' PHC they can involve themselves in initiatives that tackle ill-health, or at least its symptoms, without challenging the status quo and the underlying social causes of disease. Some commentators show the links between the West's economic recipes for Third World countries, especially structural adjustment policies, and the promotion of social initiatives that do not challenge the status quo: the encouragement of selective rather than comprehensive PHC is a good example (Kanji 1989). As often, there is here a close fit between a medical view of disease and symptom-focused interventions and the interests of those who at present profit from the status quo. It is important for health workers in the field, perhaps especially in South Africa, to realize that some seemingly praiseworthy health programmes, stressing the short-term technical interventions of selective PHC, can be serving interests that are positively against any social change. The arguments are rarely spelled out in this fashion. Selective PHC, when promoted, is always put forward as being the most rational option for health intervention, the most feasible, and the most appropriate.

No sooner had the conference of Alma Ata finished (and its approach been brought to international attention and indeed begun to find its way into national health documents) than the scope of PHC as proposed by the conference began to be whittled down and its challenge eroded.

There was little criticism of the aims of PHC, as presented by Alma Ata, but voices were raised, arguing that these objectives were too idealistic. There was need to be selective, to target conditions of ill-health which could be perceptibly and cost-effectively improved upon. We cannot do everything all at once, it was argued. Let us target those most at risk, specific diseases with high morbidity and mortality and amenable to non-costly interventions. Also, some proponents of this approach argued that poorer countries lack the institutional capability to implement a comprehensive PHC approach. 'The strategy to improve health must be selective. Success will depend heavily on correctly identifying the most important problems in each population group, selecting the most cost effective interventions, and managing the services efficiently.' (Warren 1988: 892)

UNICEF has been prominent in promoting selective PHC, for instance in its programme 'The Child Survival Development Revolution' (the word revolution, interestingly, has been dropped in some countries that adopted the programme because it had unpalatable connotations). PHC becomes GOBI and GOBI–FFF: a series of simple, cost-effective solutions to major problems. G is for growth monitoring, O for oral rehydration, B for breast feeding, I for immunization, FFF for food supplements, female education and family planning. In later years water and sanitation were added by some programmes. Many health workers find in this simple formula a manageable and effective interpretation of PHC. Manageable it may be, but in what sense can it be said to be effective?

Poverty, and the web of socio-economic conditions linked to it, are at the root of many health problems in poor communities. Is it possible to make a significant difference in the health status of communities by focusing on individual diseases, through selective PHC? It is perfectly understandable that the medical profession would be drawn to such an approach, in the light of what has been said already about the medical model and the search for technico–medical solutions to health problems. With its doctrine of specific aetiology, allopathic medicine seeks to knock out the causative agent of particular diseases in the body: a pill for every ill. There is a predisposing attitude to the simple technical solutions of selective PHC as strategies for dealing with the enormous health problems of poor countries. Huge efforts have been put into the targeting of one disease at a time. Smallpox eradication seemed a great success and such targeting a model to follow. Unfortunately, the targeting of other individual diseases like malaria has proved wholly unsuccessful. Franco-Agudelo (1983: 61) cites the example of the Rockefeller Foundation's anti-malarial programme in Latin America, which adopted a technico–medical approach to the disease. The exclusion of the social determinants of ill-health from this programme made sure that the health programme did not imply any structural change towards justice. The medical model fitted well with this approach. All the efforts against the disease, 'focused first on the fields of biology and physiology, and then on chemistry and chemotherapy. At the same time, all possible social determinants were relegated to a secondary, barely scientific role. In other words, this meant the rise of the individual-biology aspects' preponderance at the expense of socio-structural ones.' In spite of anti-malarial programmes, the disease is on the increase in many countries. This should have alerted health service providers to the flaws inherent in selective technico–medical approaches, but unfortunately, the medical model of PHC is alive and well.

A striking argument in favour of thinking and planning in terms of comprehensive rather than selective PHC comes from the work of the Kasongo Project Team in Zaire (see Kasongo Project Team 1981). Measles was targeted and successfully eradicated in an entire district of around 200,000 people. This seemed like a success story. Morbidity figures and measles-related mortality figures improved. But, it was found that the targeted intervention had only a short-term impact on *overall* mortality figures. Although the targeting of one disease was successful in terms of removing the condition (measles), it was unsuccessful in terms of improving the overall life chances of the children involved. After a relatively short time the children who had not died of measles died of some other infection, linked to malnutrition and certainly to the underlying poverty of the communities involved. Selective targeted programmes are seductive to aid agencies anxious for short-term observable results, but they are programmes of primary *medical*, rather than primary *health*, care.

When the conditions that cause ill-health are not addressed the benefits are illusory. Selective PHC can be seen as an attempt to alleviate some of the worst consequences of failing to provide a comprehensive health-care system. The basic demands of PHC are almost totally removed: equity, people's participation and intersectoral collaboration get shelved. As a document overviewing the period since Alma Ata says (WHO 1988: 44), 'the selective approach fits the technological and political orientation of some donor agencies who look for concrete objectives and measurable outcomes, achieved in a relatively short period of time; in embracing these characteristics of selective programmes, they might ride roughshod over fundamental principles of community-based PHC.'

Quick technical fixes as promoted by some practitioners of selective 'PHC' are far from the spirit and approach of Alma Ata. As Farrant

(1989: 8) puts it: 'The effect of this promotion of SPHC under the PHC umbrella is to keep health interventions firmly within medical control and to detract from the need for long-term social, economic and political change.'

South Africa has important decisions to make, not least concerning the health of its population and the shape of its future health services. Crucial to these decisions, I think, is the notion of PHC: what is actually meant by policies that claim to be PHC promoting; likewise, have all the actors involved appreciated the full force of the consequences of the choice between selective and comprehensive PHC? Activists from a variety of backgrounds have highlighted the socio-economic causes of ill-health in South Africa: they are hard to ignore. There is clearly a move towards a more just, more participatory health-care system and the interest in comprehensive PHC is genuine and strong. But will the promoters of PHC be able to resist the medicalization of PHC entailed by the adoption of the selective option, the darling of so many medical professionals and aid agencies?

REFERENCES

ANC (African National Congress) (1992) *Ready To Govern*, ANC Policy Guidelines

Banerji, D (1984) 'Primary Health Care: Selective or Comprehensive', *World Health Forum*, vol 5

Engel, G I (1976) 'The Need for a New Medical Model: A Challenge for Bio-medicine', *Science*, vol 196, no 4286

Farrant, W (1989) 'Health Promotion and the Community Health Movement: Experiences from the UK', paper presented at the International Symposium on Community Participation and Empowerment Strategies in Health Promotion, Biefeld University, Germany, June

Franco-Agudelo, S (1983) 'The Rockefeller Foundation's Antimalarial Pro-gramme in Latin America: Donating or Dominating?', *International Journal of Health Services*, vol 13, no 1

Kanji, N (1989) 'Charging for Drugs in Africa: UNICEF's "Bamako Initiative"', *Health Policy and Planning*, vol 4m, no 1

Kasongo Project Team (1981) 'Influence of Measles Vaccination on Survival Patterns of 7–35 Month-Old Children in Kasongo, Zaire', *Lancet*, 4 April

Lankester, T E (1991) 'Primary Health Care: Delivery or Participation?', Editorial, *Tropical Doctor*, vol 21, no 1

Macdonald, J (1993) *Primary Health Care: Medicine in its Place*, London, Earthscan

Maglacas, A (1984) 'Health for All: A Framework for Action', *Philippine Journal of Nursing*, vol 54, no 3

McKeown, T (1976) *The Role of Medicine: Dream, Mirage or Nemesis?*, London, Nuffield Provincial Hospitals Trust

Robb, D (1992) 'Development Approaches to Health', *1992 Report*, Cape Town, Alexandra Health Centre and Institute of Urban Primary Health

Tarimo, E and Creese, A (eds) (1990) *Achieving Health for All by the Year 2000: Midway Reports of Country Experiences*, Geneva, World Health Organization

Warren, K (1988) 'The Evolution of Selective Primary Health Care, *Social Science and Medicine*, vol 26, no 9

WHO (1986a) *Intersectoral Action for Health*, Geneva, World Health Organization

—— (1986b) 'Report of the Working Group on the Concept and Principles of Health Promotion (1984)', *Health Promotion*, vol 1, no 1

—— (1986c) *Ottawa Charter for Health Promotion: An International Conference on Health Promotion, 17 November 1986*, Copenhagen, World Health Organization

—— (1987) *Health Promotion: Concepts and Principles in Action: A Policy Framework*, Copenhagen, World Health Organization

—— (1988) *From Alma Ata to the Year 2000: Reflections at the Midpoint*, Geneva, World Health Organization

WHO/UNICEF (1978) *Primary Health Care: The Alma Ata Conference*, Geneva, World Health Organization

Wisner, B (1988) *Power and Need in Africa*, London, Earthscan

Yach, D, Martin, G and Jacobs, M (eds) (1993) *Towards a National GOBI–FFF Programme for South Africa*, Seminar held in Cape Town, 21 January 1993

Chapter Eleven

AIDS in South Africa: A Wild Card?

Alan Whiteside

This chapter considers the growing AIDS (acquired immune deficiency syndrome) epidemic in South Africa and assesses its implications for development in the region. It begins by examining the data on HIV and AIDS available from the country, and the response to the epidemic. This includes information from the sero-surveys carried out over the past two years. The chapter then argues that South Africa is at special risk of a rapid spread of the disease, both because of the socio-economic structure of the society and the legacy of the apartheid system. The implications are then examined under the headings of demographic, financial and economic, macro-economic, and social and political. Data from South African sources are supported by examples from other countries of the region. The chapter concludes that the looming HIV/ AIDS epidemic will have severe consequences for the country. Unfortunately there has, to date, been little success in slowing the spread of the disease. It should be placed high on the national agenda. Certain specific measures should be adopted immediately, including the ending of the migration of single males.

AIDS AND HIV IN SOUTH AFRICA

At the Sixth International Conference on AIDS in Africa in Dakar in 1991 Dr Michael Merson, director of the World Health Organization's Global Programme on AIDS (GPA) declared, 'The 1980s were the decade of HIV in Africa; the 1990s will be the decade of AIDS in Africa.' In 1992 some South African decision makers finally began to wake up to the threat AIDS poses. Unfortunately the response is still fragmented and the spread of the virus continues unchecked.

HIV and AIDS Data

Why has the response to AIDS been so poor in South Africa? There are two identifiable reasons: firstly the epidemic is in its early stages and there have been comparatively few deaths; and secondly the type of people infected has confused the response. The first case of AIDS was seen in South Africa in 1982. Up to 30 October 1992 a cumulative total of only 1517 cases had been reported. By comparison, during the period January to November 1992 there were 2591 cases of malaria and 64,950 of tuberculosis (*Epidemiological Comments* 1992). Furthermore the situation seemed so much better than in South Africa's northern neighbours. Tanzania had reported 27,396 cases of AIDS to WHO up to 31 August 1991; Zimbabwe 12,514 up to 30 June 1992 and Malawi 12,074 up to 31 October 1990. As Table 11.1 shows the disease was, up to 1992, spreading comparatively slowly in South Africa.

Table 11.1 : AIDS in South Africa since 1982 (by year of diagnosis)

Year	Cases	Deaths*
1982	2	2
1983	4	3
1984	8	8
1985	8	8
1986	24	23
1987	40	33
1988	91	56
1989	175	97
1990	318	88
1991	436	105
1992	411	52
Total	1517	483

Note: *Deaths that occur outside the medical system are not recorded.
Source: *Epidemiological Comments* 1992.

The pattern of spread of the epidemic also moulded the response. Up to 1987 the vast majority of cases were in the white male homosexual community. In Calvinist South African society these people were regarded as a deviant minority, and the epidemic a punishment from God. From 1987 the greatest number of cases were in the black community and again the response was confused. Many white people saw the disease as a punishment for promiscuity, while others regarded it as 'the

solution and not the problem' — an answer to the burgeoning population and black demands. Just how confused South African society was
can been seen in work done by Joffee in which she found that young
whites regarded AIDS as a black disease, while young blacks saw it as a
white disease (reported in *AIDS Analysis Africa*).

Table 11.2 : AIDS Cases by Race Group and Mode of Transmission

	White		Black		Not		Total
	Male	*Female*	*Male*	*Female*	*known*	*Other*	
*Pattern**							
Homo/Bisexual	370	–	3	–	–	25	398
Drug Abuse	1	–	1	–	–	–	2
*Pattern***							
Heterosexual	15	4	374	390	12	26	821
Paediatric	–	–	138	114	4	–	256
Other (2)	26	4	7	–	–	3	40
Total	412	8	523	504	16	54	1517

Notes: * Includes the population groups classified as coloured and Asian.
** Includes infection through transfusion and of haemophiliacs.
Source: *Epidemiological Comments*, vol 19, no 12, December 1992.

Addressing and assessing the HIV/AIDS epidemic is made problematic
by the lack of data and the unreliability of what data there are. This is
compounded by the nature of the disease — the long incubation period
before an infected person falls ill. Reported AIDS cases reflect the levels
of HIV infection of five and more years previously. It is believed that in
most of Africa only 10 per cent of cases are reported.

South Africans used to believe that the quality of data in South Africa
was reasonably good. Events in September 1992 call this into question. A
hospital in Empangeni, Natal, reported 153 AIDS deaths for the year to
date. At this point the official statistics had recorded only 26 deaths for the
whole country up to the end of June 1992. There is other anecdotal
information indicating that there may be many more cases than are
officially reported. While cases may be recorded at the hospital level, they
are not reflected in the official statistics.

Of crucial importance are data on HIV prevalence, for they show the
level of infection in the population; indicate the number of cases that might
be expected in the years ahead; and, if surveys are done in a consistent
manner at regular intervals, can provide the basis for information on the

spread. South Africa probably has the best data on HIV incidence in the developing world.

There have been three national HIV surveys of women attending antenatal clinics in South Africa. The first was in October/November 1990, and they have been carried out annually since then. The surveys were done in a scientific manner with over 14,000 samples, and data are available from the first two. The results make alarming reading. It was found that the HIV prevalence had risen from 0.76 per cent to 1.49 per cent over the year from October/November 1990 to October/November 1991. This means that the number of HIV infected persons in South Africa rose from between 74,000 and 102,000 to approximately 191,000 in 1991. The highest levels of HIV prevalence are Natal/Kwazulu 2.87 per cent, followed by Kangwane with 1.71 per cent. The lowest level is in the Cape at 0.3 per cent. The highest incidence by race group is the black population 1.84 per cent followed by the coloured 0.14 per cent and Asians 0.11 per cent (*Epidemiological Comments* 1992).

This confirms the view that the epidemic in South Africa is now, as in the rest of Africa, a predominantly heterosexually transmitted disease with a substantial number of infants being infected. This is not to say that any group is immune from infection, but rather that socio-economic circumstances make some groups more vulnerable.

South Africa — At Special Risk

The spread of HIV in the region is being exacerbated by social and political stresses which lead to a breakdown of societal norms and a greater incidence of risky behaviour. Some of these stresses have a long history in the country while others are comparatively new. They are detailed below.

Cross-Border Migration

The movement of people in search of employment has been going on for decades. In South Africa there are approximately 250,000 foreign men employed on contract of up to two years. Most are housed in single quarters and none are able to bring their families with them. In addition, apartheid legislation made millions of South Africans migrants in their own country, as they crossed the 'borders' of the national states. They lived in similar circumstances to their foreign counterparts. Single men are more likely to have multiple sexual partners, including prostitutes. Many South African migrants have both an urban and a rural family.

Refugees
The conflict in Mozambique resulted in over a million people fleeing across international borders in search of sanctuary. Of these 200,000 fled to South Africa and are living in refugee camps in the eastern Transvaal. In addition the apartheid regime meant that nearly 30,000 South Africans fled the country. Most ended up in camps in Zambia, Tanzania and Uganda, all areas of high HIV prevalence. Displaced people within countries do not appear in official statistics as refugees, but the low level conflict, particularly in Natal, accounts for thousands of additional displaced persons.

Conflict and Civil War
As well as creating refugees conflict means that people cannot be reached by government health and education services, which in any case lack credibility. There is also an unwillingness to listen to messages about AIDS when issues of survival are imperative.

Militarization
Armies are known to have high levels of HIV prevalence and, unless carefully targeted, to contribute to the spread of the disease. South Africa has to address this problem in the South African Defence Force and paramilitary forces, the homeland armies, and the armed wings of the liberation movements.

Drought
The 1991/2 drought in Southern Africa caused large-scale movement of people in search of food and incomes. It also increased poverty. Movement of people will lead to greater pressure on urban infrastructure and social breakdown.

Poverty
Anything that reduces the body's immune response and general level of health makes it easier for the HIV virus to enter the bloodstream and infect a person. These 'co-factors' include malnutrition, endemic diseases, lack of sanitation and potable water, the inability to receive or understand messages about behavioural change, and lack of resources to make the changes. Most South Africans are poor.

High Levels of Sexually Transmitted Diseases (STDs)
The incidence of STDs in a population greatly increases the probability of HIV transmission during sexual intercourse, and STD levels are high. It

is estimated that between 15 and 26 per cent of the sexually active black population in South Africa currently has or has had an STD (Doyle 1993).

Rural-Urban Linkages
Movement between rural and urban areas will ensure a more rapid spread of HIV in a country. Davies, writing about Zimbabwe noted: 'People from all socio-economic groups retain their links with "home areas" and travel there relatively frequently. This would tend to make the virus spread more uniformly throughout the population. In addition the high number of workers whose wives live in rural areas will tend to increase the number of partners and thus the rate of spread.' The same pattern of linkages is found in South Africa, due, among other things, to the system of apartheid.

Status of Women
The low status of women and their comparative lack of power make behaviour change more difficult and leave them victims of cultural obligations.

Implications

What does the spread of HIV and AIDS mean for South Africa? Will it result in a decline in the population as early AIDS literature suggested? Could economic growth be adversely affected? And will labour become scarce? It is difficult to predict these things with any certainty, for nowhere in the world has the epidemic run its full course. None the less certain predictions can be attempted. It is probable that because of the level of development and the legacy of apartheid, the effects will be much worse than in the lower income developing countries.

In trying to assess the effect of AIDS South Africa has certain advantages. First we can learn from the experiences of other countries, where the progress of the epidemic is more advanced; in particular many of Zimbabwe's experiences may be applicable. Secondly, the country has a considerable research capacity, both in academic institutions and in the private sector. This makes sophisticated assessment possible, not only in terms of potential numbers, but also in regard to effects.

The Demographic Picture

There is a general consensus among South African model builders that the number of HIV positive people in the sexually-active population will not exceed 20–40 per cent at the peak, and the South African population will not decline. But the seriousness of the epidemic should not be underestimated. The most reliable modelling is done by Peter Doyle and his colleagues at the Metropolitan Life Assurance Company in Cape Town. His projections for two scenarios are shown in Table 11.3.

Table 11.3 : Summary of Model Projections

	1991	1995	2000	2005
HIV-infected				
Scenario 60	97 000	970 000	4 112 000	6 410 000
Scenario 61	97 000	970 000	3 700 000	4 762 000
AIDS sick				
Scenario 60	1 190	25 000	259 000	743 000
Scenario 61	1 190	25 000	255 000	618 000
AIDS deaths				
Scenario 60	1 350	23 000	203 000	525 000
Scenario 61	1 350	23 000	197 000	429 000
Cumulative deaths				
Scenario 60	2 200	47 000	602 000	2 588 000
Scenario 61	2 200	47 000	594 000	2 321 000

Source: Doyle 1993.

Scenario 60 is calibrated to data available from other African countries. Scenario 61 is less pessimistic and assumes that there will be significant behaviour change 12 years into the epidemic. Whether this will indeed be the case remains to be seen; so far there has been little cause for optimism. Doyle (1993: 105) concludes that, 'the epidemic is predicted to peak at a prevalence rate of approximately 27 per cent of the adult population by the year 2010 in the absence of behaviour change. If we assume such changes will occur, a peak prevalence is predicted of approximately 18 per cent to be reached, between 2000 and 2005.'

The Financial and Economic Cost of AIDS

Most studies on the implications of AIDS have concentrated on the financial costs of the disease. The costs may be divided into direct and indirect costs. The direct costs are actual expenses incurred in dealing with the disease.

Some can be measured quite easily, for example those related to health care. From the time a person is first tested HIV positive to the point when he or she dies, a measurable amount of money will be spent on health care. These costs may be incurred by the individual, the family, the medical-aid society or insurance company, or the public health system. These costs vary greatly from case to case depending on the resources the individual can command and his or her access to health care.

It appears from worldwide experience that there is a close correlation between a country's Gross National Product (GNP) and expenditure on AIDS. Put simply, the richer a country the more will be spent on each case. It should also be noted that AIDS does not necessarily cost any more than any other long-term or chronic illnesses. What makes it different is that it hits people at the peak of their productive years, when they would not normally require medical care, and that cases are likely to increase rapidly.

Other easily measurable direct costs include testing — now being done by blood transfusion services, insurance companies and doctors; research by both scientists and social scientists; and the extensive and potentially expensive education programmes that have been put into place. More difficult to measure are items such as time spent waiting for appointments, transport costs for patients and their families and, of considerable importance, the emotional anguish, pain and suffering. Some estimates of the cost of AIDS to South Africa are given in Table 11.4.

Table 11.4 : Total Costs of HIV/AIDS, Unadjusted
(1991 R, rounded billions)

	1991	%	1995	%	2000	%	Cumulative Costs 1991–2000
Indirect	0.30	72	2.01	62	9.35	48	34.11
Direct							
Low	0.08		0.69		4.71		14.85
High	0.11	28	1.26	28	10.01	52	30.08
Total							
Low	0.37		2.70		14.06		48.96
High	0.41		3.27		19.35		64.19

Source: Broomberg et al 1993.

Alan Whiteside

Table 11.5 : Total Replacement and Lost Production Costs if only the Unskilled and One-Half of the Semi-Skilled Personnel can be Replaced ('Adjusted') Assuming Ten Working Years Lost (1991 R Million)

	Replacement	Lost Production	Total
1991			
Assumption (A)	5.1	257	262.1
Assumption (B)	2.5	32	34.5
Assumption (C)	8.4	651	659.4
2000			
Assumption (A)	2 049	41 112	43 161
Assumption (B)	325	5 038	5 363
Assumption (C)	6 254	103 825	110 079

Source: Trotter 1992.

Many of the reviews of the effect of AIDS on national economies to date have concentrated on the costs to the economy and to the health service. For example Broomberg et al estimate that in 1992 AIDS will account for between 0.85 and 1.37 per cent of total health expenditure. This could rise to between 18.76 and 39.83 per cent in the year 2000. The estimate of the total current costs of AIDS to the GNP in 2000 is between 5.1 and 9 per cent. In Malawi it is estimated that by the year 2000 AIDS may account for between 27 and 38 per cent of the Ministry of Health expenditure (personal communication).

Apart from the sheer size of expenditure there is a very great danger that the rise in AIDS cases may result in the crowding out of other health-care problems — something which could have an adverse impact on the health status of a nation.

The indirect costs arise from the loss of productive members of society. They include morbidity when people are ill and mortality when people die and years of production are lost. It is estimated that the indirect cost of an AIDS death is between 65 and 75 per cent of total costs (Broomberg 1992: 42), and 90 per cent of the indirect cost will be accounted for by premature death rather than disability or morbidity. Calculations on the indirect cost in South Africa estimate the total cost as being between R34.5 million and R659.4 million in 1991, rising to between R5363 million and R110,079 million in 2000. This is shown on Table 11.5.

157

The Macro-economic Consequences

It is now becoming apparent that the AIDS epidemic will have a negative effect on economic development and growth at a national level. This is particularly serious when the already poor performance of South Africa's economy is considered. In 1992 the real GDP was expected to fall by 2.5 per cent, the third year in a row that the fall would have occurred. The reasons for the negative impact of AIDS have been well analysed by Mead Over (1992) of the World Bank. Two important points to emerge from this work are:

- The skills base of the average African economy is small. The more skilled people are infected, inevitably the worse the effect on the economy.
- If AIDS care is financed out of savings then this will reduce funds available for investment, and if the shortfall is not made up by foreign investment then future growth will suffer.

Over (1992) looks at a number of possible scenarios and concludes that AIDS will reduce the annual growth rate of GDP by between 0.56 and 1.08 per cent in 30 African countries and by 0.73 and 1.47 per cent in the ten worst affected, depending on the level of skilled people infected and the amount of AIDS care funded from savings.

The projected impact of AIDS on economic growth has also been assessed by Anderson et al (1991: 49) who conclude that 'the HIV epidemic will have serious repercussions for economic growth and the provision of health care in Sub-Saharan Africa and may exacerbate other factors that constrain economic growth in the region.'

In a recent special report on Zimbabwe, the Economic Intelligence Unit examines the effect of AIDS on its development scenario. The report notes (Riddell 1992: 84):

> The worst effects [of AIDS] on the economy are likely to occur in the medium to long , rather than short term ... For the purposes of the main scenario, it is assumed that as a result the problem of AIDS, the lower of three national projections of population growth is likely to be most accurate ... As for the effect on the economy, it is assumed that this could have the effect of reducing economic growth rates by a negligible 0.01 per cent in 1992, but this increases to a more significant 0.2 per cent by 1996.

The mechanisms include lower productivity leading to depressed demand and lower exports, imports of drugs squeezing out other more productive imports and the potential fall in investor confidence.

SOCIAL AND POLITICAL CONSEQUENCES

The divisive effects of this disease could be considerable. AIDS has resulted in blame and prejudice. In a society as divided as South Africa, there is a real danger that the epidemic may magnify existing divisions. For example, the private medical care system may continue to treat those who can afford it, while the state system may adopt a no or low-cost treatment regime. This would be seen as inequitable and would cause a great deal of resentment. The political consequences can only be guessed at. If the epidemic causes growth to falter at the same time as the demand for state services increases then politicians will have a difficult path to tread.

REFERENCES

Anderson, R, Rowley, J, Konings, E, Wan Ng, Boily, M-C and Garnett, J (1991) 'Potential Demographic and Economic Impact of AIDS in Sub-Saharan Africa', Report to the Overseas Development Administration, mimeo, Imperial College, London

Broomberg, J, Steinberg, M, Masobe, P and Behr, G (1992) 'The Economic Impact of the AIDS Epidemic in South Africa', in Cross and Whiteside, qv

Cross, J and Whiteside, A (eds) (1992) *Facing up to AIDS: The Socio-Economic Impact in Southern Africa*, Macmillan, London

Davies, R (nd) 'The Political Economy of AIDS in Zimbabwe', Harare, mimeo

Doyle, P (1993) 'The Demographic Impact of AIDS on the South African Population', in Cross and Whiteside, qv

Over, M (1992) 'The Macroeconomic Impact of AIDS in Sub-Saharan Africa', Population and Human Resources Department, World Bank, mimeo

Riddell, R (1992) *Zimbabwe to 1986: At the Heart of a Growing Reaction*, Economist Intelligence Unit, Special Report No M205, London

Trotter, G (1992) 'Some Reflections on a Human Capital Approach to the Analysis of the Impact of AIDS on the South African Economy', in Cross and Whiteside, qv

Whiteside, A (1991) *HIV Infection and AIDS in Zimbabwe: An Assessment*, Harare, Southern Africa Foundation for Economic Research

PART III: EDUCATION AND THE MEDIA

Chapter Twelve

People's Education and 'Nation Building' for a New South Africa

Steve Randall

This chapter[1] restates the continuing relevance of 'people's education' as a necessary mobilizing dynamic in the project of social emancipation in South Africa today. My concerns are threefold: that the transformatory potential of education is being replaced with a 'skills' paradigm; that as a consequence of this and other factors, the mobilizing element of people's education is in danger of being usurped by its converse — a demobilizing or immobilizing of the movement; and — related to this latter vis-à-vis the requirements of 'nation-building' in a land despoiled by the ravages of apartheid — that this skills-based notion of national development is misconstrued.

This instrumental approach to education, with its stress on vocational training to meet the skills needs of the market echoes many of the themes in the government's Educational Renewal Strategy document (Department of National Education 1991). It likewise resonates with similar preoccupations in other quarters. Hence, according to Tony Morphet (1991: 81), Bernie Fanaroff of the National Union of Metal Workers of South Africa 'has put the need directly — education and training must become "a national obsession" if we are to make any progress towards an economy which can grow and deliver benefits to the mass of the population.'

This new-found convergence of concerns about educational interests extends to the parameters — the precepts and prescriptions — with which educational issues are discussed. Thus a Joint Working Group (JWG) comprising senior government ministers and leading figures in the opposition camp — including African National Congress and

---

1. A fuller version of this chapter is in the *Review of African Political Economy*, no 58, autumn 1993.

National Education Crisis Committee representatives — has been established to explore the educational requirements of the future South Africa. One newspaper (*The Argus*, 9 September 1991) describes this development as a 'Patriotic Front on Education'. The same paper rounds off its report of this gathering thus:

> The JWG agreed that the social and educational plight of the marginalized youth ('lost generation') was a very serious problem, South Africa is, at least, shifting emphasis on academic education to technical training and this fresh approach could provide an answer to the 'lost youth'. Business said it clearly: 'Empower them with technical skills to enable them to compete in the job market'.

I am not saying here that the development needs of South Africa's people will not be the overriding imperative of any government inheriting the callous legacy of apartheid. Using figures culled from various researchers (Cherrett and Harding 1990; Unterhalter 1990; Chisholm 1991; Pillay 1990) we can build a profile of the 'educational damage' done to South Africa's population.

In South Africa today 60 per cent of those under 30 are not engaged in formal employment and most of those have never been so on a regular basis. A staggering 64.4 per cent of the black population is functionally illiterate and, as Chisholm (1991: 2–3) notes, 'what is startling about this figure, is that the highest number of illiterates occur within the generation schooled by apartheid, those between the ages of 16 and 34.' Of those at work, 66 per cent have not gone beyond primary education. There is a pool of unskilled labour (7.5 million) chasing 1.5 million jobs. At the other end of the labour market one third of 1.8 million managerial and professional posts are unfilled owing to a skills shortage. Related to this shortage of higher level personnel is a staggeringly high failure rate of black students — a legacy of decades of 'Bantu' mis-education — at both school and university.

Black students are grossly under-represented at the tertiary level compared with whites. For example, whites account for the vast majority of those receiving technical education, and there are only 2.6 African university students per 1000 head of population compared with 31.1 white university students per 1000 head of population.

This segmentation of educational and skills provision along racial lines is illustrated when we realize that estimates put the shortage of qualified chartered accountants at more than 7000 by the turn of the century and that of the 12,000 qualified chartered accountants in 1989, only 25 were African. Figures for the same year list blacks as constituting

3.8 per cent of all engineers, 10.9 per cent of all scientists, 12.5 per cent of all technicians and technologists, 11.8 per cent of accountants and auditors and 6.7 per cent of all administrative occupations. Against this imbalance and mismatch of skills needs is an economy in serious decline with a decelerating growth rate and a formal sector seeking to become more capital intensive, concentrating on technological innovations and so unlikely to provide an employment base for South Africa's population. Little wonder then that development is a 'national obsession'.

This turn to a 'technicist', or instrumental, sooner than 'political' definition of education and its role in society quickens the perception that 'people's education' is no longer relevant. It is said that the agitation in the classrooms has eroded the 'culture of learning' — hence the drastically low performance rates of black pupils — and that 'the struggle is no substitute for study'.

The notion is gathering ground that people's education has failed the community by turning its students into 'failures'. So there is a reorientation to more orthodox educational strategies as a means of upliftment.

The prescriptions for people's education were neither sufficiently developed nor sufficiently precise. Hence it was insufficiently emphasized that, in the words of the educationist Bernstein (1970: 104), 'education cannot compensate for society.' Having invested unwarranted faith in the term's magical powers as a catalyst, concerned parents, firstly disorientated then demoralized, became educational apostates. This conceptual confusion became a political confusion.

Adrian Blunt (1988) talks of Western models of education which, when transplanted to a developing country, create social and cultural inconsistencies. One consequence of such inconsistencies is the formation of a very small educated elite who command key positions in government, business and industry and who enjoy an urbanized, metropolitan lifestyle resourced by the labours of the rural poor. But it is not just the 'ideology' of formal education that militates against the interests and needs of the mass of the people; the delivery mechanisms, the structures and ethos of conventional knowledge-pursuit, are likewise inappropriate. Thus in the schooling system there is no discrete, specific terminal goal that corresponds to each activity. Rather, learning is a long-term deferral, each activity being a trailer for the next, more abstract, stage. Each phase is little more than a protracted admissions test for the following stage. With usually inflexible age-specific entry and exit points, if students miss these they miss out on all that has gone before or after. Similarly if students drop out then all efforts hitherto go unrecorded and so unacknowledged. There is a set pattern in a set sequence to which students must mould themselves. This endlessly preparatory and abstract or academic education neither equips with skills nor can it demonstrate its immediate applicability. Its main function — other than the reproductive one described above — is as an initiation rite into a status-conferring 'brotherhood' (*sic*).

This self-perpetuating brotherhood is responsible for the phenomenon of urban drift whereby the successful ones mimic the metropolitan life-styles of the West, becoming, in effect, a class of mandarin drones, thus depopulating the regions of skilled human resources. The necessary corollary of this status-conferring ceremony is systemic and large-scale failure which, in the context of a developing nation, also means large-scale waste. This Western model of schooling is not just wasteful of human talent, it is also wasteful of financial resources.

Hulme and Turner (1990) inform us that the cost of educating a pupil rises almost exponentially as he or she progresses from primary to tertiary levels. Thus in New Guinea it is reckoned that for the cost of training 3000 university students 160,000 primary students could be catered for. Because most underdeveloped nations suffer a chronic shortage of higher and medium-level personnel, as in South Africa, post-colonial governments are tempted to concentrate resources in the first instance on the tertiary sector. Yet, because of factors that should not need rehearsing (poverty, inadequate communications and other infrastructures), the rural poor, with disproportionately high school absence and drop-out rates, are not represented at this level. In the words of Clift Barnard (1980: 35) — 'the group entering higher education is bound to be largely made up of middle- and upper-class children. To subsidize education at this level out of federal government funds is therefore to transfer resources from the poor to those who need subsidies least.' But that is not all.

The previously noted phenomenon of urban drift serving as a trans-mission belt of talent from the towns to the cities works at both a national and global level to take skilled graduates out of their countries in search of bigger rewards elsewhere. Thus, between 1984 and 1987, 30,000 graduates emigrated from the sub-Saharan countries (*Times Higher Educational Supplement*, 19 July 1991). This, as other commentators have observed, represents a transfer of skills from the poorer to the wealthier nations. The educational policy-makers of South Africa might respond to the above alarms by stating that they are not working to a scholarly-academic but a skills and nation-building paradigm. They might thus maintain that their educational vision is not a reproductive but a truly functional one. But is this development planning model in fact capable of delivering?

It is traditionally supposed that a nation's development is determined by the rate of growth of its Gross Domestic Product (GDP) and that the role of its human resources in this process is to lubricate the levers and mechanisms of the market to facilitate this output. In this world view, education is seen as a component, even a precondition of development. (In particular, non-formal education, which is thought to be cheap, effective — at the level of basic skills — and, because non-institutionalized, endlessly adaptable, is seen as appropriate for underdeveloped countries with remote and rural populations.) It is the gear lever that motors the economy, which can only proceed as planned if there are sufficient people with the requisite technical, supervisory and vocational skills. The right skills in the right quantity at the right time will guarantee continued wealth generation. Hence the vocabulary of human capital, skills gaps, and manpower (*sic*) resource planning.

Hulme and Turner (1990) question such an approach, claiming that 'evidence indicates that high educational levels have not been a prerequisite for the onset of rapid economic growth'. They point out that universal primary education came to Great Britain 100 years after the onset of the industrial revolution. They mention the phenomenon of educated unemployment — a by-product of the diploma disease first remarked on by Dore in 1976 whereby education becomes the pursuit of qualifications rather than the acquisition of skills. Similarly, Webster (1984) reminds us that educational criteria sometimes serve a guild function in restricting rather than widening access to many professions.

Andrew Webster (1984) points out that qualifications make people eligible for jobs but tell us nothing about their potential productivity or on-the-job proficiency. 'Education becomes obtaining qualifications in order to get a job rather than learning to do a job.' (Hulme and Turner 1990: 134.)

The argument is akin to the debate on whether skills-training of itself provides jobs. This intrusion of skills training into the educational sphere has an established if relatively recent pedigree in England, where it is known as the new vocationalism. It is interesting that De Lange's proposals for restructuring education in South Africa (HSRC 1981) carry echoes of the British Manpower Service Commission's (MSC) prescriptions for redressing the imbalance in skills deficits and labour market needs.

The new vocationalism had its origins in the so-called 'great debate' on education initiated by the then Labour prime minister, James Callaghan, in an address given in 1976 at Ruskin College, Oxford. Here Callaghan called for a tighter fit between the production needs of the economy and the grade and composition of higher education graduates.

As Andy Green (1983) convincingly established, it was the dramatic increase in unemployment, particularly youth unemployment with its attendant risks of social disaffection, which provided the motivation to act on Callaghan's nostrums, rather than any enlightened rationalization on the part of Britain's employers. Hence in 1981, coinciding with large-scale rioting by inner-city youth in virtually all of England's major cities, the MSC announced its new training initiative (NTI). A few years later its themes were incorporated into a government white paper titled 'Training for Jobs' (1984). Green shows how the NTI is not about skilling people for jobs so much as deskilling the labour force so as to make it both more pliable and less valuable — that is, cheaper. It is instructive that soon after the introduction of the first in a long line of Youth Training Schemes (YTS) the industrial apprenticeship system was effectively discontinued. Similarly, the industrial training boards, which exacted a training levy from the big employers and on which the trade unions had a significant voice, were reduced from 16 to 7.

Examining the YTS syllabus, Green illustrates how the students are instructed into cultivating transferable generic skills rather than being offered precise and specific actual competencies; hence it is a process of deskilling rather than reskilling. He cites a survey undertaken by the Industrial Research Unit of the major employers — the A–Z Study (1981) — which revealed that employers valued certain behavioural and attitudinal qualities in job applicants as much as operative qualifications.

As well as socializing a generation of young people who would otherwise not experience the labour discipline of work — there being no jobs for them — these training schemes serve to keep wage levels down (an employer paid by the government to provide work experience placements is unlikely to offer a wage to a young worker). In addition, they enable the politicians accountable to an electorate to claim that they are doing something about unemployment.

The fact is that it is not training that provides jobs but, rather, the structural requirements of the market, which determine what jobs are needed and at what pace. This belief in the beneficent self-regulation of the job market has been called the 'vocational fallacy' (Foster 1968).

The deficit model of training, whereby the individual is perceived as lacking the desired skills, puts the cart before the horse — it is the market that is defective. In many Western capitalist countries homelessness is rife while thousands of construction workers are unemployed. In this context, the slogan advertising the employment training scheme (the latest in a long string of government-employment programmes), 'we'll train the workers without jobs to do the jobs without workers,' becomes something of a non sequitur.

These various training schemes constitute a dirigisme executed in the name of free enterprise to camouflage the fact that, left to itself, the free market would not deliver. According to the *Times Educational Supplement* of 24 January 1992, 'The South African Chamber of Business predicted that only about 7 per cent of black school-leavers would find jobs immediately in the formal sector.' Remarking on how vocational training schemes in the Western world tend to take the form of state-led pre-service work preparation rather than in-service training linked to employer sponsorship, Bennell and Swainson (1990) comment on how the ideologues of market-led training schemes are unable to produce empirical evidence of either employer efficacy or sincerity of intention in this endeavour.

The volume of a country's GDP tells us nothing about the per capita participation in its consumption. Indeed population disaffection can increase in inverse proportion to the increase in national wealth if access to this wealth is not structurally underwritten. Large-scale disaffection amongst the nation's human capital can ultimately threaten the economic growth rate itself.

If the demands and directives of formal education are perceived as being inappropriate to the developing nations, then learning as a non-formal and continuous pastime is to replace it. Adrian Blunt (1988: 46) quotes the Faure report of 1972 as declaring that learning was 'a more fundamental intellectual discipline than education, and that it ought to be established as an independent field of study.' Researchers, according to Blunt, now talk of 'global learning' as opposed to meritocratically-led educational instruction premised on the individual development of the privatized agent. This they characterize as 'consideration of the learner within the total socio-cultural context of family and community' (Blunt 1988: 46). The United Nations University of Tokyo has apparently adopted the concept of global learning in its mission statement, defined as 'the need for developing not only the individual's capacity and opportunity for learning but also the learning capacity of social groups, institutions and even societies' (Blunt 1988: 46, quoting Ploman 1985).

By transcending input–output calculations, this counter discourse questions the economics of a development that sees subjects as capital stock, and is critical of abstract nation building that does not build from the actual community base upwards. It also brings us back to the notion of popular education as global learning, in which the curriculum is rooted in and grows out of the needs of family and community. In order to make agents of subjects, non-formal education must contain a dimension that generates both autonomy and transformation.

If education is seen as the catalyst of national development, providing for the economic performance needs of a country, then I view popular education as an activity that stresses the problems and needs of people as starting points for learning — in particular, though not exclusively, of disadvantaged, deprived and powerless groups. It should increase people's capacity to discover, define, pursue and achieve common objectives and, in the process, to develop more confident relationships with one another and the outside world. It is thus about the development needs of communities and people rather than the structural requirements of the national economy. It is not curriculum-led; rather, the syllabus is the lived realities of people's needs. In this context appropriateness becomes a truer yardstick of educational usefulness than scholarly excellence.

In terms of the immediate requirements of the country and its goals of development, however, a new understanding of skills training and its role in nation building must be sought. As the Development Task Force Report drawn up by Cherrett and Harding (1990) at the request of the South Africa Namibia Project suggests, a nation cannot simply be declared; it is constituted of and by its people — however carefully defined — and must command their allegiance:

> The majority population in South Africa has had a deeply negative experience of government delivery — whether from the National Party or the 'homeland' puppet structures. They may easily and quickly turn against a new government that fails to fulfil expectations. In Zimbabwe or Mozambique we can see that even a liberation movement enjoying apparently unlimited power has only a limited period of grace. A post-apartheid government in South Africa will have a restricted window of opportunity in which to secure the support of the population around development. The first five years will be critical.
>
> (Cherrett and Harding 1990: 6)

The authors continue:

> The experience of many communities has been restricted to one of mobilization around purely political questions rather than organization around tighter productive or developmental ends. And those economic/developmental initiatives that did take root have often been ineffective and, in the end, demoralizing. The lack of skills and experience in the community around organizational development and management, coupled with the difficult context

of repression, has meant that there have been few enduring development successes from this period. Many community organizations are now making an urgent appeal for resources to train and develop people in the community in organizational and development skills.

(Cherret and Harding 1990: 10)

In short, progressive educators must argue for an emphasis on skills — albeit of a wider application — for the most pragmatic of reasons.

The structuring dynamic of such skills-based learning is not the discipline of the subject but the act of problem-solving which enables people to effect change in their environment and so make them autonomous agents rather than passive ciphers. It enables its students — in the words of Paolo Freire (1972) — to 'read the world'. It therefore necessarily generates both autonomy and transformation.

It has been stated that the crisis facing a post-apartheid government will be that of demand versus capacity. A regime that has negotiated rather than taken power will have its ability to reallocate resources across the board greatly circumscribed. There will be structural and resource constraints coupled with suspicion from the private and corporate sector. It addition, it will be difficult to sell the notion of deferred gratification to a mass population that feels it has already waited too long for its moment in the sun.

The urban classes, with their network of professional associations and contacts, as well as the employed workforce in trades unions, will be able to lobby and petition for a share of whatever resources are to be made available. But the dispossessed and excluded 65 per cent (the shanty-town and township dwellers, the unemployed and unskilled youth, the homeland denizens) may be shut out — voiceless and with no way of staking their claim. If these communities are not to remain disaffected then we must broaden the notion of skills to include community development, thereby enabling them to identify and address their needs whether these be negotiating and lobbying tactics or the pooled husbanding and marketing of local resources.

The Development Task Force report of 1990 which maintains that such skills of community advocacy and self-help are different in kind from the mobilizing skills acquired in the years of struggle, puts it thus:

One key to effective development mechanisms is the encouragement of the population to act for themselves. Above all the creation of social movements amongst the unorganized, the dispossessed is key. The 65 per cent of the population that is either rural, illiterate or unemployed must organize if their needs and priorities are to become part of a National Agenda.

(Cherrett and Harding 1990: 13)

In this way the non-metropolitan populations will be self-reliant and pro-active whilst remaining involved in the debate about their country's future and direction. Such community advocacy skills are at least as crucial as (and in the transition years perhaps more relevant than) vocational training.

REFERENCES

Barnard, C (1980) 'Imperialism, Under-Development and Education', in Mackie, qv

Bennell, P and Swainson, N (1990) *Education and the New Right in South Africa: A Critical Appraisal of 'The Long Term Future of Education in South Africa' by Elizabeth Dostal*, Johannesburg, Wits University Educational Policy Unit

Bernstein, B (1970) 'Education Cannot Compensate for Society', in Rubenstein and Stoneman, qv

Rubenstein, D and Stoneman, L (1970) *Education for Democracy*, Middlesex, Penguin

Blaug, M (1968) *Economics of Education*, London, Penguin

Blunt, A (1988) 'Education, Learning and Development, Evolving Concepts', *Convergence*, vol 14, no 3

Cherrett, I and Harding, D (1990) *Development Task Force Report*, South Africa Namibia Project

Chisholm, L (1991) 'Apartheid Education, the Legacy, the Challenge', unpublished paper

Department of National Education (1991) *Educational Renewal Strategy: A Discussion Document*, Pretoria

Foster, P (1968) 'The Vocational School Fallacy in Development Planning' in Blaug, qv

Freire, P (1972) *Pedagogy of the Oppressed*, London, Penguin

Green, A (1983) 'Education and Training under New Masters', in Wolpe and Donald, qv

Hulme, D and Turner, M (1990) *Sociology and Development: Theories, Policies and Practices*, New York, Harvester Wheatsheaf

HSRC (1981) *Provision of Education in the Republic of South Africa: Report of the Main Committee of the HSRC Investigation into Education* [De Lange Report], Pretoria, Human Sciences Research Council

Mackie, R (1980) *Literacy and Revolution: The Pedagogy of Paulo Freire*, London, Pluto Press

Morphet, T (1991) 'Post-Apartheid Education: Getting Beyond the Catastrophe', unpublished paper

Nasson, B and Samuel, J (1990) *Education from Poverty to Liberty*, Cape Town, David Phillip

Pillay, P (1990) 'The Development and Under-development of Education in South Africa', in Nasson and Samuel, qv

Unterhalter, E (1990) 'Education and Training Needs in Post-Apartheid South Africa', in *Commonwealth Secretariat (1990) Human Resource Development for a Post-Apartheid South Africa — a documentation*, Geneva, Commonwealth Secretariat

Webster, A (1984) *Introduction to the Sociology of Development*, London, Macmillan

Wolpe, A and Donald, I (1983) *Is There Anyone Here From Education*, London, Pluto

Chapter Thirteen

Building Community Capacity for Participation in Educational Governance

David Johnson

In South Africa, governance, or the system for the control and coordination of education, has historically been rigid and hierarchical, and the sole domain of the state. The undemocratic patterns in planning, financing and managing education has resulted in unequal provision and limited improvement and development. This chapter has as its central problematic the democratization of school governance. The main argument rests on the premise that a democratic system of governance would have to allow greater participation. Only then would the provision of education be improved and, more important, such improvements sustained. In such an argument educational development is based on the principles of sustainable development.

The notion sustainable development is being used widely and is based on Ogun's assumption (cited in Shaeffer 1992) that development 'depends on enhancing people's capacities as individuals and groups to improve their own lives and to take greater control over their own destinies.' Adopting a participatory approach to educational development would thus mean a fundamental change in the process of governance.

In order to address the issue of democratizing educational governance, a number of key questions must be addressed. The National Education Policy Investigation (NEPI) research group on governance and administration highlight several key issues which are revisited in this chapter. These are:

- How can we make education governance and administration more efficient and democratic?
- Should education decision-making be centralized or decentralized?

- How can we make sure that all the different levels in the education system are involved in decision-making?
- What is the role of the community in controlling schooling?

This chapter addresses these questions by providing brief notes on the following issues: the current system of education; democracy and education; centralization and decentralization; participation; and capacity building. The discussion on these issues is not meant to be comprehensive but is intended to raise questions pertinent to thinking about how governance could be democratized.

THE CURRENT SYSTEM OF EDUCATIONAL GOVERNANCE

The current system of education in South Africa is extremely complex, due entirely to the historic policies of the National Party which made for centralized control and decentralized administration. It is perhaps inappropriate to talk of a system of education. The fragmentation of education, particularly through the creation of the Bantustans and own affairs departments has resulted in 19 departments of education under 14 different cabinets, each with their own regulations. There are at least 15 ministers of education and at least 17 different authorities are responsible for the employment of teachers (NEPI 1992a). Thus it may be more appropriate to refer to the current system of education as a conglomeration of systems.

This fragmentation makes the governance of education extremely complex and uneven. While the white system of education is provincially based and allows for the participation of parents on provincial boards, this is not the case for the other systems.

The multiplicity of systems has given rise to a large bureaucracy, by its very nature fragmented and poorly coordinated. There is a paucity of research in South Africa on the nature of the education bureaucracy but there is some data on its prevailing structure. According to a study by the Commonwealth Secretariat (Commonwealth Expert Group 1991), the distribution of posts in the current public service follows the normal apartheid pattern whereby virtually all middle and higher level posts are occupied by white middle-aged men. Of about 3000 top jobs in the public service (director or above), only 4 per cent are filled by blacks and only 0.5 per cent by Africans. The bureaucracy, it appears, 'has been built on the conception that black people are the objects of administration and control rather than part of the democratic political process' (Commonwealth Expert Group 1991: 51).

A popular criticism of the current system is its failure to allow for the participation of parents, teachers and students in decision making. While this is largely correct, the notion of participation needs closer analysis. Indeed with respect to educational policy, particularly in matters such as resource allocation, the curriculum, the financing of education and so on, the influence of parents, teachers and students remains limited. However, it must be pointed out that certain forms of parent participation are allowed and that such participation varies between departments. For example, the white system of education provides for the participation of parents on provincial education boards. All the other departments make provision for limited forms of participation at the school level (usually fund-raising activities and advisory functions) through school councils and management committees. The departments have, however, retained tight control over this process through reserving the right to make final decisions and by appointing members of the school committees. Thus, in black schools these councils and management committees are largely discredited.

Recent changes in the current government's schooling policies have made provision, in white education, for the election of governing bodies with more responsibilities and decision-making powers than the old management committees. In black education there are strong indications that parent–teacher–student associations (PTSAs) may become recognized as governing bodies. It is, however, notable that in the governance of education there is still no statutory provision for the participation of mass-based educational organizations. And this really is a source of popular discontent. Given that this discontent is extremely widespread, it is necessary to examine the nature of mass-based educational organizations and their capacity to participate in governance.

The National Education Coordinating Committee (NECC) was established in response to a continuing and deepening school crisis, which had become apparent by the middle of 1985. The NECC saw its main objective as the transformation and restructuring of the education system (Levin 1991). In 1986 the notion of 'people's education for people's power' was gaining ascendancy (Sisulu 1986). During this period, the link between people's education and the national democratic struggle was stressed to the exclusion of the upgrading of skills through education and training. The overwhelming concern was the role of education in equipping people to participate in the struggle for social transformation as political agents (Wolpe 1991). Thus, education was seen as a means to achieving democracy and citizenship but given undue weight as a mechanism for social transformation (Wolpe 1991). In the present situation, these concerns have been redefined to give expression to the need for human resource development (Johnson et al 1991) and capacity building. There is, however, a danger that the new emphasis on skills development could lead to a highly technicist approach to education and training if the notions of democracy, equity and historical redress are lost.

Recognizing the urgency to build capacity, the NECC and the Education Development Trust, in cooperation with the People's Education Commission, set up the NEPI to research aspects of education and to provide a set of policy options for a democratic educational system.

The NECC has also engaged in a sustained debate about community involvement in the governance of education. Part of its remit was to establish organs of people's power in schools (Tywala 1992; Maile 1992). The debate itself was sharpened considerably at a recent NECC conference on education and democracy. The NECC clearly places much emphasis on PTSAs as a key structure for the democratic governance of education. We need to analyse this structure more carefully here.

PARENT–TEACHER–STUDENT ASSOCIATIONS: DEMOCRATIC STRUCTURES OF GOVERNANCE?

PTSAs were set up in the mid-1980s. The relative success in establishing them in a large number of schools was partly because the school management committees in black schools were largely discredited. One specific problem with management councils was that they were formed by the various education departments and imposed as local structures of governance (in a limited capacity) and as such were undemocratic. The fact that parents are appointed to management councils to the total exclusion of other interest groups like students and teachers is particularly unwelcome.

Kulati (1992) argues that in understanding the dynamic development of the NECC and PTSAs and the problems that emerged, it is useful to view their shifting role in terms of adapting strategies to suit changing contexts and demands. He identifies three phases in the struggles around PTSAs.

In the first phase, PTSAs are seen as the structures that emerged to facilitate community involvement in the education crisis. Their main function was to mediate in the crisis brought on by the marginalization of parents in the unfolding struggles by students and youth over education. During the second phase, PTSAs began to take on an overtly political function, in which the question of people's power became paramount. PTSAs began to challenge the Department of Education and

Training's authority within the schools and were increasingly seen as the alternative structures of school governance.

Finally, according to Kulati (1992), during the period after 1990, when the bans on political organizations had been lifted, questions about PTSA involvement in the day-to-day running of schools were brought to the forefront. Thus the shift from the politics of protest to the politics of transformation and reconstruction forced many PTSAs to confront difficult questions about school administration and management.

However, Kulati does not even begin to consider that the structure of the PTSA is potentially problematic in that it forges into a single unit three different constituent groupings, which have different roles and responsibilities and which participate quite differently in the educational process. Thus, the question is not only whether PTSAs have the potential to govern, but whether they could accommodate the differing demands made of each sector.

There is also the second issue of establishing and sustaining PTSAs. Establishing PTSAs is not an unproblematic task, as a regional organizer of the NECC explains (Tywala 1992): 'The process of setting up PTSA structures was not at all easy ... we encountered a lot of problems with school heads because the idea of PTSAs has been discussed in relation to the strategy of making the government unworkable.' It appears that Tywala is arguing that the role of a PTSA, at least in the current context, is to challenge the state's control over education. It would thus be important for PTSAs to recognize that their scope is beyond that of local struggles in education. In fact the NECC argues that PTSAs should become a coherent national movement with the following aims:

- to intervene in the education crisis;
- to ensure holistic participation by parents, teachers and students in the formulation and implementation of education policy;
- to empower parents, students and teachers to participate in a democratic education system and in society as a whole;
- to facilitate the transition process towards a non-racial, non-sexist education system;
- to monitor, study and provide accessible information to those it represents; and
- to embark on programmes which would facilitate the achievement of its aims.

(NEPI 1992b)

Creating and establishing PTSAs is a difficult process, but building the capacity to sustain them is an issue that has been given very little attention. According to Maepa (1991), in 410 schools contacted, the Soweto Education Coordinating Committee (SECC) had established 360 PTSAs, but by the end of June 1991, 22 of these had 'collapsed due to a lack of service.' As far as is known, there is as yet no indication of how far PTSAs are being sustained in schools across the country, but if the statistics of the SECC are generalizable, the attrition rate could be quite high. Thus, as Maepa (1991) argues, the 'need to service these Associations in order to prepare them to play a meaningful part in education is in our view crucial.'

The task for the NECC therefore appears to be twofold:

- to build, strengthen and consolidate PTSAs as local governance structures in schools throughout the country; and
- to formalize structures at different tiers of the education system (national, regional and local) to allow PTSAs to participate in policy formulation, implementation and monitoring at the national, regional and local levels of the education system.

Moreover, the NECC sees it as incumbent to consolidate their current gains before a new government is installed. This raises questions about the nature of the relationship between the democratic structures of governance (PTSAs) and the new state.

DEMOCRACY AND EDUCATION

One of the most crucial issues in the debate on governance has been the extent to which a new system of education and control would be democratic. Indeed the nature of a future system of governance will be determined by its underlying conceptions of democracy.

Education systems anywhere in the world operate within well established centres of power (Pascal 1989) but it has never been completely clear how such power and control is redistributed. In other words there has been much debate as to whether the education system becomes more democratic out of conviction or expediency.

Elite models of the distribution of power portray public institutions as dominated largely by ruling groups. The move towards democratization, they argue, is due to political necessity rather than egalitarian sentiments. Thus the democratization of school governance in this model is seen to result from the educational establishment acting in the face of a changing social and political climate in order to maintain its authority and control. Such an elite model was put forward by Bacon (1978) to describe the democratization of school boards in Sheffield (England). He concluded his study by arguing:

It is extremely naïve to assume that the pressure for greater parent, worker or community involvement in the management or government of schools present a genuine, spontaneous 'grassroots' activity. ... Rather, it seems to be apparent ... that most of the momentum has been generated by a diffuse but none the less, in part, recognizable metropolitan intelligentsia, either employed directly or indirectly, in elite roles within the nation's public education industry.

A similar argument has been offered by Beattie (1978) in his comparative study of formalized parental participation in Western European countries following the Second World War. He claims that this was largely due to:

political necessity and in particular the need experienced in different ways by Western democracies to legitimize the status quo by defining certain areas within which democratic participation can occur. In my view, the adoption by liberal democracies of formal machinery for consulting and involving parents in education has little to do with the rightness or persuasiveness of the arguments in favour of such innovations; it has a great deal to do with an underlying crisis of confidence in democratic institutions.

Thus, in this model the democratization of school government is seen as a false front behind which the old hierarchy could continue to operate within the same power structure (Pascal 1989).

In pluralist models power is seen to be contested between social movements and the state. After a long history of state repression, organizations in South Africa have recently been allowed more space in which to operate, mainly as a result of the political and economic crisis prevalent there. In this case power is distributed throughout the system between various institutionalized interests. Narsoo (1991) argues that the South African state is rapidly attempting to decentralize and is privatizing a wide range of parastatals. This would make it very difficult for a new government to alter the balance of power in the new society. In this instance, strengthening the independence of civil society does not necessarily mean greater equity or freedom. In this model power is distributed unequally, with different groups having greater access to the decision-making arena than others. Power is not, however, concentrated in certain unchangeable centres. It is distributed throughout the system and, as a result, various groups and institutions are able to exert real influence on educational leaders.

David Johnson

It is difficult to fit any model of school governance neatly into this ideal type. Evidence from the international literature seems to suggest that neither a pluralist nor an elitist view is satisfactory. The evidence seems to lean towards a more neo-pluralist view (Pascal 1989) in which the educational elite retains the balance of power in its favour, but is compelled to devolve a significant degree of power to other participants. What view is adopted as an explanation for the distribution of power within a system of school governance has important implications for policy and leads us to a number of questions about the nature of the relationship between a new, democratic state and community-based structures of governance.

The NECC (NEPI 1992a) looks at how such a relationship might be structured from three different perspectives. In the first, the governing body would be aligned to the state, which would be responsible for appointing members to the governing body, for setting the operational agenda and for providing the necessary training. In the second, the governing body is completely independent of the state. This is based on the assumption that even in a democratic state the possibilities of meeting educational needs are limited and that such needs are better served by an educational structure located within civil society. In the third, the governing body is seen as a semi-autonomous community structure which, though linked to the state, is primarily accountable to the community it serves.

Each of these three views on the degree of distance between the state and the community-based governing body has certain advantages and disadvantages. The first makes for an extremely centralized and authoritarian system of educational governance. The administration and control of education is seen to be a function of the state. The second, in which the governing body is completely independent of the state, can be more sensitive to local needs and respond more quickly to the demands of the system, but has the disadvantage of a potential conflict of interests between the state and the governing body. The third, in which there is a relationship between the state and community control of governance, has the potential for cooperation, though such cooperation would have to be negotiated very carefully. At the end of the day, the process of discussion and deliberation facilitates the process and practice of participatory decision making.

This raises two central factors — the need to define the mechanism through which people at all levels of society can have access to power and through which power and authority can be redistributed; and the need to determine the process by which people are empowered to participate more fully in the political, social and educational processes. The debate on the nature of the relationship between the state and governance structures is part of a much wider debate on whether education systems should be centralized or decentralized.

CENTRALIZATION VERSUS DECENTRALIZATION

The international literature points to two opposing forces at work in the education system. There is an argument to be made that this dichotomy is far too narrow and is inadequate to describe features of a national system of governance. After all, most systems contain both centralizing and decentralizing tendencies. But despite this argument, it is still important to explore the conditions that determine the balance. In the United Kingdom, for example, a historically decentralized system is becoming increasingly centralized. Many observers believe that this tendency has much to do with the fact that different educational priorities and varying social and economic conditions determine the extent to which countries devolve or centralize decisions.

There are two views. On the one hand, it is assumed that only greater decentralization can make for greater democracy and participation, while on the other hand is the belief that only strong central leadership can redress educational inequalities and inequities. The two views are summarized in the following quotation:

> Those who champion democratic participation in education believe that communities will be served best when decision-making is decentralized and when people ... teachers, parents and students alike ... are encouraged to participate directly in making the decisions that affect them. ... In contrast to this view, the notion of administrative leadership is one which implies hierarchical elevation of the ... principal to an extraordinary level of power, centralizing decision-making and control of resources in the hands of the few. It is assumed that strong leaders, with their expertise, technical know-how and experience, can solve administrative problems more efficiently than could cumbersome and wasteful community participation in decision-making.
>
> (Rizvi, cited in Shaeffer 1992: 19)

Arguments in favour of decentralization are normally about flexibility and sensitivity to local needs. It is argued that decentralized systems allow for greater community participation. Sander and Murphy (1984) suggest for example that:

David Johnson

A more decentralized governance structure is needed so that schools, as unique educational entities, can offer their local communities the services, programmes, and activities which they desire. ... If adults are going to develop this ownership and commitment to their local schools, the governance of education must be decentralized so they participate in decision making activities, at the local school level, which directly influence the quality and quantity of education offered to children. The school committees, school councils or parent–teacher groups established to facilitate participatory decision-making must be based on a collaborative management philosophy of governance.

(Sander and Murphy 1989: 41)

There are, however, a number of problems with the assumption that decentralization is a sufficient condition for democracy, particularly in South Africa where the legacy of apartheid has created specific conditions and features.

One such feature is contestation in the terrain of education, marked historically by different forms of opposition and resistance. Sayed (1992) argues that the highly centralized nature of the apartheid education system has meant that such resistance could be directed to the state which has overall control over the system. The danger with decentralization, he argues, is that it may become an effective way of deflecting conflict away from the central state to smaller, devolved structures.

A second feature of the South African system of education is its gross inequality. Some economists (Pillay 1991) argue that the role of the central state is crucial in redressing such inequalities, particularly with regard to the state's role in redistributing educational finance. Pillay (1991: 103) suggests that, 'If state financing is used to address some of these inequalities, education financing can function as an effective redistributive instrument.' Decentralization, certainly in the way it has been proposed in South Africa in the recent Educational Renewal Strategy, may be construed as a way of dumping the state's responsibilities for financing education onto the community. In this way decentralization may not reduce inequality but exacerbate it.

Another important feature of South African society is its multicultural, multilingual nature. Decentralization is seen as consistent with the need to accommodate cultural differences. The peculiar distortion of cultural diversity under apartheid does, however, raise the question of whether decentralization will in fact retard unity and further entrench racism and ethnic divisions (Sayed 1992).

183

Finally, there is a widespread view that decentralization facilitates a transfer of power through widening participation. In reality, the process of decentralization is often a process of shifting power from a central source to an equally powerful group at the local level. According to McGinn and Street (1986), 'Decentralization is sought not to increase participation for individuals in general but to increase the participation of certain groups.' It is in fact to the issue of participation that this chapter now turns. With respect to the debate on centralization and decentralization, it is sufficient to conclude that the advantages and disadvantages of both will vary according to the existing situation in any one country. Being aware of how decentralization may under certain conditions detract from its intended course is important for South Africa.

PARTICIPATION

One of the problems with participation is a lack of clarity and consensus over what it actually means and what it should achieve. As Lucas (1976) observed, 'Participation has come into vogue. It is on everybody's lips. But like many vogue words it is vague. Everybody wants it, but it is not at all clear what "it" is, and would be participators are often dissatisfied with all attempts to meet their demands.' Richardson (1983) begins to define participation in relation to the degree of power held by the participants. For her, the essential nature of participation is not so much in the consequences — like the redistribution of power, greater efficiency and effectiveness of services and so on — but in the fact that it is a process of bargaining, which has unpredictable outcomes. If participation is not necessarily associated with particular political or social outcomes, it may begin to explain why the concept has support from a wide and diverse spectrum of political thought.

In South Africa, as in many other countries, a new view of parental participation has emerged over the last few years in which the 'logic' of market forces enters the sphere of education. Market theory in education, according to Bowe et al (1992: 25), 'rests upon a set of relatively straightforward premises which link market functions, and particularly competition, to individual choice.' It begins by applying the notion of consumers and producers (ie parents or children and teachers or educational officials) to education. Participation is seen in terms of promoting the consumer's interests, in exactly the same way as if the consumer were shopping for a commodity.

A market-oriented view of participation also employs the rhetoric of democracy and choice. Parents (as individual consumers) would have the right to choose which schools their children should attend and the right to assess the quality of the 'product' they are purchasing. An inherent contradiction in this model of participation is that consumers and producers are brought together in the decision-making process. This is atypical of the market situation in which the two are traditionally kept apart.

There are a number of problems with the market-oriented approach to participation, particularly when applied to South Africa. First, it rarely acknowledges that the market is inherently unequal and hierarchical. Not all consumers have the same power to purchase or the requisite knowledge to participate equally. Second, it does not take account of relationships forged between teachers, parents and students. And third, it appeals to parents as individual consumers. Given these criticisms, the market-oriented approach to participation in educational governance is fundamentally flawed. Participation devised along such lines would not bring about a system of governance that is able to effect historical redress (Sayed 1992).

PARTNERSHIP AND COLLABORATION IN THE GOVERNANCE OF EDUCATION

Recent research in South Africa suggests alternative options for participation in education. One such option is a model of collaboration and partnership. According to Ki-Zerbo, cited in Shaeffer (1992),

> The education system should not be regarded as a branch of the bureaucracy. Instead, it should be a subsystem highly interactive with other parts of the social whole. The point is to give pupils, parents and teachers responsibility for their own affairs, to the point of enabling them to administer the educational system on their own within the context of natural or contractual communities. The assumption of responsibility must necessarily embrace three indispensable areas: participation in design and decision-making processes; regular structured involvement in the processes of management and evaluation; and finally, financial accountability with regard to income and contributions.'
> (Shaeffer 1992: 14 citing Ki-Zerbo 1990: 86)

The school governance perspective starts from the assumption that central government is responsible for planning and administration. It proposes, however, that the formulation of policy is discussed within (and is accessible to) public forums at every level of the system. Essentially, it argues that it is the responsibility of the state to ensure adequate educational provision and it is indeed within this domain that the management function of governance should be located. However, this perspective also provides for the participation of key interest groups (such as organized parents, teachers and students) in the bodies responsible for management and execution of policy. To ensure 'transparency' the approach suggests that policy forums should have the right to discuss and assess the implementation of policy and make recommendations on how such policies could be operationalized.

The important contribution of this approach to the debate on governance is in its proposals for separate modes of participation and representation. It is contended that participation in school governance can be separated into two different though interrelated modes, namely the management mode and the representative mode. The management mode is understood to be primarily the domain of the government and involves the day-to-day management of schools. The representative mode is largely the domain of the key interest groups (such as organized parents, teachers and students) and is concerned with relaying the concerns and interests of organizations or groupings into the structures that make up the management mode. The representative structure is largely concerned with challenging the policies of school management and representatives are accountable to the organizations or groupings they represent. Each body at each level has a combination of members of whom some are present in a management capacity and others in a representative capacity. The two modes of participation in the governance process would permit the contestation of school governance both from within the system (management mode) and from outside the system (representative mode). The difference is between the different or multiple identities of the individuals concerned. One identity is as a student, parent or teacher (management mode), while the other identity is as a member of a student, parent or teacher organization (representative mode).

What the approach fails to consider is that the achievement of participatory democracy depends on more than just a political ideology and on the creation of appropriate institutions. Participatory democracy is dependent on people, through their local or mass-based structures, with the capacity and capability to participate equally and effectively. The next section of this chapter will thus concentrate on education and training for participation and democracy.

Building Capacity — Education and Training for Democracy

'It is clear that transformation of the current system of governance into one that is more participatory and accountable is not possible unless there is commitment of substantial resources to building capacity at schools, local and regional levels.' This quotation from NEPI (1992a) suggests that the question of training and the commitment of resources to such training is a crucial prerequisite for broadening the basis of participation in educational governance.

Training Needs for Community-Based Organizations

As far as I know, there are very few training programmes designed to build the capacity of community-based organizations to participate in governance. The effectiveness of a joint NECC/University of Bristol training programme aimed to help NECC regional organizers meet their training obligations will be known in the near future. There is a great need for programmes to prepare people for 'leadership and decision-making roles and for positions in their communities, to equip them for greater participation in political and social processes, and to provide them with the knowledge they need to be able to create, manage and maintain a democratic society' (Ellis 1993: 23). Ellis goes on to argue that it is important to scrutinize training programmes very carefully and to assess the extent to which they are capable of contributing to participation and democracy.

An important aspect of training is clearly adult and non-formal education. In South Africa, provision for adult education is varied and on the whole fragmented (NEPI 1992b). The objectives of the training curricula are also unclear in most cases. There is therefore some concern about those who do complete training courses remaining ill-equipped to participate effectively in their communities, particularly with respect to the governance of schools.

It will, however, be crucial for programmes aimed at building community capacity to be based on the principles of adult learning. The training itself will need to be more participatory, ensuring that the trainees themselves play a more active role in identifying needs, discussing and solving problems, and evaluating results.

A second important, though often neglected, point to consider in discussions about capacity building is how to equip the bureaucracy with the skills it needs to manage institutions more democratically. According to Ellis (1993: 31), such training could 'help to reorient their thinking, to increase awareness of their own need to learn and to continue learning, to be more flexible and open to change, and to be willing to change their attitudes and their way of relating to people and functioning.' Ensuring effective collaboration in managing the system of education in a future South Africa is to ensure a comprehensive training programme aimed at all levels of the system and at a wide range of needs. The first task therefore would be to conduct a national audit of

training needs. Research elsewhere (Shaeffer 1992) points to some generic needs which may exist in South Africa too.

The Needs of a Future Bureaucracy

It is inconceivable that the current bureaucracy will be dispensed with in
its entirety. It is clear too that it cannot be retained in its current form.
Urgent training of new people for key posts in a post-apartheid civil
service is of fundamental importance to the process of transformation. Of
more significance, however, is the need to intervene and change the
culture of the existing bureaucracy. This is more of a challenge. There is a
popular belief that bureaucracies are unwilling or unable to change. The
conclusions of a workshop with members of the civil service in South
Africa suggests that this may not be the case and, as such, intervention or
training should take this factor into account.

Thus two things would have to happen — a possible intervention with
high-level administrators committed to change, and large-scale training
of staff. It is likely that such training would have to be incremental. In
thinking of the training needs of bureaucracies, Shaeffer (1992) further
suggests follow-up training 'through specific projects in which new skills
and attitudes can be carried out; ... and a support system of sorts to
continue to encourage and help those newly trained in performing their
tasks differently.'

Training Needs at the National Level

At the national level, the new ministry would have to be sensitized to the
rationale for (or potential of) wider participation in educational development. According to Shaeffer (1992) several methods might be useful in
this regard, namely 'well-chosen case studies concerning the role of
collaboration in solving educational problems; the dissemination of
information about successful experiences elsewhere in the world; the
implementation of policy seminars on these issues; and the development
of high-level task forces and pilot projects using more participatory and
collaborative approaches.' The suggestion is clearly that training programmes aiming to build capacity for participation must themselves
apply methodologies and techniques that encourage participation.

CONCLUSIONS

A number of issues have been raised in this chapter including notions of
power and power distribution, effective participation and whether the
nature of a system (centralized or decentralized) inhibits or facilitates
participatory democracy. I finally argue that the quality of participation

David Johnson

largely depends on the degree to which people acquire the appropriate knowledge, attitudes and skills needed for active and meaningful participation.

REFERENCES

Bacon, W (1978) *Public Accountability and the Schooling System: A Sociology of School Board Democracy*, London, Harper Row

Beattie, N (1978) 'Formalised Parent Participation in Education: A Comparative Perspective', *Comparative Education*, vol 14, no 1

Bowe, R, Ball, S and Gold, A (1992) *Reforming Education and Changing Schools: Case Studies in Policy Sociology*, London, Routledge

Commonwealth Expert Group (1991) *Beyond Apartheid: Human Resources in a New South Africa*, Cape Town, The Commonwealth Secretariat/David Philip

Ellis, P (1993) 'Training for Democracy: Adult Education Practices', *Convergence*, vol 26, no l

Johnson, D, Unterhalter, E and Wolpe, H (1991) *Formal and Non-Formal Structures of Human Resource Development for a Post-Apartheid South Africa*, London, Commonwealth Secretariat

Kulati, T (1992) 'An examination of the Historical Evolution of the Notion of Community Participation in South Africa', unpublished article

Levin, R (1991) 'People's Education and the Struggle for Democracy in South Africa, in Unterhalter and Wolpe, qv

Lucas, J (1976) *Democracy and Participation*, Harmondsworth, Penguin

Maepa, D (1991) 'Report of the Soweto Education Coordinating Committee', unpublished report

Maile, M (1992) 'Community Participation in Education: An Option for South Africa in Transition', unpublished manuscript, University of Bristol

McGinn, N and Street, S (1986) 'Educational Decentralisation: Weak State or Strong State?, *Comparative Education Review*, vol 30, no 4

Narsoo, M (1991) 'Civil Society — A Contested Terrain', *Work in Progress*, no 76, pp 24–7

NEPI (1992a), *Report of the National Education Policy Investigation Educational Research Group*, Cape Town, Oxford University Press/NECC

—— (1992b) *Report of the National Education Policy Investigation Adult Education Research Group*, Cape Town, Oxford University Press/NECC

Pascal, C (1989) 'Democratised Primary School Government: Conflict and Dichotomies', in Glatter, R (ed) *Educational Institutions and the Environment: Managing the Boundaries*, Milton Keynes, Oxford University Press

Pillay, P (1991) 'Financing Educational Transformation in South Africa', in Unterhalter, E, Wolpe, H and Botha, T, *Education in a Future South Africa: Policy Issues for Transformation*, London, Heinemann

Richardson, A (1983) *Participation*, London, Routledge & Kegan Paul

Sander, B and Murphy, P (1989) *Administration and Management of Education: The Challenges Faced*, Paris, IIEP

Sayed, Y (1992) 'A Critique of the Decentralisation of Educational Administration: Reconceptualising the Governance of Schools', unpublished article

Shaeffer, S (1992) *Collaborating for Educational Change: The Role of Teachers, Parents and the Community in School Improvement*, Paris, IIEP

Sisulu, Z (1986) 'People's Education for People's Power', *Transformation*, no 1

189

Tywala, P (1992) 'Setting up Parent, Teacher, Student Associations: Problems and Pitfalls', unpublished manuscript, University of Bristol

Unterhalter, E and Wolpe, H (eds) (1991) *Apartheid Education and Popular Struggles*, Johannesburg, Ravan

Unterhalter, E, Wolpe, H and Botha, T (1991) *Education in a Future South Africa: Policy Issues for Transformation*, London, Heinemann

Wolpe, H (1991) 'Reproduction, Reform and Transformation: Approaches to the Analysis of Education in South Africa', in Unterhalter and Wolpe, qv

Chapter Fourteen

Redefining Adult Education in South Africa's Changed Politics

Paul Fordham

The idea of using adult education as a tool for social transformation has long been influential in South Africa's liberation movement. In his 1976 court testimony, Steve Biko made a direct link between black conscious-ness and ideas about 'conscientization' derived from Paulo Freire (Biko 1979: 28; Freire 1972a and 1972b). The adult literacy project then being pursued by Biko and his colleagues in the South African Students' Organization, was designed to help 'blacks grapple realistically with their problems ... to develop ... an awareness of their situation to be able to analyse it, and to provide answers for themselves. The purpose behind it really being to provide some kind of hope.' (Biko 1979: 26–8, 117, 233)

The increased state oppression of the 1980s did not dim the pursuit of black conscientization, or the link between political goals and the educa-tion of adults. What happened was a diversion of some of the political energy into the 'civics', many of which had education programmes with similar purposes (Matiwana et al 1989).

With the opening up of a new political agenda, there is once again explicit and now much more detailed debate about the link between adult education and social transformation, and about the ways in which conscientizing education will engage with new kinds of state provision and with the new political order. Some of the debate, and the new thinking which accompanies it, is taking place within university adult education departments. The aim of this chapter is to situate this new thinking within the international adult education 'movement'; and to comment on its possible contribution to sustainable development in the new South Africa.

ADULT EDUCATION AS 'MOVEMENT'

In the 25th anniversary issue of *Convergence* (1992), experienced adult educators were asked to reflect on the role of adult education in social transformation. Adult education is here seen as having its 'roots in social activism and democratic values'. As Hall (1981: 5–6) puts it: 'I did not begin with the question of what is the potential of adult education? I began with questions about the failure of democracy in the US, with global injustices resulting from colonialism ... and the conviction that change at all levels was necessary.'

Gayfer adds a further dimension by linking adult education with development and refers to the 1976 conference on 'Adult Education and Development' in Dar es Salaam, which stressed adult learning as an essential element of all development strategies (Hall and Kidd 1978: 17–18). For the first time at an international conference, adult educators were making a strong link with the theory and practice of Paulo Freire (especially in literacy) and with the education-in-development practice of Nyerere's Tanzania. As Nyerere himself put it at the time:

> Adult education should promote change, at the same time as it assists men to control both the change which they introduce, and that which is forced upon them by the cataclysms of nature ... In that case, the first function of adult education is to inspire both a desire for change and an understanding that change is possible.
>
> (Nyerere 1973)

International adult education was also at the same time promoting the democratization of research through the idea of participatory research, in which research, learning and action are intertwined; where 'people who are experiencing a social situation, identify, analyse and act upon their problems' (Hall 1981). It is within a frame of discourse that emphasizes the purposes of education as facilitating social transformation, and which emphasizes learner participation, that the new thinking in South African adult education is best considered.

ADULT EDUCATION PRACTICE: THE 'LIBERAL' UNIVERSITIES

Adult education in the older English medium universities of South Africa is strongly influenced by the traditions of their counterparts in England. But for the UK, it is many years since the practice of educating adults was seen as part of any kind of social or political 'movement'. Field practice in this sector of education is always closely tied to context (political, social, economic, cultural); and in context as well as dominant values, the UK today is no place for an adult education linked to wider social or political movements for change, particularly those that look to change in the direction of greater equity.

It was not always so. The establishment of adult education departments in the 1920s was deliberately linked both to working-class emancipation and to the reform of their parent universities in the direction of wider access. For some, this also meant a change of curriculum, so that economics, for example, would begin from the workers' wages, living conditions and the aims of their trades unions (McIlroy and Spencer 1988; Fordham 1984). In the 1970s there was a brief resurgence of this kind of practice in various community-based projects (Lovett 1975). While government itself was persuaded to fund similar small-scale activities in the 1980s under the REPLAN (adult unemployed) programme (Fordham 1992; Johnston 1987). There was also a significant contribution to the education of women (Thompson 1980 and 1983). While the real achievements were certainly less than declared aims, there has also been a sense of continuity in practice and some development of a consistent professional ideology; this is seen much more clearly at the international level than in the UK itself.

As Millar (1984) records, much of current practice is well within the UK originated extra-mural tradition of sharing academic knowledge 'with a wider adult community. ... Its emphasis tends to be on the humanities and the social sciences, its dual values those of personal enrichment and enlightened citizenship. ... It serves the needs of those who have experienced extended formal education.' Perhaps the best example of this kind of programme is the well regarded annual summer school of the University of Cape Town, which attracts enrolments each year of some 5000, mainly white middle-class students. As well as citizenship and personal enrichment, one might also add that part of the traditional rhetoric is a sometimes neglected commitment to equality of opportunity for all adults.

While the apartheid state remained firmly in place, this democratic concept was confined largely to those who had benefited most from the existing educational system. As the state begins to change, there are attempts to increase non-white participation in existing programmes. Whether these attempts are any more successful than similar attempts to increase working-class participation in the UK remains to be seen. Much more important is likely to be the pressure for more non-white entry to undergraduate and graduate study, with concurrent pressure for curriculum change. New publics knocking at the door of the university are likely to want entry to the main gate, not the side entrance via adult education. And there is likely to be as much political pressure on the curriculum of primary education as on adult access.

However, in the same paper, Millar is already taking tentative steps towards a reification of the democratic part of professional adult education ideology when he speaks of 'development projects ... [which] ... attempt to promote community education goals as part of wider social goals.' Eight years later and in the same department there has been a vigorous attempt to shift practice in the direction of new programmes and new participants in response to the changed politics; similar changes can be found in other universities. Such shifts include 'community adult education' (see below), policy orientated research and 'protected' space for the discussion of 'civic issues' where 'leadership skills can be transmitted, policy issues debated, citizenship reconstructed, historical and social contexts contested, and access to university intellectual resources secured' (Fiske 1992). In most of the liberal universities, the search for greater political relevance seems to have developed around the idea of outreach to different publics via some form of 'non-formal' education.

NON-FORMAL AND COMMUNITY-BASED ADULT EDUCATION

The non-formal idea[1] in education grew up around World Bank (1974) development strategies in the 1970s. 'Questions of employment, environment, social equity and, above all, participation in development by the less privileged now share with simple growth in the definition of objectives (and hence the model) of development toward which the effort of all parties is to be directed. These changes have their counterpart in the education sector.' Although now seen by some as a 'fashion' of the 1970s and by others as education for other people (or other people's children), it is now being promoted anew by UNICEF and others as part of the follow-up to the World Conference on Education for All (WCEFA 1990).

The De Lange Report (HSRC 1981) gave renewed prominence to the non-formal idea in South Africa and was the subject of extensive debate in the 1980s (Millar et al 1991). In terms of university practice in the 1990s its main expression has been in the promotion of various

---

1 . The idea embraces a vast range of educative services such as health and agricultural extension, post-primary skill training, adult literacy, and women's groups aimed at income generation or consciousness raising. They have their roots in attempts to answer specific development needs, though the degree of learner participation in programme development is both enormously varied and crucial to the quality of outcomes.

'community-based' programmes. These are not in the main concerned with the provision of subject-based courses, but with training community leaders, action research, production of teaching materials (for example in adult literacy) and acting generally as resource centres for non-university activists. Examples are the Zenex Adult Literacy Unit at the University of the Witwatersrand and similar work in Natal. All are in varying degrees motivated by the sense of a democratizing mission and most see development related research opportunities as part of the package they offer. There is also a strong sense that adult education should be involved in 'change', although the purposes are not always clearly defined or the underlying values articulated.

Internationally, non-formal education (NFE) is often defined in terms of relevance to the needs of the poor, flexibility in organization and methods, carefully targeted approaches and specificity in objectives (Fordham 1980). In the 1970s it was thought that the idea would help to give coherence to existing diverse practice. Except in a small number of countries this did not happen. What it did do was dramatically extend the horizons of educators beyond the school, so that significant policy attention was given to the 'neglected area' of adult and community education (King 1988).

The Department most clearly aligned with the liberation struggle is the relatively new (1985) Centre for Adult and Continuing Education (CACE), at the University of the Western Cape (UWC). Its mission is to serve 'the poor and the oppressed individually and organizationally, with an overall commitment to the attainment of a non-racial democratic society' (Samuels 1992). Its non-formal programme is focused entirely on support for the work of non-white community groups (the 'civics'), offering debate, resources, research, training and capacity building within community organizations.

In the process, CACE seems to be redefining NFE more specifically in terms of disadvantaged target groups and also close alliance with their political demands; with little emphasis on particular methods or a specifically out-of-school approach. For example, the CACE programme includes computer literacy as well as organizational skills training and lectures which are 'non-formal' only in the sense that they do not lead to qualifications. This is absolutely appropriate in the current political context, and underlines that for CACE, NFE is 'socially transformative ... aimed at those involved in anti-apartheid struggles.' The form that this kind of education has taken responded to the expressed needs of those anti-apartheid groups through development projects, short courses, lectures, conferences and seminars.

The participatory research influence is strong, linking the 'three inter-related processes of investigation, education and action' (Samuels 1992). One practical result of this research approach was a study of community organizations in greater Cape Town, which was possible only with the close cooperation of those same organizations (Matiwana et al 1989). This is a source book of information about these organizations, at once useful to other researchers and to the organizations themselves.

One feature of education-for-liberation at CACE is the clear linkage established between oppression based on race and oppression based on gender or class. Seminars (gender and popular education workshops) held in 1990 challenged participants to analyse and relate all forms of group oppression; and there was a deliberate attempt to facilitate the exploration of differences as they faced individuals and group members. The educators were involved in a particular form of Freirean dialogue with learners, recognizing differences and commonalities of experience and knowledge at different points (Walters 1992).

Since the early 1970s, adult educators involved in learning for change have tended to invoke Paulo Freire as a source of inspiration (Freire 1974). Often they are simply reinforcing older ideas derived from successful practice: namely that dialogue with students and negotiation with potential learners are central to effective programme planning. Because adult education is a voluntary activity, the intended learners cannot be motivated to attend unless content and methods are seen as relevant. Nevertheless, there are consistent themes in a situation of oppression which point to the value of a Freirean curriculum for the oppositional educator.

Starting from the background of group experience, generative themes (for example poverty, segregation) are used to motivate, increase under-standing and develop the group's capacity to change and improve the quality of their own lives. Whatever the topic, the basis of curriculum planning in this approach becomes the environment and experience of the group itself. Moreover the idea of what is useful knowledge is also challenged. It gives rise to an epistemology where experience and the creation of knowledge are part of one process. As Freire once said in a conversation in Birmingham, 'the act of knowing is there on the table between the teacher and the learner.'

An important and unanswered question is what happens when Freirean educators move from programmes designed for liberation to ones where social and economic development themes become the new purposes, and where the 'civics' and other NGOs are no longer solely oppositional.

Both Millar (1991) and Morphet (1992) have begun to explore tentative answers to this question, while others (for example CACE at UWC) are also reflecting anew on current practice. Morphet (1992) talks of the recent past as having a:

> foundational place for adult educators, linking small-scale action with larger visions of social change. However, the Freirean foundation always had problems of internal coherence, but now it has ... fragmented. ... It was a theory of a divided world ... 1989–90 (whatever its final outcomes) shifted that ground under our feet. The patterns of legitimacy and legality which had until then been locked in conflict, were reordered and brought at least within sight of each other. This has changed not only the way we see the social world but the way we understand our professional purposes.'

How will these purposes be applied to new kinds of practice, and how will that practice change in the immediate future?

For adult basic education, Millar derives from an analysis of COSATU's policy papers a tentative outline of the main trends. He identifies: the power struggle for resources and legitimacy in both industrial training and basic education by unions and by NGOs, a struggle which will produce some formalization of NFE; a great emphasis on exchange value (access for non-traditional students: the integration of formal and non-formal); renewed emphasis on human resource development. For the last named, education becomes an 'expert system' of social technology leading to measurable skills and competencies.

The questions which have to be answered include how the 'professional purposes' referred to above will be adapted to meet these new challenges. Above all, will a new 'foundational place' be developed to replace the Freirean model? These are important question for non-formal and community educators in all countries; but they have particular prominence and urgency in South Africa.

THE CURRICULUM OF TRAINING

Reviewing the curriculum of training provides a framework within which the larger issues can be addressed, and this was a major theme at the 1992 'Conference of University-based Adult Educators' (Hemson 1992).

At UWC, the diploma course has a Freirean foundation which aims to 'serve the needs of the poor and oppressed and work towards the attainment of a non-racial, non-sexist democratic society'. There is also a research approach designed to produce 'reflective practitioners', and this relates particularly well to the organization development and management part of the course. Thus while the present theoretical base is oppositional, the course is also grounded in the work of the changing local social/political organizations from which the students come. There is flexibility for change to meet changed circumstances. The certificate course at UWC has a similar orientation, but its inclusion of 'contextual studies' in the first year gives additional rootedness in current NGO practice.

Other universities have curricula closer to those in many English-speaking countries, based on a foundation disciplines approach (psychology, sociology, philosophy, history), but modified by the professional practice of trainees, the ideology of meeting needs and elements from other adult education theorists (for example Knowles 1980).[2] As always the danger here is that curricula become decontextualized and, eventually, remote from the socio-political realities they were originally designed to serve; although there is no evidence that this is a present danger in current South African curricula, for example, the *adult learning* component of the diploma course at University of Cape Town shows a sharp awareness of contextual realities (Millar 1992). However, while it is difficult to decontextualize a Freirean curriculum, the same is not true of an approach from the traditional foundation disciplines.

PROFESSIONAL ADULT EDUCATION AND SUSTAINABLE DEVELOPMENT

It was suggested in the first section of this chapter that the new South African thinking could best be considered within a frame of discourse which emphasized social transformation. But the question has also been posed of what happens when an exclusive concentration on liberation gives way to a more complex political and social situation; where the emphasis is on various kinds of 'development'. Can we situate the new South African thinking within an international adult education 'movement' which has hitherto also emphasized transformation and opposition to the socio-political status quo? Is there a professional ideology which underpins Morphet's 'professional purposes' and can this help professionals to develop a new foundational place on the shifting ground which is the new South Africa?

'Adult education' as an idea derives from at least six different but related areas of international practice: the right to literacy for all, community development, extension education (for example agriculture), folk

2 . For a full discussion of the theoretical issues see Usher in Bright (ed) 1989

---

high schools (Scandinavia, Germany), liberal university adult education (UK, USA), *'educación popular'* (Latin America). While these have not yet produced the new foundational place, they do offer a set of shared perspectives and attitudes which could be helpful in developing and locating it.

It is not so much a question of agreed knowledge and skills into which all must be inducted, but is rather concerned with professional attitudes. These may conveniently be considered in relation to democracy, culture and development. The first is based on a belief that, ideally, all adults should be actively involved in forming and implementing public policy, and that adult education can help maximize human potential in decision making. The second sees adult education as a major means for the preservation, development and transmission of culture (for example the national regeneration of language and tradition in late nineteenth century Denmark).

Perhaps most importantly in South Africa, there is the idea of adult education as the hand of development: as a change agent (back to Nyerere again). Both the idea of adult education and its operational provision imply a continuing closeness to public policy formation and implementation; to politics as this may variously be defined (Fordham and Fox 1989). This sensitivity is a current strength. In the struggle to reform the future, the substantial resources of university adult education in South Africa also have a strong and constructive relationship between activism and academe. If new foundations can be devised which build on this relationship, then there will continue to be long-term influence on the developing educational system as a whole.

REFERENCES

Biko, S (1979) *The Testimony of Steve Biko*, London, Panther Books
Bright, B (ed) (1989) *Theory and Practice in the Study of Adult Education*, London, Routledge
Fiske, I (1992) 'Recent Developments: Extra Mural Studies at UCT', in Hemson, qv
Fordham, P (ed) (1980) *Participation Learning and Change*, London, Commonwealth Secretariat
—— (1984) 'A View from the Wall', *International Journal of Lifelong Education*, vol 2, no 4
—— (1992) 'Replan 1984–91', *Studies in the Education of Adults*, vol 24, no 2
Fordham, P and Fox, J (1989) 'Training the Adult Educator as Professional' *International Review of Education*, no 35
Freire, P (1972a) *Pedagogy of the Oppressed*, Harmondsworth, Penguin Books
—— (1972b) *Cultural Action For Freedom*, Harmondsworth, Penguin Books
—— (1974) *Education the Practice of Freedom*, London, Readers and Writers Publishing Cooperative

Hall, B (1981) 'The Democratization of Research', in Reason and Rowan, qv

Hall, B and Gayfer, M (1992) 'The Role of Adult Education in Social Transformation', *Convergence*, vol 25, no 4

Hall, B and Kidd, R (1978) *Adult Learning: A Design for Action*, Oxford, Pergamon Press

Hemson, C (ed) (1992) *Proceedings of the Conference of University-Based Adult Educators*, University of Natal

HSRC (1981) Provision of Education in the Republic of South Africa: Report of the Main Committee of the HSRC Investigation into Education [De Lange Report], Pretoria, Human Sciences Research Council

Johnston, R (1987) *Exploring the Educational Needs of Unwaged Adults*, Leicester, NIACE/REPLAN

King, K (1988) *Aid and Educational Research in Developing Countries*, London, Overseas Development Administration

Knowles, M (1980) *The Modern Practice of Adult Education*, Cambridge, The Adult Education Company

Lovett, T (1975) *Adult Education, Community Development and the Working Class*, London, Ward Lock

Matiwana, M, Walters, S and Groener, Z (1989) *The Struggle for Democracy*, Belleville, University of the Western Cape

McIlroy, J and Spencer B (1988) *University Adult Education in Crisis*, Leeds, University of Leeds

Millar, C (1984) 'The University and Continuing Education', *South African Journal of Education*, vol 4, no 1

—— (1990) 'Curriculum Evolution in University-Based Adult Education Programmes, *South African Journal of Higher Education*, vol 4, no 1

—— (1991) *New Rules for Educating the Educators*, Cape Town, University of Cape Town

—— (1992) 'Adult Learning in the Diploma Course', in Hemson (ed), qv

Millar, C et al (1991) *Breaking the Formal Frame*, Cape Town, Oxford University Press

Morphet, T (1992) 'Thinking about New Foundations', in Hemson (ed), qv

Nyerere, J (1973) *Freedom and Development: A Selection of Writings and Speeches, 1965–1973*, New York, Oxford University Press

Samuels, J (1992) 'Non-Formal Education at CACE', in Hemson (ed), qv

Thompson, J (ed) (1980) *Adult Education for a Change*, London, Hutchinson

—— (1983) *Learning Liberation*, London, Croom Helm

Usher, R (1989) 'Locating Adult Education in the Practical', in Bright, qv

Walters, S (1992) 'Gender and Adult Education', in Hemson (ed), qv

World Bank (1974) *Education Sector Review*, New York, World Bank

World Conference on Education for All (1990) *World Declaration and Framework for Action*, New York, WCEFA

Chapter Fifteen

The Press in Post-Apartheid South Africa

Benjamin Pogrund

The press in South Africa has suffered like everything and everyone from apartheid. When the Afrikaner Nationalists came to office in 1948 the press was free, enjoying rights gained as a result of a struggle, 120 years earlier, against an autocratic British governor of the then Cape Colony. That said, how the press applied its freedom was another matter: in practice, with only few exceptions, it restricted itself to the existence and concerns of the white minority.

Blacks featured in the news as the accused in criminal trials, or as anonymous statistics in road or mining accidents — the usual style in reporting the many gold mining accidents was along the lines: 'Two miners, Mr P van der Merwe and Mr J Kotze, and six natives were killed in a rockfall on X mine. ... Production was not affected.' Very occasionally black names were seen in the political sphere, but essentially only in relation to the dominating white tussle between English- and Afrikaans-speakers. Not until the end of the 1950s did the mainstream 'white' press begin to report meaningfully on the disabilities of the majority of the country's people and to treat blacks as normal subjects of news. In its behaviour the press was reflecting the society in which it operated; it did so without questioning why and what it was doing.

The press has changed profoundly during the past 45 years that Afrikaner Nationalists have been in government. First, as the Nationalists imposed racial apartheid policy, extending and institutionalizing existing racial divisions and discrimination, they attacked personal liberties. The press was caught up in this and suffered the same loss of freedoms as every individual South African. Additionally the press suffered from specific legal restrictions, harassment and intimidation. Second, standards have suffered. Government repression helped to make journalism unpopular; there has also been management shortsightedness about pay and conditions and a downgrading of editorial quality; too few talented people have been drawn into the profession and significant numbers of experienced journalists have emigrated.

Now, as white minority rule nears an end, the damage inflicted on the press has to be repaired. The first and most fundamental question is: what sort of press is the new South Africa to have? There is agreement on the desirability of press freedom. A declaration about freedom of information is in the new constitution and Bill of Rights. But this in itself is insufficient: there is, unhappily, no shortage of instances in the world where fine words have not been enough to keep tyranny at bay, and indeed have even been used as a figleaf for oppression. The former Soviet Union provides an awful warning; Stalin's constitution of 1936 said in Article 125: 'the law guarantees the citizens of the USSR freedom of speech of the press.' Closer to home, even the National Party (quite unblushingly) declares its belief in press freedom.

In the new South Africa, if the intention is indeed to ensure freedom of the press in the fullest sense, in the same sense that democracy is intended, then it needs to be buttressed by as much practical detail as possible. Implementing the detail will also further the process of repair, and strengthen the press so that it can better fulfil its functions.

An appropriate conceptual framework exists in the Windhoek Declaration adopted in 1991 at a seminar sponsored in Namibia by the United Nations and UNESCO and attended by journalists from 35 African countries. It has particular relevance because it came after the years of conflict over UNESCO's New World Information and Communication Order. Out of this argument has emerged widespread acknowledgement of the tie between democracy and freedom of information, and as a corollary, that talk of placing the media at the service of the state is inimical to freedom.

The Windhoek Declaration is founded on the 'free flow of ideas' and calls for 'an independent, pluralistic and free press'. Those are the key phrases, and they are rightly described in the declaration as 'essential to the development and maintenance of democracy in a nation, and for economic development.'

How to put them into practice in South Africa? Any thought of a quick overnight fix — of destroying everything at one fell swoop to create something new and beautiful — is unrealistic; that is not the way the country is evolving, and in any event the press as an institution does not lend itself to such instant reform. At the same time, there is urgency in ending the artificiality of the establishment press which belongs to a dying era. A combination of interlinking actions is needed, to break with the past and to use what is good for the present and future.

First, getting rid of restrictive laws and rules enacted by the Nationalists. The emphasis during their rule was on the interests of the state, at
the expense of individual freedom. A democratic South Africa should
have no need for laws such as those imposing sweeping prohibitions on
publication of information about defence, police or mental hospitals,
never mind the previous, now repealed, restriction on information about
prisons. Nor should there be any need to conceal details about nuclear
matters and fuel supplies. Nor can there be justification for laws giving
police the power to order journalists to leave scenes of unrest, or magis-
trates wide rights to exclude public and press from criminal proceedings.
Where such laws still exist they need to be speedily reformed.

There are some thorny issues: should publication of racial incitement — 'hate' propaganda — or incitement to violence, continue to be
illegal? On the face of it, a society as polyglot as South Africa needs such
protective laws, and especially because of the existence of malignant
forces which are set on undermining a non-racial democracy with violent
words and deeds. On the other hand, South African experience with
these laws has not been a happy one: the Nationalists had them in their
armoury and used them as a means of suppressing dissident views.

Rather than tempt future governments to do the same, the country
should attempt to do without them; at the very least, if such laws are to
exist, they should be as circumscribed as possible with the onus firmly
on the state to prove wrongdoing.

Second, enacting a Right to Know law, with positive affirmations of
the right of every citizen — and hence of the press — to obtain information from both the government and private sectors. Several countries
have freedom of information laws and South Africa can draw on their
experience. A campaign for such legislation is under way in Britain and a
full-fledged model law is available for South Africa in the Right to Know
Bill introduced by Mark Fisher MP, which had its second reading in the
House of Commons in February 1993. The Bill, with careful detail about
both rights and safeguards, seeks to create a right of access to official
records held by public authorities, to reform official secrets legislation, to
create a right of access to employment records, and to require companies
to publish more information in their annual reports.

Third, even while noting that journalists cannot lay claim to being
above the laws which determine the rights and liberties of everyone in
society, for the sake of ensuring maximum disclosure of important
information consideration needs to be given to a 'shield' law, as it is
known, which would give journalists a right to protect the anonymity of
sources of information.

Fourth, journalism training must be extended, with a special emphasis on helping those already in jobs to upgrade their qualifications. It is worth bearing in mind that this will bear fruit well beyond the bounds of the press: people trained in journalism often move into government and private business, carrying communication attitudes and skills with them. Training has a particular task in overcoming the deficiencies among black South Africans created by Bantu Education, widespread disruption of education, and the years-long neglect by the white-run press. The emphasis will naturally be on domestic training, but international assistance needs to be sought for expensive placements abroad, to run for six months to a year for maximum benefit.

Fifth, the monopolistic control of the press is one area that has to be dealt with, to end the control by four newspaper groups, two of them committed to Afrikaner Nationalists and the other two owned by the Anglo American Corporation. Nor is it healthy to have the Argus Group's domination and influence in so many related fields. The extent of the problem was indicated in a report[1] in *South* newspaper which noted that the four English and Afrikaans newspaper groups account for about 93 per cent of all urban dailies and weeklies. They also own or control about a third of the press in country districts, more than 80 per cent of free sheets and nearly half the magazines.

In another report,[2] the *Weekly Mail* said that the Argus Group:

has come to dominate not just the English-language newspaper business, but also its main rivals (Times Media and Caxtons), the major distribution agency (Allied Publishing) and the major printing presses (Johannesburg Printers, for example). And Argus — or its sister companies — now has a major hand in the companies that overwhelmingly dominate the book industry (CNA and the Literary Group), the record industry (Gallo), television (M–Net), radio (702) and the film industry (NuMetro). It also has links, through its sister companies, with a video production studio, a major ink producer, a major paper producer.'

'Unbundling' is the phrase used in calls to end these ownerships which are contrary to the interests of a society intent on democracy and a free flow of ideas. There has to be swift change, hopefully voluntarily, or else by law, with clear limits, too, on cross-ownership. An independent press

---

1. 'Press freedom not cut and dried', by Moegsien Williams, *South*, Cape Town, 17 May 1990.
2. 'Media-nopoly!', by Anton Harber, *Weekly Mail*, Johannesburg, 30 May 1991.

means a press free both of government and of monopolistic private ownership.

But in breaking up the whole, who is to own/control the parts? Should substantial sections of the whole, at least in regard to newspaper conglomerates, be allowed to remain in the interests of efficiency and economic survival? If so, who will the owners be? These are difficult issues because effecting change should not mean inflicting damage on what is worthwhile. At the other extreme, vesting ownership in a government-directed media trust, as for example in Zimbabwe, is equally to be avoided. The essential point must be made time and time again: whatever the good democratic intentions and promises of government, political leaders and their officials must be kept as far away as possible from the press; in the nature of things, they desire to control and to direct the press, always of course with the highest possible motives to serve society and the people.

The way out of these dilemmas could be sought by a combination of methods, with trusts consisting of eminent individuals responsible for senior editorial appointments and maintaining editorial integrity and freedom, operating together with a commercial company whose stock is owned by public investors and with a ceiling on the amount of stock that any person or company can own..

Sixth, there has to be a levelling of the playing field between the 'established' press, which has enjoyed the benefits of white domination to create its niche, and the 'alternative' press which, despite its fine record in recent years, in general lacks capital and skills. The alternative press needs financial help to extend its coverage, increase its paging and upgrade standards by hiring the best possible journalists — all so that newspapers and magazines can aim at becoming commercially self-sufficient and competitive.

The Swedish method — of government funding, derived from the general tax, which is shared among the press — is unlikely to be appropriate for South Africa if only because it can be expensive and financial resources will be severely limited. The new South Africa is going to have to spend every available cent on overcoming the heritage of neglect and discrimination left by the Nationalists in education, housing, health and social security.

A creative method for securing funding would be to draw on the experience of two Afrikaans press groups, Nasionale Pers and Perskor, which have grown financially fat with the help of large printing plants built on the certainty of getting government contracts to print official documentation. The financial benefits they have enjoyed — in effect, a licence to print money — have enabled them, among other things, to run newspapers at a loss until the good times come. One example is the *Citizen*, which was originally founded through misuse of taxpayers' money: Perskor was able to garner enough millions to ensure that the newspaper's life was maintained.

This Nationalists' cosy setup has to be speedily ended. It must be transformed into serving a wider benefit. Plants to print the vast amount of government documentation will be needed as much in the new South Africa as before: from parliamentary Hansard through blue books and magazines. Ownership of the printing plants could be vested in the press as a whole, with a proportion of income devoted to assisting the alternative press and to pay for other improvements, such as training for journalists. Whether the existing printing plants are taken over, and on what financial basis, is a matter for political debate. An additional particular plus for this system is that the government would not be the direct provider of funding. It would not have immediate involvement, reducing the temptation to use subsidies as an excuse for interference.

A second major source of income for the alternative press lies in profitable television advertising: the M–Net channel is currently controlled by the establishment press. It was a government gift to them, to bolster them against the loss of advertising to television. It is now time to change the owners, and beneficiaries, of M–Net to ensure a wider spread of the benefits.

Helping the alternative press means giving assistance to existing newspapers and magazines, as well as encouraging the launch of new publications, especially at grassroots community level. Pluralism means encouraging the broadest possible range of newspapers and magazines, allowing freedom of expression for different shades of opinion and different approaches to journalism.

Seventh, the South African Broadcasting Corporation: its television and radio have been totally under the control of Afrikaner Nationalists and have been used with cold calculation as powerful weapons in support of the ruling elite. The way forward was agreed at Codesa 2 with details set out of an independent body 'to regulate the telecommunications sector' to ensure 'political neutrality of, and for access to' state-controlled media. Turning the SABC inside out has to start at the top, and the process of achieving this has been under way. Percolating a new professional approach throughout the organization can be speeded up, as proposed by the Film and Allied Workers organization, by splitting the SABC into a core unit with responsibility for public broadcasting within specified limits, and the hiving off of other sections into either community or privately owned units, with the same protection against monopoly and cross-ownership as should apply to newspapers.

Radio is a key medium for South Africa. It has to be with different authorities estimating the level of illiteracy among blacks at anything from 25 to 50 per cent or more. At the same time, no less than nine out of ten black households have a radio.[3] The significance of the medium carries its own caution for the restructuring process: it would not, for example, be helpful to the new South Africa to have the set of political zealots who have controlled radio and television merely replaced by zealots from another part of the political spectrum who are convinced in their own way that theirs is the one and only proper message for the people. Rather, public mediums deserve as much old-fashioned journalistic orthodoxies as possible, with professional striving for telling the story as it is with the least possible embellishment.

Eighth, and finally, there is the responsibility of the press and of individual journalists for their own wrong behaviour — for transgressions of a different order than ordinary contravention of common law, whether untruthful reporting or gross intrusion into a person's privacy. The obvious method — a press code of conduct enforced by the industry's own council — has a shadow over it: the Nationalists used a code and a council as part of their web of intimidation. Yet it is the way in which the press must watch over itself as changes are made. Rather leave the press to police itself, to redress legitimate complaints by the public, than precipitate intervention by the state.

Even with the energetic pursuit of these various remedial measures the press does not exist in isolation but can only be what society wants it to be. That places responsibility on the political leaders to give the lead in ensuring practical expression for the concept of a free press, even to the extent of tolerating the backsliding, mistakes and excesses which are bound to be thrown up as the press grapples to overcome its inherited deficiencies in attitudes, training and professional experience. Then, too, officials of government have to be schooled in the notion of freedom of information: even if Right to Know legislation is enacted it could be nobbled from within unless the bureaucracy is imbued with the spirit of openness.

The political leaders have to be clear about what they want, for the climate of intolerance of the view of others which has developed in South Africa endangers all hope of democracy. Intolerance puts freedom of the press in mortal danger.

Despite the hazards and magnitude of the problems there can be cause for hope. However poorly press freedom has been applied in

3. Market Research Survey, MRA, reported in *Weekly Mail*, Johannesburg, 30 May 1991.

South Africa, there is yet a tradition of a belief in freedom. The aspiration was kept alive during the dark years, and it is alive. There is, too, a history of struggle — imperfect and flawed as it was — by journalists for the public's right to know what was being done by the Nationalists. The belief in press freedom, and the commitment to free publication, provide a basis for the future.[4]

---

4 . Since writing, Argus has responded to criticisms of its monopoly control, first by selling a majority shareholding in the *Sowetan*, the daily newspaper aimed at black readers, to a consortium of black businessmen; second, it has sold effective control of its major newspaper interests to Ireland's Independent Newspapers whose head, Tony O'Reilly, is a friend of the African National Congress leader, Nelson Mandela. Argus retains its other extensive media holdings. These moves will, hopefully, contribute to the regeneration of the English-language press and towards bringing about a press which is more in tune with majority aspirations.

PART IV:
SUSTAINABLE
DEVELOPMENT: AN
OVERVIEW

Chapter Sixteen

Sustainable Development and the Peace Process in Southern Africa: The Experience of Mozambique and Angola

Barry Munslow

There are many similarities between Mozambique and Angola which make a comparative review appropriate. The two ex-Portuguese colonies share a common legacy of a poorly educated population with the bulk of skilled and semi-skilled occupations the restricted preserve of the settlers. Both have experienced 30 years of war, the first half of which involved an anti-colonial struggle and the second half responding to serious destabilization orchestrated primarily by the South African government. Angola and Mozambique were the two countries in the forefront of supporting the struggle for majority rule in Zimbabwe, Namibia and South Africa. The cost of this support has been heavier for the people of these two countries than for any other peoples in the region. The two countries are large and have a rich and relatively pristine natural resource base yet their people are amongst the poorest on earth. They are endeavouring to make the hazardous transition to peace with many setbacks along the way. In this chapter I will examine the peace process and sustainable development opportunities for each country in turn and attempt finally to draw some more general conclusions which may have some relevance for South Africa.

ANGOLA

For a while the prospects for Angola looked good. The peace agreement was signed in May 1991 and the agreement held until the election results were announced in October 1992.

In the National Assembly elections the MPLA (the Popular Movement for the Liberation of Angola) won 53.74 per cent of the vote and UNITA (National Union for the Total Independence of Angola) 34.10 per cent. In the Presidential elections José Eduardo dos Santos (MPLA) won 49.67 per cent and Jonas Savimbi (UNITA) 40.07 per cent of the vote. Because the Presidential winner did not poll over 50 per cent, under the election regulations a run-off ballot was required between the two leading candidates. The restart of the war put paid to these final niceties of the electoral arrangements. That the war recommenced was not the result of a rigged election, as the UN declared the result to be generally free and fair, rather it was the outcome of an unfortunate juxtaposition of factors.

The crucial problem seemed to be that UNITA was determined to take power at any price, irrespective of election results, and it was not sufficiently warned off such a strategy by the United States. Furthermore the United Nations peace-keeping and electoral supervision mission had insufficient finance and personnel to ensure that the electoral process would stick. It also reflected the inadequacies of the UN to cope with the new responsibilities being placed upon it and the need for a drastic overhaul and streamlining of procedures. The crucial missing elements in Angola were the effective demobilization of the soldiers of the two rival armies and the successful integration of a truly national army. Patrick Smith (1992: 102) has captured the problem well:

> Despite the hopeful signs that the Angolan people and many of the soldiers were desperate for peace and national reconciliation, the demobilization process and the military integration process had not advanced far enough to give them the confidence that it would succeed. Key indicators of success would have been provision of jobs and retraining for demobilized soldiers (from both armies) and decent joint training facilities for members of the integrated force, Forcas Armados Angolanas (FAA), which would have inspired confidence in the process and given it a much needed momentum.

Although the peace agreement was signed in May 1991, it was not until March 1992 that troops from the rival armies began to enter the 49 designated assembly points. Instead of the two months originally envisaged to place all of the troops into the assembly points, it took almost five times as long even to begin the process — a fatal flaw as it turned out. A second difficulty was that less than two thirds of the expected 160,000 troops actually entered the assembly areas. The reasons were various: inaccurate initial numbers, troops simply going home being fed

212

up with not receiving pay or adequate food and perhaps some troops were deliberately kept back. Troops should have been assembled in good time, have been demobilized properly and be given an economic stake in the future peaceful development of the country. It was essential that a single unified army be created well before elections took place. This would have effectively disarmed the parties to the conflict. However, the USA forced the election to go ahead before all the conditions of the peace agreement had been implemented.

The crucial lesson to draw is that any strategy for sustainable development in a conflict situation, be it in Angola, Mozambique, South Africa or elsewhere, must start by guaranteeing the peace. The space created by the brief respite of peace in Angola, a period of 17 months as it turned out, allowed some initiatives to be taken to raise the agenda of sustainable development. Preparations for the Rio Earth Summit played an important catalytic role. The fact that Brazil, the host nation, was part of the Portuguese-speaking community meant that the profile of sustainability was raised in Angola. A national report was prepared which began to create a belated awareness of the issues (Government of Angola 1991). There then followed a World Conservation Union (IUCN) initial environmental profile of Angola (Munslow 1992). The picture that emerged of the situation in Angola was mixed.

The war has had both positive and negative effects upon the environment. On the negative side has been the enormous cost of human suffering and social dislocation; the stalled development efforts; the high rate of urbanization in the search for security by displaced populations, creating unsupportable localized pressure on the natural resource base and basic service provision; war pillage of valuable commodities such as ivory, skins and hardwoods; the complete absence of effective planning for the sustainable utilization of the resource base; policy uncertainty in the move towards multi-party democratic elections; neglect of environmental education at every level and a generally low level of awareness of the issues. The fact that the war has greatly restricted the scope for human activity has had some positive effects on the flora and some of the fauna of the country, acting as a *de facto* conservation policy. The restriction on human economic activity has allowed both a natural regeneration and a restriction on land clearance for such things as settlement, agricultural production and mining.

Immediate areas for future concern include: wildlife and parks, as all forms of protection have collapsed and the men with guns have taken a heavy toll on the animal population; coastal zone management; and in particular the urban environment where there are serious pollution and service provision problems. Major efforts will be required in environmental education, institution building and inter-agency cooperation, training, research, policy formulation and legislation. At present there is no effective policy or legislative framework, no natural resource management planning, no enforcement capability and no capacity for undertaking environmental impact assessments.

The brief period of peace allowed a more detailed environmental assessment to be carried out (IUCN 1992). This began by examining the broad socioeconomic parameters. Prior to the restarting of the war in October 1992, it is estimated that a significant proportion of the population of 13 million had been forced out of their home areas. Estimates will now have to be considerably upgraded given the intensity of more recent conflicts which totally destroyed the second largest city of Huambo early in 1993, amongst other dire events. Given the likelihood of a major resettlement exercise with the eventual onset of peace, the IUCN (1992: 10) report stresses 'it is important that specific programmes be initiated to assist the rural population to resume their productive activities so as to prevent an unsustainable harvesting of resources for survival in the short run.'

Even before the resumption of the war, the overall context in Angola was not conducive to optimism concerning the prospects for sustainable development initiatives. Environmental concerns were barely visible as an issue in Angola, either amongst the political parties or the people and for understandable reasons. Survival is the dominant concern followed by a desperate desire for peace and economic reconstruction. The low level of environmental consciousness makes establishing a sustainable development agenda all the more difficult. Yet sustainable development should be all about guaranteeing peace and human survival, linking development initiatives with the wise management of the natural resources base.

This lack of awareness is reflected at all levels of government. The institutional context is very weak. Responsibility for these matters has always rested with the Ministry of Agriculture, and within this Ministry more recently with the Institute for Forest Development (IDF). Environment concerns are pigeonholed with wildlife and forests and sit in a ministry responsible for creating a number of the country's environmental problems through its earlier state farm policy and neglect of the family farming sector. As awareness has grown of environmental issues, institutional conflicts have emerged, with IDF being seen as trying to assume a monopoly of environmental concerns by other sectors, just at the time when there appears to be some status and potential lucrative benefits attached to being associated with taking environmental initiatives.

There is a general malaise amongst government institutions which means they have very little development impact. The reasons are complex and various: the lack of trained people; an ethos of government employees occupying a post rather than doing a job; low pay; no resources; the absence of any policy direction, accountability, work performance assessment or incentives; all of these impediments are wrapped up in the insecurities of a war psychosis. Mozambique shares many of the same problems in government.

The political stalemate has created a power vacuum and the birth of an active and vibrant civil society has been painstakingly slow. There has never been the legal or political space for civil society to emerge and consolidate. With the exception of the churches no independent organizations or associations were allowed to exist until recent times. The IUCN report (1992: 22) concludes:

> From a political perspective, there are thus few chances that a sustainable development strategy can be popularly defined and implemented in Angola in the immediate future. Those who are likely to support such a strategy — a few isolated individuals that are spread throughout the government administration, some NGOs, and the people if they were organized — do not have much effective power, and those who hold power seem to have little interest or incentives to pursue such a strategy.

Yet stopping the war alone would mark the most enormous step forward. Peace would release significant sums of money from defence expenditure (45 per cent of total government expenditure) and permit investment in development. Such development initiatives as are taken will no longer be wantonly destroyed. Much of the most highly skilled labour in the country is currently tied up in the two armies and peace would release desperately scarce skilled labour for development. Highly qualified people who have fled the country in considerable numbers would be tempted to return.

It is important to give some indication of the extent of the human costs of the war up to the signing of the May 1991 peace agreement. Approximately 900,000 Angolans died, of which probably 90 per cent were non-combatants, there were 70,000 amputees, 50,000 orphans, and countless numbers were affected by all of the emotional and psychological traumas associated with a civil war (Sogge 1992: Chapter 2). Facts are one of the first casualties of war, so all figures should be treated with caution. It has been estimated that a quarter of the civilian population has been either displaced within the country or has fled to neighbouring countries and that the total cost to the country through war damage and lost production was US $35–40 billion (De Carvalho 1992: 6).

Surviving the War

A recent publication drawing upon the experiences of many Angolan people provides revealing insight into the ingenuity with which people survived the deprivations of the war (Sogge 1992: Chapter 3). Denied access to much agricultural land by the perils of mines and ambush, people intensified production on smaller plots. Millet and sorghum, the hardier grains, once again became more commonly used; cassava and sweet potato became far more popular spreading to the south of the country; both require little attention. In central and western zones people planted more bananas. People generally relied far more on fishing, hunting and gathering. People worked for food, used traditional mutual-aid systems and some stole when other avenues were closed. Trade became a way of life for all Angolans. Artesanal production increased with cottage industries making bricks, wedding cakes, clothes and providing services such as hairdressing. Nearly everyone had more than one job. Fuelwood and charcoal provision were common avenues of employment to meet urban energy needs. The struggle for survival according to Sogge (1992: 51) meant that: 'Solutions for oneself and one's personal network came first. Solutions for the public at large became nobody's business.'

MOZAMBIQUE

Sustainable Livelihood Rehabilitation and the Peace Process

Like Angola the greatest single impediment to sustainable development in Mozambique has been the war. Guaranteeing the peace is the best way of ensuring a more sustainable development future. Ensuring the sustainability of programmes for the demobilization of troops and relocation of displaced people will make in turn a vital contribution to peace.

Drought and the war have placed enormous strains on the country's economic and social recovery programme and there has been an overall decline in growth rates. The Economist Intelligence Unit (1993: 3) gives the following figures for real GDP growth: 1988 (5.7 per cent), 1989 (4.0 per cent), 1990 (1.5 per cent), 1991 (0.9 per cent) and 1992 (–2.0 per cent). The imperative now is to go for growth almost at any price, to attract as much foreign and national investment as possible and to avoid any impediments to this process.

The two immediate sustainable development challenges are to ensure effective troop demobilization and to relocate rural peoples in a process of social and economic reintegration. Instituting the right kind of programmes to support sustainable livelihood rehabilitation may provide the key to success. An effective process of demobilization would ensure that former troops would be able to sustain their livelihoods without resorting to the use of the gun. A programme of purchasing weapons has an important role here and the immediate destruction of the weapons is essential. This process also requires a programme of sustainable livelihood rehabilitation both for the demobilized troops and also for the huge number of people relocating in rural areas. *Efforts to date have ignored the knowledge base required for sustaining livelihoods.* Initiatives are needed to improve knowledge of good practices of natural resource management amongst the groups who will be re-entering peasant production. These should emphasize strategies of risk minimization (against, for example, drought), ensuring increased and long-lasting improved productivity and basic needs provisioning for poverty alleviation.

It needs to be a national programme but functioning at the district and locality level and administered from the provinces. The approach adopted should involve:

* identifying indigenous knowledge of good natural resource management practices and the local people who have this knowledge. The latter will become the educators with incentives and support provided; and
* identifying simple messages and techniques and back-up support that will help people secure their livelihoods.

Since the signing of the peace accord in October 1992, there has been far greater access to the interior of the country than was at first thought possible. This has led to a massive effort by many people to move back to reclaim their land. The relative abundance of land gives grounds for optimism, but there will undoubtedly be many struggles at the local level over access to the natural resource base. Security of access to land and other natural resources and access to knowledge of best management practices are necessary to secure livelihoods. They should be seen as important contributions to the decentralization process.

Sustainable livelihood rehabilitation in the context of the poorest country in the world, recently destroyed by war, means targeting first those who could destroy the peace (the former troops) and next those whose lives have been most disrupted by massive displacement from the base of their former livelihoods — peasant production.

Summary of Objectives

Primary
- Ensure sustainable livelihood rehabilitation;
- Prevent the re-emergence of war;
- Protect the natural resource base.

Secondary
- Develop local leadership and organization;
- Contribute to the democratization process through decentralization, empowerment and ensuring human survival and restoration of dignity.

Tertiary
- By securing rural livelihood rehabilitation contribute to the broader process of national integration and development.

The Challenges of Demobilization and Sustainable Livelihood Rehabilitation

Approximately 70,000 to 100,000 troops were scheduled to be demobilized, leaving a standing army of 30,000. The process involved getting all the troops into 49 assembly points scattered strategically around the country. The troops would also have their families with them, between two to three dependants each; between 300,000 and 400,000 people in total would have to be transported back to their homes, although for most this would mean moving to places within the same province as their assembly points or to immediately neighbouring provinces. The four main priority provinces concerned were in the centre of the country: Manica, Sofala, Tete and Zambezia. Next in importance was Nampula in the north, followed by Gaza and Maputo provinces in the south.

Of the demobilized troops it was estimated that 50 per cent would become farmers and the rest would rely on other employment, of which half would be involved in public employment projects, rebuilding bridges, schools and health posts. The sustainable livelihood rehabilitation programme to be considered here focuses only on those going into agriculture. The total number involves between 100,000 and 200,000 people (troops and dependants). Those troops who expressed their preference to go into agricultural production were farmers before and still have some land. For the RENAMO (Mozambique National Resistance) troops in particular, reintegration into their former communities depends upon the way in which they departed from those communities and their ability to be reintegrated as a part of the healing process.

Massive social disruption has occurred as a result of the length and intensity of the war combined with the effects of drought. Up to half the total population of the country has been affected. As Table 16.1 shows, it can be categorized into the following groups, with estimated population numbers given for each category (Green 1992a: 7–8).

Table 16.1 : Categories of Uprooted Peoples and Estimated Numbers

Categories	*Estimated Numbers*
International refugees	1 500 000
Internal refugees (in camps)	1 800 000
Internal displaced persons (not in camps)	3 000 000
Urban war flight	500 000
Pauperized in place	1 000 000
Total	7 800 000

Source: Green 1992a.

The figures in the table are indicative as there are no accurate statistics. Mozambique's government has taken the position that support should not be differentiated between these groups as all are in need of help. It aims, on paper at least, to have a decentralized reconstruction strategy that will incorporate all groups. The problems in implementing such a strategy are daunting, not least because of donor diversity and lack of coordination and the tendency of aid agencies to weaken government capacity at the national level (Hanlon 1991; Brochmann and Ofstad 1990). However, the institutional weaknesses in government are not simply the result of structural adjustment induced government cutbacks and donor dominance, although both play a part. There is also the strong legacy and mentality of over centralized government.

The package necessary for rural reconstruction is clear: access to land, transport home, tools, seed, food until the harvest, access to basic health, education and clean water, local physical infrastructure, market access, household cash incomes and the chance to build a home. This applies equally to effective troop demobilization and to the relocation of displaced rural populations.

Attention thus far has focused in the main on material packages and programmes required to aid livelihood rehabilitation (Green 1992a and 1992b). Whilst no-one would deny that these are of major importance, alone they are not enough, nor is it possible to provide all of the material aid calculated to be necessary. The problems with such an approach are:

- The size of the material package being requested appears far greater than is likely to be forthcoming from the international community.
- The capacity to distribute such large quantities of material resources effectively is very limited given weaknesses in the communication, transport and banking systems.
- Administrative capacity at the provincial and district levels is very limited.
- The willingness and capacity to decentralize resources has proved to be a serious stumbling block in the past. Decentralization means a willingness to forgo possibilities for accumulation at the centre.
- By placing undue emphasis upon the material components rather than on local knowledge and local human resource capacity, the existing mentality of dependence on outside aid can be reinforced.

People have become accustomed to devising their own survival strategies, with some more adept at this than others. A recent survey of the literature on displaced Mozambicans by Ken Wilson (1992: 10) for the Swedish International Development Authority concludes:

> The most important finding is that it is the survival strategies of the refugees themselves that are key to survival. They simply are not passive victims waiting for aid, in danger of becoming dependent ... Study after study demonstrates the phenomenal ability with which refugees deploy their social networks, available resources and energies in order to carve out protection and a livelihood.

Whilst it is certainly true that the survival imperative is very powerful, the way in which food relief has become so institutionalized in Mozambique and in the surrounding refugee camps means that in some cases the dependence mentality has been inculcated.

All the evidence from Africa and elsewhere shows that generally refugees take responsibility for their own repatriation, local reintegration and livelihood sustainability (Allen and Morsink 1993). Ken Wilson's (1993: 2) important research in the Refugees Studies Programme at Oxford stresses that as formal repatriation programmes do not usually work then assistance can be enhanced 'through the identification of means of supporting refugees own return initiatives,' by targeting the key constraints encountered by the refugees themselves. It is useful to summarize Wilson's outline of the reasons why refugees prefer to self-repatriate:

- they control their own lives and options;
- formal programmes are generally inadequate, assistance arrives too late and plans are flawed; and
- too little assistance is offered.

All the evidence from Mozambique points to the fact that refugees have indeed returned themselves and that the official agencies and the government have no effective strategy other than to sanction this. Wilson (1991) suggests that the emphasis should be on linking the process of returning home to development, in other words relief programmes must provide a bridge to development. Secondly, aid agencies can help build peace by 'absorbing the energies of the former belligerent parties and bringing them under their patronage' (Wilson 1993: 18). Goods have to be delivered to the parties concerned if there is to be an alternative to war as a means of livelihood. Specifically the aid agencies must wean RENAMO from the outside forces that nurtured it for so long. Its methods had so alienated most of the international community that there was a reluctance to engage with RENAMO. This must now be overcome and the norms of civilized behaviour inculcated as the prerequisite for international support.

There is a knowledge base for survival which is already decentralized and widely dispersed. It is in place. It has not yet been tapped or released to meet its full development potential. What follows is an attempt to elaborate some ideas about how this could take place. The aim is to put the *sustainability* into *livelihood rehabilitation*. That requires human resource capacity building. It is about training and transferring knowledge. It is also about institution building, but this time institution building in civil society and at the decentralized provincial and district levels of government. Demobilized troops and the various categories of uprooted peoples should be targeted jointly in a community reintegration process. A training and consciousness raising programme will help build capacity for the restitution of viable peasant farming. It will use as a powerful and hitherto untapped development resource, local traditional knowledge and good practices of natural resource management to ensure sustainable livelihoods. Those possessing this knowledge should be identified and used as trainers. However, current levels of indigenous knowledge alone are inadequate for historical and other reasons. Hence the need to disseminate advice on best practices. Given the ever present threat to their lives and the disruptions engendered, survival today rather than sustaining livelihoods for the future has been people's priority.

The best peasant farmers in Mozambique have developed a range of risk minimization and coping strategies in the face of climatic variations which produce frequent periods of drought. Pre-existing indigenous forms of adaption provide a foundation on which to build to minimize risks. Whilst the current drought may have helped create the conditions in which both sides in the conflict wished to secure peace, a future period of drought could induce a return to armed banditry by people whose agricultural livelihood has been destroyed. The ability of farming families to adapt depends on their knowledge, skills and resources. Learning risk avoiding strategies becomes ever more important given the prospect of global climate change.

The three main ways of coping with drought in Mozambique have been most usefully described by Julian Quan (1992) — (1) flexibility within farming systems; (2) off-farm income generation; and (3) increased reliance on wild resources.

1. Flexible farming system adaptions include: staggered planting times; diversifying crops (for cash, subsistence and insurance) and mixes of varieties; scattering plots over different terrain; insurance plots; incremental irrigation and soil conservation; maintenance of carry-over stocks and seeds; mixed farming and small animal husbandry. Outside inputs can also offer appropriate technological options for raising yields and strengthening system flexibility. People also sell their assets, cut spending, go into debt and look for jobs.

2. Migrant labour has been a traditional off-farm income generation option in Mozambique. Internal markets for casual labour also provide sources of support in times of stress. Larger and more productive farmers absorb surplus seasonal labour in exchange for food or a share of the produce. A recent study commissioned by the Ministry of Agriculture (Van Vugt 1992) has provided a survey of traditional systems of mutual help which include *tsima, cofunana, tsone, mbelelo* and *xitique*. In addition to mutual help there are various forms of salaried help such as *kurimela, ku thekela* and *mugwazo*. By working for other local farmers people acquire inputs to restart farm production of their own, such as cuttings, seed and tools. It also helps build a sense of community.

222

3. People rely far more on hunting, fishing and gathering a variety of products. The countryside provides food resources in lieu of agricultural production in the form of edible roots, leaves and insects. Woodlands provide fodder and browse for livestock and fertilizer from leaf litter and cattle manure. Trees aid soil moisture retention and help erosion control and tree products provide sources of fruit, fibre, fuel, construction materials and habitats for game.

Natural ecosystems are relatively more resilient in the face of drought and climate variability than agro-ecosystems. The important point, however, is to learn how to manage both wisely.

The aim is to identify local people who have the knowledge and skills of good farming practices to spread the word. Additional inputs of good practices must be conveyed through national health, education and water networks, which, along with agricultural extension, are the only branches of government that exist in most districts of the country. Appropriate technologies will have an important role to play.

The Challenges

- A culture of dependence amongst some, relying on food handouts rather than production. The drought has exacerbated this tendency.
- The youth in the urban areas will not return to the rural zones in any numbers, only their parents. Youth has become urbanized, has lost agricultural skills and interest.
- The lack of rural services, a production and commercialization network and continuing fear of the war restarting will slow the process of permanent rural resettlement.
- Those in government and the aid agencies are not yet using the language of sustainability to inform their programmes and activities.

By identifying local people/leaders with the indigenous knowledge and expertise to disseminate models of good practice, an education process can begin that is low cost, relies on local resources and is based on the principles outlined above for the demobilization of troops.

The greatest danger currently in Mozambique is that once again, as in Angola, we are witnessing inadequate levels of international support for the peace process. The peace agreement was signed in October but it was not until 17 December 1992 that the UN Security Council gave its approval for a force of 7500 troops as well as police and civilians to be made available to monitor and ensure the ceasefire. Only several months later did these forces arrive. There is evidence already of widespread desertions given delays in demobilization (*Africa Confidential* 1993: 7).

Troops without food and pay are a dangerous element and can upset the peace process: a rebellion by the presidential guard was crushed in March 1993. Freelance banditry as a survival strategy will do little to consolidate peace and economic reconstruction. The UN Secretary General explained in his report of December 1992 that it is of 'critical importance that the elections should not take place until the military aspects of the agreement have been fully implemented' (*Indian Ocean Newsletter* 1992).

LESSONS FOR SOUTH AFRICA

The people of Mozambique and Angola have suffered more than anyone in the region from the struggle against apartheid and white minority rule, even compared with the black population of South Africa itself. Undoubtedly South Africa faces profound economic problems in the future. But a brief comparison of the GNP per capita figures of $2500 for South Africa and $80 for Mozambique shows the enormous regional disparities in standards of living, notwithstanding the fact that the gross inequalities existing within South Africa are masked by the average GNP per capita statistic. A future democratically elected government of South Africa incurs an enormous moral debt to the people of Mozambique and Angola, whose land was turned into killing fields under the white minority South African government's 'Total Strategy' policy of regional destabilization. There is an unspoken obligation on South Africans to ensure that in the process of moving to majority rule any continuing support for destabilization is rapidly curtailed from whatever source inside South Africa, and secondly that every effort is made to compensate Angola and Mozambique for the intolerable burden that they have carried for volunteering to be the rear base for the anti-apartheid struggle. The relative economic affluence of South Africa makes this a possibility, notwithstanding the internal pressures to concentrate on alleviating the poverty conditions inside South Africa.

The next lesson is the absolute priority of making the compromises for securing peace. This means finding ways of diffusing the various armed forces involved in the conflicts inside South Africa prior to the elections. The leadership and organizers of the armed groups have to be bought off and given a role in the democratic process and other means of livelihood must be found for the foot soldiers to pre-empt any return to arms.

A third lesson is that to secure a sustainable development future it is necessary to cultivate an open and democratic civil society. This will permit powerful voices to be raised in defence of the environment, of poverty alleviation and of the special concerns of women who are inevitably at the forefront of any prospects for sustainable development.

Barry Munslow

Mamphela Ramphele (1991: 201–2) has captured well a number of the South African issues. Apartheid, she says:

> has forced large numbers of people into unsuitable environments, putting disproportionate pressure on natural resources and carving deep fissures into valleys and hillsides. It has broken urban areas into fragments ... In the wider region, it has wreaked ecological havoc by sponsoring wars and undermining economies ... What is called for is a reversal of the philosophy of separation in favour of a more holistic approach. A renewed awareness of the interdependence of human beings and their environment ... will grow with the empowerment of ordinary people ... participatory democracy is a vital prerequisite for the upgrading of the environment, enabling people to reclaim control and to hold authorities accountable to the communities they purport to serve.

For this to happen education must be the *number one priority*. A necessary, though not sufficient, condition for empowerment is enlightenment. Sustainable development is all about improving the human resource base through understanding, so that the natural resource base can be managed more wisely, thereby looking after our future welfare as well as today's survival. Nothing should be done in the final phase of the struggle to consolidate majority rule which will impede the education of the black majority population. A successful transitional strategy from war to peace relies on human empowerment: the key is the kind of education that incorporates an environmental understanding of the process of accelerating development to alleviate poverty whilst not undermining the natural resource base upon which survival and prosperity ultimately depends. The educational effort should not ignore the pools of traditional knowledge of good environmental practices where they still exist, indeed it should build upon these if appropriate.

REFERENCES

Africa Confidential (1993) vol 34, no 1
Allen, T and Morsink, H (eds) (1993) *When Refugees Go Home*, London, James Currey
Brochmann, G and Ofstad, A (1990) *Mozambique: Norwegian Assistance in the Context of Crisis*, Bergen, Chr Michelson Institute
De Carvalho, J (1992) *Economic Memorandum on the People's Republic of Angola*, translated by Marga Holnes, London, Embassy of the People's Republic of Angola
Economist Intelligence Unit (1993) *Mozambique Country Report No 1*, London, The Economist

Government of Angola (1991) *National Report for the UNCED Conference*, Luanda, Government of Angola

Green, R (1992a) 'The Four Horsemen Ride Together: Scorched Fields of War in Southern Africa', paper presented to the Refugees Studies Programme, Queen Elizabeth House, University of Oxford

—— (1992b) 'Human and Livelihood Rehabilitation After War: Reconstruction, Structural Adjustment and Transformation in SSA', Addis Ababa, paper presented to the Inter-Africa Group Second Annual Symposium

Hanlon, J (1991) *Mozambique: Who Calls the Shots?*, London, James Currey

Indian Ocean Newsletter (1991) 26 December

IUCN (1992) *Angola: Environment Status Quo Assessment Report*, Harare, IUCN

Munslow, B (1992) *Environmental Profile of Angola*, Harare, IUCN

Quan, J (1992) 'Security and Change in the Southern African Environment: The Case of Mozambique', MSc thesis, University of London

Ramphele, M (ed) (1991) *Restoring the Land: Environment and Change in Post-Apartheid South Africa*, London, Panos

Smith, P (1992) 'Angola: Free and Fair Elections', *Review of African Political Economy*, no 55

Sogge, D (1992) *Sustainable Peace: Angola's Recovery*, Harare, Southern African Research and Documentation Centre

Van Vugt, A (1992) *Estrategias de Sobrevivencia*, Maputo, Serie: Communidade rural, Ministerio de Agricultura

Wilson, K (1991) 'Linking Returning Home and Development in Northern Mozambique: Some Preliminary Suggestions', unpublished paper, Refugees Studies Programme, University of Oxford

—— (1992) *Internally Displaced, Refugees and Returnees from and in Mozambique*, SIDA Studies on Emergencies and Disaster Relief, Report no 1

—— (1993) 'Assisting Repatriation: Recent Lessons from Self-Repatriation in Mozambique', draft paper, Refugees Studies Programme, University of Oxford

Chapter Seventeen

Ideologies of Sustainable Development

Ken Cole

All of a sudden the phrase Sustainable Development (SD) has become pervasive. SD has become the watch-word for international aid agencies, the jargon of development planners, the theme of conferences and learned papers, and the slogan of development and environmental activists ... [but] 'What *is* SD?' is being asked increasingly frequently.

(Lélé 1991: 607, emphasis in original)

Sustainable development as an idea links environmentalism and development, and has come to the fore as people's concern for the environment has achieved greater prominence. It is beyond the scope of this chapter to explore the rise of modern environmentalism, but see Pepper (1986). What is of concern here is the political nature of the environmental debate. Ideological differences between environmentalists crucially reflect conceptions of 'how' and 'why' consumption and production should be regulated or restricted to ensure a viable natural environment. At issue here is how far environmental reform implies political, social and economic reforms. In this regard there is a whole spectrum of thought ranging from the conservative reactions of privileged people anxious not to share their advantage, whether resources are diminishing or not, to the beliefs of those who hold that a sustainable environment is contingent upon a society based upon fairness, justice and cooperation and that this can only be achieved through challenging the power of the ruling class. In between lie those who think that such a society can emerge through a pluralist process of rational, technical reforms.

The quest for a sustainable environment raised development issues, as the loss of natural habitat and the breakdown of indigenous social systems were increasingly linked to development projects. As Adams (1990: 1) states: '"Save the rainforest" campaigns, or the articulation of opposition to investment in large projects like dams, follow logically enough from concerns about pollution, whales or First World rural environments.'

From the early 1970s the phrase 'sustainable development' has become increasingly the focus of the development debate. And now such diverse bodies as the United Nations Environmental Programme (UNEP 1978), the International Union for Conservation of Nature and Natural Resources (IUCN 1980), the World Commission on Environment and Development (Brundtland 1987), the British Ministry for Overseas Development (Patten 1987), and the World Bank (Hopper 1988) can all embrace the goal of 'sustainable development'. That conservative development agencies and environmental groups and organizations can apparently sing the same song suggests that the term is so ambiguous as to have little meaning. The commonest definition of sustainable development is to be found in *Our Common Future*, the report of the World Commission on Environment and Development (Brundtland 1987: 43): 'Sustainable development is development that meets the needs of the present without compromizing the ability of future generations to meet their own needs.' But precisely because this definition leaves out of consideration *how* this is to be achieved it can be embraced by conservatives and radicals. As Adams (1990: 4) puts it, 'Development bureaucrats and politicians have undoubtedly welcomed the opportunity to fasten onto a phrase that suggests radical reform without actually either specifying what needs to change or requiring specific action.'

We now turn to *how* different interpretations of sustainable development variously conceive of development and the environment, and how people are seen to interact socially in their use of the natural environment in the development process. Levins and Lewontin (1985: 267) explain that 'Scientists, like other intellectuals, come to their work with a world view, a set of preconceptions that provides the framework for their analyses of the world. These preconceptions enter at both an explicit and an implicit level, but even when invoked explicitly, unexamined and unexpressed assumptions underlie them.' The 'unexplained and unexpressed assumptions' in social analysis refer to the assumed *dynamic* of social activity — the *motivation* for social behaviour, *why* people do things. The significance of 'facts' is only to be understood in terms of their relation to other facts. It is not the events themselves that are important so much as the implied relation *between* events. Colclough

(1982: 490, emphasis added) argues that 'the state of confusion in policy, and indeed amongst academic theorists, stems from sharp disagreement over the real *causes* of ... phenomena, and the ways they can best be addressed.'

Development implies a change in people's behaviour, and it is the assumed source of human motivation that provides the dynamic of the development process, indicating the appropriate emphasis for development policy. The 'unexamined assumptions' that underlie development theory, and hence understandings of sustainable development, are assumptions about human nature. As Harbour (1982: 52) says: 'Questions about what man should strive to be, the structure of the good society, the meaning of justice, the distinction between political right and wrong, and how to bring about a better society can have no adequate answers until one has some idea about what man is in the first place.'

That there are assumptions about human nature (rather than 'facts') is a reflection of human social existence. *All* people live in some form of society and it can never be clear if their behaviour ultimately reflects their genetically-determined innate characteristics (nature); if they have been socialized into acceptable behaviour patterns (nurture); or if their biological potential and social experience are dialectically interdependent (praxis). Because there are no asocial individuals to act as a control group, the nature/nurture/praxis debate is a perennial one in social science. Or, as Smith (1983: 3) writes, the enterprise of confronting 'the various views of human nature with the "facts" ... is doomed from the start, since there exists no neutral body of empirical information that lends itself to being divided into facts and irrelevant pieces of information ... what is evidence for one view of human nature is irrelevant for another.'

All analyses of human behaviour must start from some conception of people's nature. And these conceptions amount to *beliefs*. Everyone has to have a belief structure in order to understand their environment and make sense of their experience. But importantly, beliefs about human nature justify particular forms of social organization as conforming to the *real* nature of humankind: the concept of human nature implies a political assessment of social existence.

> Explanations in society are not simply scientific responses to a problem. They are weapons in a fight, the basis for praise or blame. It is for this reason that social science can contribute least where the social and political significance of the problem is the greatest. The study of economics has its 'black holes', but they are not the blindness of economists so much as the blindness of the

social order. For blindness serves its function too, protecting and
defending a status quo.

(Harris 1983: 5)

Hence, in considering alternative theoretical analyses of sustainable
development it is not simply a question of *choosing* which is empirically
right and which is empirically wrong, but of *comparing* the underlying
assumptions. The implied social and political bias of the particular interpretation of social experience has to be made explicit. Certainly theories
have to be empirically validated: but potentially a number of coherent
interpretations of social behaviour can fulfil this criterion, each of which
has an ideological, and ultimately a political dimension. Redclift (1989:
201–2, emphasis added) points out that 'different perceptions of the
environment are neither more or less "rational" — they merely reflect
the way we look at the world ... divergent views are not necessarily
correct or false and are unlikely to be consistent as long as people have
different *interests*.'

It is commonly argued that there are three different approaches to
social analysis in general (see Cole 1993), and it has been observed that
there are three approaches to the analysis of sustainable development in
particular. According to Seidman and Anang (1992: 23) 'the three categories include: (1) "mainstream" which ... in the 1980s generally
underpinned the policies of the International Monetary Fund and the
World Bank; (2) "basic needs/structuralist" ...; and (3) "transforming
institutionalist"' and, as Redclift (1989: 37) states, 'several different
approaches to economic behaviour and environmental values are examined: differences within neo-classical economics, "deep" ecological positions and Marxist theory.' The three perspectives conceive of sustainable
development quite differently, having different intellectual parameters
for the understanding of phenomena. That is, the various interpretations
are informed by differing beliefs about human nature: the 'unexamined
and unexpressed assumptions' that underlie the analyses.

If it is believed that people reflect their innate capacities and drives,
behaviour is assumed to be biologically determined. Society is merely
the sum of the individuals who compose it and the dynamic of social
change and hence development is individuals who, in their motivation,
are essentially *independent* of society. The *form* of social organization is
irrelevant to the analysis. But, as we shall see, for other perspectives on
development society is *more* that the sum of the individuals, and the
form of social organization is a variable relevant to the analysis of
people's behaviour. However, for biological determinists the relation
between culture and the environment is not a meaningful question.

230

Because society is seen as no more than the sum of the individuals who compose it, social change derives from either the slow process of human evolution according to the survival of the fittest, from a changed social environment as a result of individuals struggling to be 'free' to express their unique personalities, or from more people entering society, ie population growth, in which case sustainable development is fundamentally about the 'carrying capacity' of the planet.

Where independent individuals are understood to be the development dynamic, the 'mainstream' or 'neo-classical' approach, sustainable development is about the conservation of the natural environment in the face of individuals' ever greater consumption demands. Adams (1990: 49) explains how 'development and conservation are defined in such a way that their compatibility becomes inevitable. Development is presented as "the modification of the biosphere" (IUCN 1980). ... Meanwhile conservation is "the management of human use of the biosphere".' The result is that the victims come to be blamed for environmental degradation. Referring to the South African experience, Mamphela Ramphele (1991: 13) writes, '"Overpopulation" has been identified as the main problem, and black people have been held responsible for destroying trees and creating waste.' This is in spite of the fact that black people have been coerced into living in overcrowded 'homelands' by the Land Acts of 1913 and 1936, which reserved only 13 per cent of land for the use of the African majority. And the repeal of the pass laws in 1986 opened the floodgates to African urbanization; it is estimated that 1000 people per day migrate to urban areas (see Ramphele 1991: 5), with little or no investment in the urban infrastructure (for example, housing, roads, water, sewage and power).

However, it is thought by some theorists that with appropriate economic policies society can adapt to rising population. Although humans are motivated to want 'more', with economic incentives, human technical ingenuity is almost limitless, and production can be expanded to meet increased consumption demands. Khan and Wiener (1967: 116) refer to our 'capacities for and commitment to economic development and control over our external and internal environment and concomitant systematic, technological innovation, application, and diffusion ... these capacities are increasing, seemingly without foreseeable limit.'

People are motivated by sensuous expediency in the drive to be happy (or what economists call 'maximizing utility' according to individual's 'subjective preferences') and will respond to price signals. And the environment can be given a monetary value. As it is degraded people will be willing to pay for services and amenities to ameliorate their deteriorating living conditions, and entrepreneurs will see opportunities to make a profit, and invest in the environment. Mellos (1988: 54) writes: 'In the case of pollution, the economically sensible choice of means for handling it, Beckerman contends, is "optimum" pollution as "the level at which the social costs of reducing pollution ... just equals the social benefits of doing so".' 'Optimum' pollution is determined by what consumers are 'willing to pay' for an acceptable lifestyle. And as resources are depleted there will be shortages and their prices will rise, reducing consumption and acting as an incentive to entrepreneurs for substitutes to be developed. Inequality begets incentives and becomes the 'mother of invention'.

Khan (1979: 60–1) holds that 'the increasing disparity between ... the richest and the poorest nations ... [is] a basic "engine" of growth. ... The great abundance of the resources of the developed world — capital, management, technology, and large markets in which to sell — makes possible the incredibly rapid progress of most of the developing countries.' The integrity of the natural environment depends upon the institution of 'free' markets, and those who are poor will become the most environmentally disadvantaged. The implied political programme is conservative.

Alternatively, rather than human nature being thought to be biologically determined, people can be seen to be malleable beings, who can be 'moulded' to the needs of society. Individuals are culturally conditioned, socialized, nurtured.

> Man is innately programmed in such a way that he needs a culture to complete him. ... Man is like one of those versatile cake mixes that can be variously prepared to end up as different kinds of cake ... just as a cake has to be baked, so a baby has to be exposed to a specific, already existing, culture.
>
> (Midgely 1978: 286)

People are no longer *in*dependent from society, but *de*pendent upon society. To produce their livelihoods people have to cooperate through a technical division of labour. And society has to be managed through pluralist political institutions, through which people are consulted, to create a cooperative environment within which to produce (not a competitive one orientated towards consumption). Free markets, the rationale for which is individual choice, are unable to respond to the technical needs of social cooperation in production. Society is now *more than* the sum of the individuals who compose it.

Such a cooperative environment cannot coexist with extremes of poverty and wealth, and there has to be a degree of distributional equality. Crucially there is a technically defined common interest. As Howe and le Roux (1992: 15, emphasis added) write: 'The economic crisis that faces South Africa calls for a fundamental restructuring of *both* the political and economic system ... the apartheid policy, which was originally intended to benefit white South Africans, eventually harmed *us all*.' Social institutions evolve to meet the needs of a changing technology, and sustainable development is a problem of the incompatibility of the institutional structure of society and the technology of production. On the one hand this can imply scaling down technology to systems manageable within existing cultural institutions — Schumacher's 'small is beautiful'. As Schumacher himself (1974: 147) puts it: 'If the purpose of development is to bring help to those who need it most, each "region" or "district" within the country needs its own development.' For such theorists decentralization is the key to sustainable development. The organization of the economy has to be on a scale which can be grasped by the majority of people.

However, for some theorists within this perspective, economic growth is seen as necessary to relieve poverty, reducing pressure to use the environment in an unsustainable way to survive. For example, Brundtland (1987: 59) asserts that 'economic growth is ... the only way to tackle poverty, and hence achieve environment–development objectives. It must, however, be a new form of growth, sustainable, environmentally aware, egalitarian, integrating economic and social development.'

Apartheid essentially is an institutional structure inimical to economic growth; hence it ultimately declines, though not without privileged interests attempting to hold onto their advantage. People, shortsightedly, allow their short-term personal interests to supercede long-term social considerations. For such theorists South African industries are unable to compete on the world market because of limited home demand. Those Africans who are able to work in the modern industrial sector are paid extremely low wages, effectively denying industry a home market upon which to build economies of scale and lower the costs of production. 'Consequently', Howe and le Roux (1992: 17) argue, South Africa 'did not develop the economic base from which to launch an assault on world markets.' And this failure to develop both home and export markets meant that South Africa was unable to develop a capital goods sector, adversely affecting the balance of payments.

Also, Bantu education, a product of apartheid, denied Africans a technical education, depriving the economy of an educated workforce (literate, numerate and skilled). Overall, the social institution of apartheid was, and is, inappropriate to economic development and contrary to the technically defined common interest.

In the end even those who were supposed to benefit from apartheid, the white workers and capital, suffered the consequences. ... South Africa has two different futures. ... It can be transformed into a democratic society with a successful and thriving economy, or it can become a disaster area. ... Either we are going to get things right, and there will be a great future for *all* of us. Or ... *we* are going to destroy ourselves.

(Howe and le Roux 1992: 19, emphasis added)

The approach is utopian and assumes a political will to reach a compromise between conflicting, at least in the short term, economic interests. The basis for a compromise exists because of people's dependence upon a technical division of labour, implying cooperation rather than competition.

We seek to present the first steps towards solutions that could be realized *given that the corresponding political will existed. The stimulation and organization of the will is the task of Green politics.* We must help forge coalitions at both national and international levels that will increase the chance for realizing an ecological global economy based on solidarity.

(Group of Green Economists 1992: 7, emphasis added)

The politics of this approach are reformist and elitist. There is an assumed common social interest (defined by the exigencies of technical progress). Development is essentially a *technical* process to be managed by 'experts'. The political imperative is social democratic.

There is a third interpretation of human nature. People are not passive, essentially being determined and moulded by genetic (biological) or social (cultural) forces beyond their control, but they are active participants in the shaping of their lives. People are *inter*dependent, *creative* beings. While being born with a biological potential, this can only be realized through social activity. As creative beings, people are driven to fulfil their potential as individuals, but this is neither fixed nor static. Having, through social interaction, achieved an ambition or fulfilled a need, individuals widen their horizons to embrace new objectives and meet new expectations and realize new needs. People change over their lifetime. Biology and social experience are dialectically interactive: praxis. As Marx (1936: 124) said, 'all history is nothing but a continuous transformation of human nature.'

An individual's changing potential provides the dynamic of the dialectical process of social change. People live in societies, the structure of which tends to protect a status quo, maintaining the privileges of a ruling elite. The social structure cannot ultimately accommodate people's changing potentials as these become new 'needs', the fulfilment of which implies a changed social division of labour potentially challenging entrenched political interests. Further, the social structure is riven with contradictions with the interests of a ruling class dominating the regulation of society and the social use of the natural environment. It is where the social structure constrains an individual's creativity that frustration is generated; people might be unemployed, or denied access to social services or educational provision. If people are aware of shared constraints then there is the basis for collective action to change society, collective action in which people actually *participate* rather than partake of the consultations typical of social democratic impetuses to change.

People interact socially with the natural environment (ie not merely as individual consumers, or rationally according to technically defined priorities). And if we are to change the way we relate to the environment to realize sustainable lifestyles, then patterns of social behaviour have to change, where existing patterns reflects the power structure of competing class interests. Ramphele (1991: 11, 16) states that: 'Past experience in South Africa indicates that effective ecological protection will not be achieved without democracy and an equitable distribution of power. ... Ending the exploitation of both people and the environment involves the total transformation of South African society. Trade unions have a crucial role to play in this process.'

In a country where decent housing, adequate medical provision, and a living wage are denied to the majority, with 5 per cent of the population owning 80 per cent of the wealth, it is not surprising that the essentially conservative environmental politics of the white elite, focusing on conservation, are not a priority for the black majority. For the disadvantaged the relevant environmental issues have to do with where they live, work and play. Concerns which cannot be divorced from the social order which requires the black majority to suffer disadvantage and want, and the struggle for better housing, health care, education provision, workers rights, and the fight for a democratic constitution, are fundamental to the achievement of sustainable development.

There is an emerging 'new environmentalism' in South Africa which addresses the political and social dimensions of protecting the environment, and links these to analyses of sustainable development through such issues as land use, urbanization, workplace safety, employment, food policy, education and democracy. Trade unions and environmental organizations have begun to work together. Lena Slachmuijlder (1993) reports that since 1990, Earthlife Africa and the Chemical and Industrial

Workers Union have waged successful campaigns against Bayer-owned Chrome Chemicals for hazardous toxic dumping and working conditions; and Thor Chemicals, who were forced to close part of their recycling operation because of working conditions in their mercury processing plants. Also, in struggles against air, water and noise pollution, Earthlife has been able to mobilize researchers, doctors and academics to help the residents of several townships build stronger cases against the authorities (see Slachmuijlder 1993).

If people are understood to be creative beings who are socially inter-dependent, then attempts to build alliances between competing social interests may go some way to resolving the problem of sustainable life-styles. But this can only be *tactically* valid, for the ultimate *strategic* objective must be to empower people to participate in controlling their own lives. As Chambers (1988: 3) puts it, 'Development below is an approach, not a package. The approach suggests that for success, development must be not only innovative and research-based, but locally conceived and initiated, flexible, participatory and based on a clear understanding of local economics and politics. ... The poor are not the problem, they are the solution.' Adams (1990: 196, 201, 202) goes on to argue that '"Green" development is not about the way the environment is managed, but about who has the power to decide how it is managed.' The implied political programme is socialist.

The purpose of the above analysis has been to highlight the irrelevance of seeing sustainable development as a 'rational problem' which can be resolved in the common interest. If people are to succeed in their struggle for a sustainable lifestyle, then the political implications of alternative policy prescriptions have to be addressed. The different perspectives derive from quite different ways of conceiving of the development process, ways which have distinct political implications.

REFERENCES

Adams, W (1990) *Green Development*, London, Routledge
Brundtland, G (et al) (1987) *Our Common Future*, Oxford, Oxford University Press
Chambers, R (1988) 'Sustainable Rural Livelihoods', in Conroy and Litvinoff, qv
Colclough, C (1982) 'Lessons from the Development Debate for Western Economic Policy', *Foreign Affairs*, vol 58
Cole, K (1993) 'The Intellectual Parameters of the Real World: Experience, Reality and Ideology in Economic Analysis — Implications for the Teaching of Economics', Development Studies Discussion Paper no 234, University of East Anglia, Norwich
Conroy, C and Litvinoff, M (eds) (1988) *The Greening of Aid*, London, Earthscan
Forbes, I and Smith, S (eds) (1983) *Politics and Human Nature*, London, Frances Pinter

Group of Green Economists (1992) *Ecological Economics*, London, Zed Books
Harbour, W (1982) *The Foundations of Conservative Thought*, London, University of Notre Dame Press
Harris, N (1983) *Of Bread and Guns*, Harmondsworth, Penguin
Hopper, W (1988) *The World Bank's Challenge: Balancing Economic Need with Environmental Protection*, Godalming, 7th Annual World Conservation Lecture, World Wide Fund for Nature, UK
Howe, G and le Roux, P (eds) (1992) *Transforming the Economy*, Durban, Indicator South Africa
IUCN (1980) *The World Conservation Strategy*, Geneva, International Union for Conservation of Nature and Natural Resources
Khan, H (1979) *World Economic Development: 1979 and Beyond*, Boulder Colorado, Westview Press
Khan, H and Wiener, A (1967) *The Year 2000: A Framework for Speculation on the Next Thirty-Three Years*, London, Macmillan
Lélé, S (1991) 'Sustainable Development: A Critical Review', *World Development*, vol 19, no 6
Levins, R and Lewontin, R (1985) *The Dialectical Biologist*, Cambridge Massachusetts, Harvard University Press
Marx, K (1936) *The Poverty of Philosophy*, London, Lawrence and Wishart
Mellos, K (1988) *Perspectives on Ecology*, London, Macmillan
Midgely, M (1978) *Beast and Man*, Brighton, Harvester
Patten, C (1987) 'Aid and the Environment', *Geographical Journal*, no 153
Pepper, D (1986) *The Roots of Modern Environmentalism*, London, Routledge
Ramphele, M (ed) (1991) *Restoring the Land*, London, Panos
Redclift, M (1989) *Sustainable Development*, London, Routledge
Schumacher, E (1974) *Small is Beautiful*, London, Abacus
Seidman, A and Anang, F (eds) (1992) *21st Century Africa: Towards a New Vision of Self-Sustainable Development*, Trenton NJ, Africa World Press
Slachmuijlder, L (1993) 'What it Means to be Green in South Africa', *Capitalism, Nature, Socialism*, vol 4, no 1
Smith, S (1983) 'Introduction', in Forbes and Smith, qv
UNEP (1978) *Review of Areas: Environment and Development and Environmental Management*, Nairobi, United Nations Environmental Programme

Index

Printed in the United States
by Baker & Taylor Publisher Services